Dear Reader,

I grew up in a small, predominantly Roman Catholic town in rural western Massachusetts. When I was very young, my grandmother took me to church every Sunday. I had some difficulty understanding everything that was going on during the service. As most children can relate, I was bored, which made me antsy and often got me into a bit of trouble.

As I grew older, I began to realize that much of the scriptures that were being read to us were, in fact, stories of things that happened long, long ago. Attending catechism class on Monday nights expanded my knowledge of the Bible, and after many years, I finally had a pretty good grasp of its basics.

What pleases me most about writing this book is my creating something for children who are in the same boat I once was in. This book will allow parents and children to read famous stories from the Bible together in an easy-to-understand form.

I owe thanks to many for their inspiration to write this book, especially my grandmother who took me to church every Sunday, the priests of the various churches I used to attend, and the teachers of several courses and lectures I have taken over the years. Above everything, the Bible itself deserves a big thanks. It seems every time I open its pages, I find something new. In fact, gathering the words for the pages of this book has taught me more than I ever thought possible. Enjoy!

Michael A. Pagdos

EDITORIAL
Publishing Director: Gary M. Krebs
Managing Editor: Kate McBride
Copy Chief: Laura MacLaughlin
Acquisitions Editor: Bethany Brown
Production Editor: Khrysti Nazzaro

PRODUCTION
Production Director: Susan Beale
Production Manager: Michelle Roy Kelly
Cover Design: Paul Beatrice and Frank Rivera
Layout and Graphics: Colleen Cunningham,
Rachael Eiben, Michelle Roy Kelly,
Daria Perreault, Erin Ring

An Everything® Series Book.
Everything® and everything.com® are registered trademarks of F+W Publications, Inc.

Published by Adams Media, an F+W Publications Company
57 Littlefield Street, Avon, MA 02322 U.S.A.
www.adamsmedia.com

ISBN: 1-58062-547-9
Printed in the United States of America.

J I H G F E D C B

Library of Congress Cataloging-in-Publication Data
Paydos, Michael.
The everything Bible stories book / Michael Paydos.
p.   cm. --   (An everything series book)
ISBN 1-58062-547-9
1. Bible stories, English. I. Title. II. Everything series.
BS550.3 .P39 2002
220.9'505--dc21
2002010015

This publication is designed to provide accurate and authoritative information with regard to the subject matter covered. It is sold with the understanding that the publisher is not engaged in rendering legal, accounting, or other professional advice. If legal advice or other expert assistance is required, the services of a competent professional person should be sought.

—From a *Declaration of Principles* jointly adopted by a Committee of the
American Bar Association and a Committee of Publishers and Associations

Illustrations by Kurt Dolber and Barry Littmann.

This book is available at quantity discounts for bulk purchases.
For information, call 1-800-872-5627.

Visit the entire Everything® series at everything.com

THE

EVERYTHING®

BIBLE STORIES BOOK

Timeless favorites from the
Old and New Testaments

Michael Paydos

Adams Media Corporation
Avon, Massachusetts

Contents

PART I The Old Testament......1

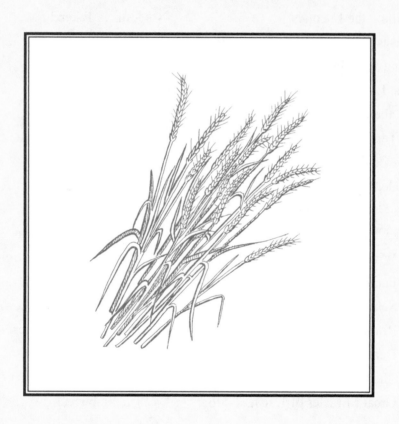

Introduction

THE CHRISTIAN BIBLE as we know it is actually a collection of sixty-six books divided in two parts. The first part, known as The Old Testament, contains thirty-nine books, which are the scriptures of the Jewish faith. The New Testament's twenty-seven books lay the foundation for Christianity. The entire Bible was written over a period of over 1,500 years, beginning about 3,500 years ago.

The first five books of the Old Testament—Genesis, Exodus, Leviticus, Numbers, and Deuteronomy—are known as the Torah to Jewish people. Torah means "teaching." Christians often refer to these same five books as the Pentateuch, which is a Greek word meaning "five books."

Since the invention of the printing press, almost as many Bibles have been printed as there are people! The Bible is the most printed book ever written. It is also the most translated book ever written with versions in 2,200 different languages, including dozens of English translations. The main differences among these versions is the style of language they use. I have used the New International Version (often abbreviated NIV) as a source for this book.

The Bible has perhaps had more influence over the history of the world than any other written text. Whether you view the Bible as a collection of folk

tales or the Word of God, you need to know something about its content to truly understand our society today.

This collection of stories brings to life some of the events, people, and adventures in the Bible. I have simplified the language and provided explanations and definitions where they are needed. But I have added nothing new or invented, other than some descriptions that do not alter the meaning of the text.

Each story is intended to stand alone, and almost every one of them can be read in less than five minutes. Reading these stories together is an ideal bedtime activity for parents and children. The chapters and verses the stories come from are also included in case you want to read the Bible version of the story. Parents and children alike should be able to enjoy these stories together. 📖

The Old Testament

Genesis	2 Chronicles	Daniel
Exodus	Ezra	Hosea
Leviticus	Nehemiah	Joel
Numbers	Esther	Amos
Deuteronomy	Job	Obadiah
Joshua	Psalms	Jonah
Judges	Proverbs	Micah
Ruth	Ecclesiastes	Nahum
1 Samuel	Song of Songs	Habakkuk
2 Samuel	Isaiah	Zephaniah
1 Kings	Jeremiah	Haggai
2 Kings	Lamentations	Zechariah
1 Chronicles	Ezekiel	Malachi

1. The Beginning
Genesis 1–2

n the beginning, God created the earth and the heavens, but they were without form. They had no shape, nothing to separate one from the other, and it was very dark. God's spirit floated above it all.

Then God said, "Let there be light!" A great big light appeared, causing the darkness to disappear. When God made light, he saw that it was good and separated it from the darkness. He called the light "day" and the dark "night." Then darkness came again, the first night. After that the light came back again. It was the first morning. It was the first day.

Everything was still shapeless, all mixed together so that you couldn't tell the difference among things. "Let there be a space above the waters, to separate things," God said on the next morning. The sky formed around the world. The world was a great big ocean, with a blue sky full of clouds above it. Then night came again, the second day ended.

God collected the waters together. "Let the waters under the sky be formed together," he said, "and let dry ground rise between them. Let plants and trees grow out of the land." The oceans separated as the continents and islands rose in-between them. In the dry ground God planted all sorts of plants and trees. They started to grow and made seeds that would sprout into more plants and trees. The world became green and full of life. That was the third day.

The next day God said, "Let there be lights in the sky to separate the night from the day, and to show the different seasons." The light that God had already created was gathered and

2

made first into two big lights: the sun and the moon. The sun was the brighter light, and was made to watch over the day. All the other little lights in the night sky were also made—the stars, comets, and other things far away that twinkle in the night sky. Because of this we know when it is day, and when it is night. The sun set and the moon rose for the first time, marking the end of the fourth day.

"Let the oceans be filled with living things and let birds fly in the skies above the earth," God said on the next morning. Birds appeared and flew high in the sky. Fish and all the other sea creatures filled up the ocean. God made the trees and other plants bear fruit for the birds to eat. God blessed all the creatures he made and told them to spread out around the earth and multiply. The sun set and night came. That was the fifth day.

"Let living creatures walk on the land," he said. And with that God made all the animals that walk on the earth, including squirrels, monkeys, bears, cows, dogs, and all sorts of bugs. God also created humans.

God wanted humans to be special, so he said, "Let us make humans in My image and they will watch over the earth and all the plants and animals living on it." God formed the shape of a man out of the dust on the ground and breathed life into his nostrils. God made humans in his image to watch over the world for him. God blessed all he created that day and sent them out into the world to multiply. Soon the world was filled with every sort of living creature. Then evening came and the day ended. That was the sixth day.

On the seventh day God looked at everything he had made. He saw that it was all very good and he was happy. This was the seventh day. On the seventh day God rested. This is why on Sundays we take the day off in honor of all that God did in the beginning of the world.

2. Adam and Eve in the Garden of Eden

Genesis 2

n addition to wildlife and wonderful creatures God also made a very special place. Around a big river he created a spectacular garden, full of beautiful trees that had all kinds of delicious fruits. It was called the Garden of Eden.

In the middle of the garden were two special trees. These were the tree of life and the tree of knowledge. Anyone who ate from the tree of life would live forever, and anyone who ate from the tree of knowledge would know about the difference between good and evil, and right and wrong.

God named the man "Adam," which means "the man" in Hebrew. He put the man, his favorite creation, in the garden. Adam was put in charge of taking care of it. When God put him in the garden, he told Adam, "You can eat fruit from any of the trees in the garden, except for the Tree of Knowledge. If you eat from that tree, you will die."

"It is not good for Adam to be alone," God said one day. "I will make a partner for him." He rounded up all the animals, and brought them to Adam one by one. As Adam saw each animal he gave it a name. Adam named all of the animals, but none of them was the perfect match for him. God decided to create the perfect companion for Adam. He put Adam in a deep, deep sleep. God took out one of Adam's ribs, and formed it into the shape of another person. Except this person was a little bit different, she was the first woman!

When Adam woke up, he was so happy to see his new companion! He named her Eve because she was to become the mother of all humankind. "Eve" means "the giver of life" in Hebrew. Adam and Eve became complete as husband and wife.

3. Adam and Eve's Sin

Genesis 3

dam and Eve were very happy in the Garden of Eden. They took care of the land, tended the trees, and always had plenty of food to eat. They ate from many of the trees in the garden, except for the fruit from the Tree of Knowledge, which grew in the center of the garden. God had forbidden them to eat from that tree, and they did as they were told.

Of all the animals God had created, the serpent was the most clever and devious. He was jealous of Adam and Eve because they were God's favorite among his creations. One day, the serpent asked Eve, "Did God really order you not to eat any of the fruit in the garden?"

"Oh no!" replied Eve. "We can eat the fruit from any tree in the Garden, except for the fruit from the tree in the center of the garden."

"Why not?" asked the serpent.

"God said if we ate the fruit from the Tree of Knowledge we would die."

"You definitely would not die," said the serpent. "God is trying to trick you because he knows that if you eat the fruit from that tree you will gain the knowledge to know the difference between good and evil. If you know that, you will be just like God."

Eve looked at the tree. On its branches were the most beautiful, most delicious looking apples in all of the Garden of Eden. With the serpent goading her on, she took an apple and ate some of it. Adam was with Eve while this was happening. He took the apple and ate some of it as well.

When Adam and Eve ate the fruit, they suddenly felt more aware of everything around them. They realized that they were both naked so they took a bunch of leaves from a nearby tree and stitched them together to cover themselves.

As they did this they saw God coming near. Feeling ashamed, Adam and Eve hid in the bushes so God wouldn't see them. Of course, God knew where they were and called out, "Adam, where are you?"

"I saw you coming so I hid because I was naked," Adam answered.

"How did you know you were naked? Did you eat the forbidden fruit from the Tree of Knowledge?"

"The woman you put here with me gave me some of the fruit. So I ate it." God turned to Eve and asked, "Is this true?"

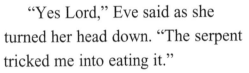

"Yes Lord," Eve said as she turned her head down. "The serpent tricked me into eating it."

God was very upset. He had given his most loved creation the most beautiful place on earth to live. The only rule he had made was for them not to eat from that one tree. The rule was made to protect Adam and Eve from the difficult knowledge they would obtain. Also, by obeying God's law, Adam and Eve were showing their love and appreciation for all he did for them.

God first turned his attention on the serpent. As punishment he cursed it so that it would have to

crawl on its belly to move around. Then he turned to Adam and Eve. He told them that from then on they, and all their children and grandchildren, would have to work hard for their livings. They would be forced to grow their own food on bad land that would make mostly weeds. God also made clothes out of animal skins for them to wear.

What the serpent said to Eve wasn't a complete lie. After Adam and Eve ate the fruit from the Tree of Knowledge, they did gain the ability to understand the difference between good and evil.

God banished Adam and Eve from the Garden of Eden. No human being would ever be allowed to enter it again. To make sure nobody ever got near the Tree of Life again, God left an angel with a giant flaming sword at the garden's gateway as a guard.

4. Cain and Abel
Genesis 4

od banished Adam and Eve from the Garden of Eden because they disobeyed his command not to eat from the Tree of Knowledge. They were forced to live on their own out in the world. But God did not abandon them. He watched over them always. After some time, Eve gave birth to a baby boy. She and Adam named their first child Cain. Not too long after Cain was born, Eve had another baby, and they named him Abel. Adam and Eve were very happy with their children and thanked God for his gift.

As Cain and Abel grew older they started to help their parents. Cain worked in a field, growing vegetables. Abel tended a flock of sheep.

One day Cain took some of the vegetables he grew and set them on an altar as an offering to God. Abel also made an offering of the best lamb in his flock. God was pleased with the sacrifice Abel had made and accepted it. A warm light shone down on Abel and his offering from heaven. Cain's offering was ignored. A sacrifice is meant to be meaningful, and in Cain's case, he simply offered a few of his extra crops that he could spare.

Cain was very angry and jealous when he saw that God liked Abel's offering and not his own. Cain clenched his hands and hung down his head.

"Why are you so angry, Cain?" God asked him. "If you do what is right, you will be rewarded. But if you let anger and thoughts of sin creep into your thoughts, you will be taken over by them."

9

Later, Cain went up to his brother and said, "Let's go out to the fields, I want to show you something." When the brothers were out in the fields, Cain attacked and killed Abel. Once he had done it, Cain got very scared and ran off to hide.

Suddenly, God appeared beside Cain. "Where is your brother Abel?" he asked.

"How should I know?" replied Cain, his voice shaking a little. "I am not my brother's keeper."

"What have you done? I can hear your brother's spirit crying out to me. From this day on, you will be cursed! You are forever doomed to wander around the earth. Whenever you plant crops, they will not grow. You will have to search among the wild plants and eat the bitter roots from the ground in order to survive."

"Why don't you just kill me?" answered Cain. "The first person who finds me will surely kill me anyway."

God placed a mark on Cain that would protect him. Anyone who tried to harm Cain would receive a punishment from God seven times worse than Cain's. After that Cain left God's presence, and his parents, and headed to a place called Nod.

Adam and Eve were very sad after that for a long time. Until one day Eve had another son. They were very happy to have a son because they missed Abel very much. They named the new baby Seth.

Cain went on to live in Nod and eventually married and had children of his own. Both Cain and Seth had children, who had children, and so on, until the world began to become full of people.

5. Noah's Ark
Genesis 5–7

Many years had passed since God created the heavens and the earth. Adam and Eve's grandchildren spread out throughout the world. People became terribly mean though. War, lying, cheating, and wickedness became common. The world had become a bad place.

In those days, people sometimes lived for a thousand years! The longer people were alive, the more evil they could do. God said, "My spirit will not put up with these wicked people for so long, I will make their lives shorter."

The world was still full of powerful and terrible people. God saw how much people loved to be wicked and evil, and he became sad. He said to himself, "I will wipe out all people from the earth, along with all the animals—everything that walks on dry land."

There was one man on earth who was good and kind. Noah was very hard working and led an honest life. Noah was a man who pleased God, and always tried to do what was right. Noah had three sons. They were named Shem, Ham, and Japheth.

God told Noah, "I am going to destroy everything that walks on dry ground. It is because of them that the earth is filled with violence. I am going to bring a great flood to the earth that will destroy every living creature on the land."

But God made a promise with Noah. God told Noah, "I will save you, your three sons, and all of your wives. You must build an enormous ark out of cypress wood. The cypress tree was very common in Noah's land. It is a kind of pine tree. Cypress was the best wood for making a boat, because it is strong and light.

"When you have finished building the ark," God said to Noah, "I want you to take into it every kind of creature, to keep them alive with you. Take two of every wild animal that walks on the land, every bird, and every creature that creeps along the ground. You must also take along food enough for you and all of the animals." Noah was not sure how he could do all that God asked, but he had faith in God and began working.

Noah and his sons neglected their crops and businesses, and focused all of their energy on building the ark, as God commanded. The people of their village ridiculed them, but they paid no attention.

When they were done building the ark the Lord spoke to Noah. "Go into the ark with your family," the Lord said, "because I have found you righteous and worthy among all humankind. Take along with you seven pairs of every kind of clean animal, both a male and female." A clean animal means one that is good for people to eat. Noah had earlier been told to bring a pair of every wild animal as well. "In seven days it will rain for forty days and forty nights, and the earth will become flooded."

Noah and his family did as the Lord told them. They put on the ark pairs of every kind of animal in the world. From elephants to mice to little insects, every creature that lived on the land went on board the ark. Two of every bird also flew into the ark. Once every animal was on board the ark, all the food was safely stored away, and Noah and his family were safely inside, God closed the door to the ark.

After the seven days had passed, it began to rain.

6. The Great Flood
Genesis 7–9

he rain continued for forty days and forty nights. God also opened up great big springs in the ground. Water gushed from the springs and added to the water from the rain. The oceans rose higher and everything was covered with water. At first it was shallow and the ark remained resting on the ground. The wicked people who had laughed at Noah and his family were now knee deep in water and very nervous and scared. God protected Noah and kept everyone away from the ark. The flood waters rose quickly, and soon the ark was floating. By the fortieth day even the tallest mountains on earth were under water!

Every creature that had lived on the land and breathed the air died. All had died except Noah, his family, and all the creatures that were on the ark. The world remained flooded for 150 days.

But God did not forget about Noah and all those living on the ark. He sent a warm wind to blow over the water. He closed the springs that gushed water deep in the oceans. God stopped all the rain. Slowly, the waters began to recede or go down. The deep water went down steadily until the seventeenth day of the seventh month, when the ark hit dry ground! The ark settled on a mountain peak named Ararat. The rest of world was still covered in water, however.

The waters continued to recede for forty more days. On the fortieth day the peaks of some other mountains began to appear.

Noah waited forty more days. On the fortieth day he opened a window of the ark and let out a raven. The big black bird flew out but had to come back because there was no dry land or food for it. Next, Noah let a dove out the window. The dove flew out but returned later that day because it could not find a good place to land either.

Noah waited seven more days. After the seven days he let the same dove out the window. That evening the dove returned with a freshly picked twig from an olive tree! When Noah saw the little leaf on the twig he knew that the world was becoming green again, and that the waters were receding. Seven days later Noah let the same dove out again. This time, it didn't come back.

Noah then removed the roof of the ark. When he did this he and his family saw that there was no longer water covering all the ground. Everything was still a bit soggy and muddy. However, as the warm dry winds God had sent continued to blow, the ground was soon completely dry.

God then said, "Noah, take your family and all of the creatures out of the ark. Come back out on to the cleansed earth and spread out."

Noah obeyed. He and his family came out of the ark. He opened the door to the ark and let out all of the creatures that had spent such a long a time in it.

The first thing Noah did when he was on dry ground was build an altar. On the altar he made a sacrifice to God, thanking him for saving their lives. God was pleased with Noah and promised that he would never again curse the earth or destroy all living creatures. God said to Noah, "As long as the earth exists, the seasons of the year will always come to pass, and the day and the night will always exist."

God then blessed Noah and his family. He told them to have many children to fill the earth with people once again. God also told them that no human being should harm anyone else. He said, "Whoever sheds the blood of another person will be punished by his or her people." God was telling people to protect one another from those who might do harm.

Noah and his family then saw a beautiful rainbow arch across the sky. God created it as a symbol of his promise to all living creatures that he would never again destroy the earth.

7. The Tower of Babel

Genesis 10–11

After the great flood, Noah's three sons, along with their wives, went out into the world and began new lives of their own. They all had many children and soon each brother had started a kingdom of his own. Soon more children were born and people continued to spread out. Because everyone was part of a great big family, they all got along really well. There were no wars, and everyone spoke the same language, so it was really easy for people from one area to go and talk with anyone else in the world.

Because the whole world had only one language, people cooperated and lived together in peace. Everyone worked together.

People continued to spread out and settle in new places as they had more and more children. One year, a group settled on a large green plain in a land called Shinar. One hundred years had passed since the great flood.

People were divided up into smaller groups called tribes. When the tribe leaders settling into Shinar got together, they realized that their tribes were spreading far apart, and soon it could become difficult for them to find each other.

The tribal leaders came up with a plan. They decided that they would build a great big city in the field with an immense tower in the center. The tower would be so tall it would reach up high into the sky, where it could be seen from miles around. One of the leaders spoke to all the people who had settled near the field and said, "Come, let us build a great city, with a tower reaching up to the heavens so we can make a name for ourselves and not be scattered all over the world."

Working together, they made very strong bricks by mixing a certain kind of mud with straw and shaping them into blocks. Then the people baked the blocks until they got very hard and very strong. They used tar to stick the bricks together.

God looked down at the people building the city and the tall tower in the center. He saw that with one language, humans were able to accomplish anything they set their minds to, and did not need to look up to God for guidance. So God came down to the city and made it so that each tribe of people spoke a different language. When the tribes could not speak to each other it became impossible for them to work together. Eventually each tribe wandered away from each other.

The tower became known as the Tower of Babel. Babel or "babble" is the word used to describe someone who is speaking in a way that we can't understand.

The Lord scattered the people all over the earth, as he originally wanted everyone to do. The city was never completed, and the tower was never finished.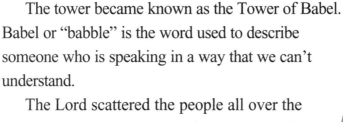

8. Abram's Journey
Genesis 11–13

ne of Noah's sons was named Shem. Two years after the flood, Shem left with his wife to start a life with his family. His children got married and had children of their own. Those children also got married when they grew up and had children as well. The family continued to grow for many generations until it had become very big and successful.

In the family was a man named Abram who married Sarai. Abram's brother had died, so he helped take care of his brother's son Lot. Sarai was unable to have children, so she and Abram did not have any of their own.

One day, as Abram was walking about on his own, God spoke to him. "Abram," he said, "you must take your wife, your servants, and all your things and leave this place. I will make you a great nation and you will be blessed."

So Abram left as God told him to. He took Sarai, his servants, and all his animals and things with him. His nephew, Lot, went with him. Many others who lived nearby also went with Abram, believing it was God's will.

Abram and his group traveled very far from the lands of their ancestors. After traveling a long time they came to the land of Canaan. While he was resting, the Lord appeared to Abram and said, "I will give this land to your children and your children's children."

After some time, a famine struck the land. A famine occurs when the food crops don't grow, usually because it doesn't rain or some kind of pest is destroying all the crops. Abram and Sarai went to Egypt. Egypt was a very powerful nation then and was more prepared for the famine than anyone else.

"You are so beautiful," Abram said to his wife, "I am afraid that once the Egyptians see you they will kill me and take you away. Tell them you are my sister so they will let us both live."

Sarai agreed. She loved Abram and was afraid of the Egyptians. When Abram and Sarai entered Egypt everyone saw how wonderfully beautiful Sarai was. Some of the palace guards went to the Pharaoh and told him about her. A pharaoh was what the king of Egypt was called. The Pharaoh invited Abram and Sarai into his palace. The Pharaoh was very nice to Abram and gave him lots of gifts, because the Pharaoh thought Abram was Sarai's brother. The Pharaoh took Sarai in as a wife.

A little while later, the Pharaoh got very, very ill. God was angry with what was happening in Egypt. The Pharaoh summoned Abram and asked him who he was, and why had the illness come. Abram told the Pharaoh the truth.

The Pharaoh was very angry. "Why didn't you tell me she was your wife?" he asked Abram. "Why did you say she was your sister? All of you, gather your belongings and leave Egypt!" The Pharaoh wanted to punish Abram, but was afraid of what might happen. Soon after, the Pharaoh began to get better.

From Egypt, Abram, Sarai, Lot, and the others in their group went back to where the Lord had appeared to him—the place where Abram had built the altar. So Abram, Sarai, their servants and flocks all settled on that land. Lot and his servants and flocks also settled there.

Lot and Abram were both very successful, and their flocks grew large. The only problem was the land that they settled on was too small to have enough grass for the sheep and cattle of both men's flocks to eat. Soon, the herdsmen of both Lot and Abram began fighting over the best places to let their animals graze.

Abram saw what was going on and realized there was a problem. One day he went up to Lot with an idea.

"We should not be fighting among ourselves. We are family," Abram said to Lot. "Here is my offer: you choose a place to settle, and I shall pick a different place in another direction."

Lot looked about and saw the plains of Jordan to the north. This area was full of rivers and streams and trees. The land was very green and lush. It was how Lot imagined the Garden of Eden must have looked. Lot went to his servants and told them to gather the flocks and all of their belongings. They then all moved out to the lush plains.

After Lot had left, God spoke to Abram, "Look out to the east, to the south, and to the west," he said. "All this land I will give to you and your children for all time. Your family will grow and be many." Abram moved his people with him to a place called Hebron, in the forest of Mamre. This forest was full of big, ancient oak trees.

God rewarded Abram for being generous to Lot. Because of Abram's generosity and good will, he was given a much larger area of land in which to live.

9. God's Promise to Abram

Genesis 15

bram, Sarai, and their servants lived by the forest of Mamre for many years. They had large herds of cattle and flocks of sheep, and they lived happily. The only thing that kept everything from being perfect was the fact that Sarai and Abram did not have any children. In those days, children were considered a special gift from God, so any husband and wife that did not have children was very sad.

One day, while Abram was in his tent the Lord appeared before him. Abram and his people lived in tents because they constantly had to move from place to place. They moved to a new place when the animals had eaten all the fresh grass where they were. The tents were very big and comfortable, and easy to move from place to place. When Abram saw the Lord he immediately knelt down on the ground.

"Do not be afraid," the Lord said. "I am your protector, and your righteousness will give you a great reward." A person who is righteous is someone who is very good to others and always obeys the Lord.

After God had spoken, Abram replied, "O Lord, what good will any of your wonderful gifts do me since I have no children to leave my wealth to? Right now, Eliezer, my servant, will be the heir of everything I own when I die."

"You will have your very own son and he will be your heir. Remember, I am your Lord, the one who brought you here and gave you everything you have."

The Lord then took Abram outside and said, "Look up at the night sky and try to count all of the stars." It was a very clear night and billions of stars twinkled all across the sky in every direction. "If you could count all of the stars, then you would know the number of offspring that you will have." God was telling Abram that he was going to have a very large family.

Abram believed everything the Lord had said to him, and he was very happy. He woke up the next day and told his wife and servants the news. He spent the day praying to the Lord, thanking him for the gift he was about to receive. Abram also made a very large sacrifice. A sacrifice was a way for people to show their love for God by giving up something valuable.

That evening, Abram fell into a very deep sleep. He had horrible dreams. He saw nothing but darkness all around him and he suddenly felt very afraid and very sad. At that point in his dream, he heard the voice of God. "You must know, Abram," the Lord said, "that you and your people will always be strangers in a strange country that is not your own. Your people will become slaves and will be unhappy for many, many years. However, in the end they will be free. After that, your people will be very prosperous. You, however, will not be a slave. You will live out the rest of your life in peace and will not die until a ripe old age."

Abram woke up and went outside of his tent. The sky was very dark until an enormous ball of fire streaked across the sky. The light was a symbol of God's promise to Abram. As the light streaked across the sky, Abram heard the voice of God say, "All this land around you will belong to your people one day."

10. Abram, Sarai, and Hagar
Genesis 16 –17

any years had passed after God made his promise to Abram, yet Sarai still had no children. She was very sad and realized that she was much too old to have children. Then Sarai got an idea.

Sarai had a servant named Hagar. Hagar was a young Egyptian girl who did work for Sarai. Sarai decided that her husband, Abram, should have a child with Hagar and then Sarai and he could raise the baby as their own.

Abram did as Sarai suggested and soon Hagar became pregnant. Once Hagar realized she was going to have Abram's child, she began to think she was very important, even more important than Sarai. Hagar began insulting Sarai and behaving as if Sarai were her servant, and not the other way around.

Sarai became very angry and distressed. She wasn't sure what to do because Hagar was going to have Abram's baby. Sarai was afraid Abram might side with Hagar. So she went to Abram and told him how Hagar was behaving and how it upset her so much. Abram still loved Sarai and simply replied to her, "You are my wife, do with your servant whatever you think is best."

Sarai was then very mean to Hagar. She yelled at her constantly and forced her to work very hard almost nonstop. Hagar became so miserable and afraid that she ran away into the desert. As Hagar wandered along a road in the desert she came upon a spring. Hagar sat beside the spring and began to cry.

Just then an angel came to the spring and found Hagar there, crying. "What are you doing here?" he asked her.

"I am running away from my mistress, Sarai. She was very cruel to me and I am afraid to go back," Hagar replied.

"Go back to your mistress and obey her as you did before," the angel told Hagar. "You will soon give birth to a son whom you will name Ishmael. His descendents will number in the millions and become a great nation."

So Hagar returned to Sarai and did as the angel had told her. Soon after returning, Hagar gave birth to a boy. Abram, who was eighty-six-years old at the time, looked at his new son and named him Ishmael.

Many years later God appeared to Abram again. "You will be the father of many nations," he said. "From now on, your name shall be Abraham." God also said, "As for Sarai, she will become the mother of many nations. So, from now on she must be called Sarah. I will bless her and she will become the mother of your son, whom you shall name Isaac."

Abraham laughed to himself. He said, "Will a one-hundred-year old man and a woman who is ninety have a son?"

"Yes, Sarah shall have a son who shall be the fulfillment of my promise to you. It will be through him that the nation of my people will spring forth."

"But what of Ishmael?" asked Abraham. "If only he could be blessed."

"I will bless him. His family will become a great nation. But my promise to you as the father of my people, I will keep through your son Isaac."

11. The Three Visitors Announce the Birth of Isaac

Genesis 18–21

t was a hot day. Abraham sat by the entrance of his tent. The great trees of Mamre surrounded his tent and gave Abraham a little shade. The day was very quiet and a gentle breeze caused the leaves of the trees to flutter just a little bit.

Abraham looked up and saw three strangers standing nearby. Abraham immediately recognized them as the Lord and his companions and rushed out to them. He bowed down to the ground and said, "My lords, if I have found any favor in your eyes, please stay with me a while and rest. I can bring you water to drink, and more to wash your feet, and some food for you to eat." The three strangers were all wearing sandals and the day was hot and dusty so washing their feet with cool clean water would be very pleasant.

"Very well," they answered. "We shall do as you offer."

Abraham hurried into his tent to his wife, Sarah, and said, "Quick, take three cups of flour and make some bread."

Then he ran out to one of his servants. "Go out to the field and find the finest calf," Abraham said to the servant, "and then prepare it for my guests." Abraham also got some curds and milk for his three visitors.

Soon, a very nice feast was prepared and Abraham set it out before the three men. He stood by them under a tree.

"Where is your wife Sarah?" the Lord asked him.

"Over there in the tent," Abraham answered.

Then the Lord said, "I will return here in about a year. By that time you and Sarah will have your very own son."

Sarah heard what the visitors said through the tent's entrance, which was open. Abraham and Sarah were very old, and Sarah was well past the age of having children. She laughed to herself and softly said, "After all these years, and with me and my husband so old, will we now really have the joy of our own child?"

Then the Lord said to Abraham, "Why does Sarah laugh and say, 'After all these years, and with me and my husband so old, will we now really have the joy of our own child?' Is anything impossible for the Lord to do? I will return in a year and Sarah will have a son."

Sarah was afraid, so she came out of the tent and went to the Lord. "I did not laugh," she lied.

But the Lord replied, "Yes, you did laugh."

So, just as God had said, Sarah had a son. Abraham was over one hundred years old when the boy was born. They named him Isaac as the Lord had instructed. Isaac comes from the word "laugh." Both Abraham and Sarah were so happy they threw an enormous feast as a celebration.

"Who would have guessed that I could have given birth at my age," Sarah laughed. "God has given me joy and laughter and everyone should rejoice with me!"

After just a couple years, Sarah noticed that Ishmael, Abraham's older son who he had with Hagar, was teasing Isaac. Sarah got very angry. "Ishmael must leave!" she told Abraham. "You must send him and his mother away from here!"

Abraham was very distressed. He was sad because he loved both of his sons very much. Not only would he miss Ishmael if he left, but also he was worried about how well Hagar and Ishmael could do out in the world by themselves. Being out alone in the desert was very dangerous and most people could not survive without a big family around them with everyone working together. As Abraham was struggling with his decision, he heard the voice of God in his head. God reassured Abraham and told him, "Do not worry about Ishmael, I will take care of him and his mother. Do as Sarah asks, because I am protecting both of your sons. They will both live to have very large families that will become great nations."

So, early the next day, Abraham gave Hagar and Ishmael food and a large leather skin full of water. He sent them off and assured them that God would be with them and protect them. He was very sad to see his older son leave, but took comfort knowing that God had big plans for Ishmael's future.

Hagar and Ishmael wandered for many days through the desert. It was a harsh, dry area. They climbed over the large rocks that were everywhere. The grass and trees were very dry. The desert had no food growing that they could eat. Soon Hagar and Ishmael had eaten all their food and drunk all their water. They couldn't find any water or food. Hagar sat off by herself and cried, because she thought she and her son were about to die.

Then Hagar heard the voice of an angel. "Do not fear," said the angel. "God will not let either of you die." Hagar looked up and saw a spring flow up from the ground. She filled up the leather skin with water and took some to Ishmael to drink. He was very weak but able to drink and quickly felt better.

Hagar and Ishmael lived in the desert for many years. Ishmael grew up strong and became a very good hunter. When he was old enough he married a woman from Egypt and then began his great life that God had foretold.

12. The Testing of Abraham
Genesis 22

braham, Sarah, and Isaac lived very happily for a few years. Abraham loved Isaac dearly and was raising him as best he could. Abraham did everything he could for his son.

While Isaac was still a young boy of five or six, God appeared before Abraham. "Abraham," the Lord said, "you must take your son, the one you love so much, and take him to Moriah. There I will show you a mountain you both must climb. When you are on the mountain, instead of a lamb, you must sacrifice your son to me."

Obeying the Lord, Abraham took his son, a couple servants, and a donkey and left for Moriah the next morning. The land they went across was dry and flat and very dusty. They traveled for three days before Abraham spied the mountains in the distance. Abraham was very sad because of what he had to

do, but God had provided him with so many blessings that Abraham was willing to obey any command.

"Stay here with the donkey," Abraham told his servants once they had arrived at the mountain. "Isaac and I shall climb the mountain to pray and make an offering." Abraham tied to wood in a bundle and slung it over his back. He also took a knife and a torch with him, so he could perform the sacrifice.

"Father," Isaac said as they were climbing, "we have wood for the fire, but how will we make a sacrifice? We have no lamb."

"God will provide," Abraham replied.

When Abraham and Isaac reached the place God had chosen on the mountain, Abraham built an altar. He placed the wood on the altar and put Isaac on top of the pile of wood. He reached for a knife and was prepared to do God's will when suddenly he heard a voice.

"Stop, Abraham! Do not harm your son," cried out an angel. "You have proven your love and devotion to God, because you were willing to give up even the one thing on earth that matters most to you—your son."

Abraham untied his son and was overjoyed. He looked off in the distance and saw a ram—a wild goat—with its horns caught in a bush. Abraham took the ram and sacrificed it on the altar instead.

The angel then said, "Because you were willing to obey God's will, you and your son and all your descendants will be blessed! Your family will grow to such a size that no one will be able to count you all. Your people will grow in number and take the cities of your enemies and become great nations. All because you obeyed the Lord."

After that, Abraham and Isaac climbed down the mountain, hand in hand. They met up with their two servants with the donkey, and headed back home. ✎

13. Finding a Wife for Isaac
Genesis 24

any years passed after God had tested Abraham. Isaac grew up to be a strong man. Sarah and Abraham were happy growing old together and watching their son grow up.

When Sarah was one hundred and twenty-seven years old, she passed away. Abraham realized that he was not going to be alive for very much longer. He was even older than Sarah.

Abraham and Isaac were living in the land of Canaan. The Canaanites were good people, but Abraham wanted his son to marry a woman from the country where he had many relatives. Abraham sent for his most trusted servant and said to him, "I am old and will soon be dead. You must swear to God that you will find a wife for my son from the land where I was born."

"What if I go there and find a woman, but she is unwilling to come back with me?" asked the servant. "Should I then take Isaac back to the country where you were born?"

"No," said Abraham. "Make sure that you do not take Isaac to the country of my birth. I have a promise from the Lord that this land will belong to my descendants, so this is where Isaac must stay. If you find a woman, but she is unwilling to return with you, then you shall be released from your oath to me."

So the servant set off for the land where Abraham was born, a place called Nahor. He took with him ten large, strong camels that were each carrying lots of treasures.

When the servant came near to the city of Nahor, he sat the ten camels down near the outskirts of the city. They were near the city's common well—a place where everyone in the city could go to get water. It was near sunset and many women were lined up at the well to get water.

Now, camels can go a long time without water, but they still need it to survive. Camels can drink a ton of water in one sitting and then not need it again for some time. It would be a lot of work and bother to get enough water out of the well for all the camels.

The servant knelt down and prayed, "God of my master, please guide me in this decision. The daughters of the townspeople are lining up, waiting for their turn at the well. May the woman Isaac is to marry show herself to me. I will ask each woman, 'May I have a drink of water?' Let the woman who not only offers me water to drink but also says, 'Here, let me get water for your camels as well,' be the chosen wife for Isaac."

Just as the servant finished his prayer, Rebekah walked by with a large red clay jar full of water on her shoulder. She was beautiful. The clay jar was very large and heavy and it was a lot of work for her to carry it all the way back to her home. To put it down would mean she would have to pick the heavy jar up again, meaning a lot more effort for her.

The servant ran up to Rebekah. "Please put down your jar so I may have a drink, I have traveled very far and I am very thirsty," he said.

"You poor man, of course you may have a drink," Rebekah said as she struggled to lower the jar to the ground. "Here, let me get water for your camels as well so they may drink."

When she finished, the servant took out a gold nose-ring and two gold bracelets. Then he asked Rebekah, "Whose daughter are you? Please tell me, is there any room at your house for me and my camels to stay for the night?"

"I am the daughter of Bethuel, Nahor's son," she answered. "We have a large home and plenty of room and food for your camels. And there is a place for you to spend the night."

The servant knelt down and praised God. "I have asked for guidance and you delivered, Lord. I have not only found a perfect wife for Isaac, but she is a member of my master's family," he said aloud. Nahor was Abraham's brother. The servant then gave the gold nose-ring and the gold bracelets to Rebekah and told her to go to her house and tell her family what he had said.

Rebekah returned home. Her brother Laban was there and saw her wearing the gold nose-ring and the gold bracelets. Rebekah told Laban everything that had happened at the well. Laban was amazed and immediately realized that this was the will of the Lord. He quickly ran to the well and found the servant with his camels standing there.

"Friend," exclaimed the man. "Come back with me to my home. We have made a special place for you."

The servant followed Laban to his home. Once there, he gave the camels to the family's servants to care for and then they went inside. Inside, the servant explained everything to Laban and Bethuel, the master of the house. He told them about Abraham's wish for his son to marry someone from his homeland and how he had prayed to God for guidance. The servant also said how if Rebekah did not wish to go, then his oath would no longer hold. The servant asked Laban and Bethuel if he may ask Rebekah to return with him.

"This is the will of the Lord," they both answered. "We have no right to oppose. You have our blessing." Rebekah agreed to go. The servant took out all the treasures he had brought with him and gave them to Bethuel, thanking him joyously.

The next morning Rebekah said goodbye to her family and went with the servant back to Canaan, to her new home and to be with her new husband. When they arrived they saw Isaac praying in the fields. He was still sad that his mother had died.

Rebekah got down from the camel and covered her face with a veil. She and the servant went up to Isaac and the servant explained to Isaac everything that happened.

Soon after, Isaac and Rebekah were married. They lived in the tent that had belonged to Sarah and loved each other very much. Isaac was comforted and felt happy again for the first time since his mother's death.

14. Jacob and Esau's Deal

Genesis 25–28

 ebekah and Isaac were married and lived together very happily. But, like Isaac's parents so long before, they were unable to have any children. One day, Isaac prayed to God for children.

God heard Isaac's prayer and Rebekah became pregnant a short time later. Inside her womb she could feel two babies, and they were kicking and jostling at each other constantly. Rebekah was worried. She prayed to find out what was happening.

The Lord said to her, "Inside you are two nations. You will give birth to two sons, and one will be stronger than the other. And the older will serve the younger."

When Rebekah gave birth, her first son was covered in red hair and was very big. They named him Esau. The second son born was much smaller and was holding on to Esau's heel. They named him Jacob.

Esau grew up to be big and strong. He was a skilled hunter and would often go off on long adventures. Esau was Isaac's favorite son, mainly because Esau would bring back meat from the animals he would kill on his hunting trips. Jacob grew up to be very thoughtful, and stayed home most of the time, helping his mother. Jacob was his mother's favorite son.

Because Esau was born first, he was the legal heir to Isaac's estate. It meant that when Isaac died, Esau would get everything Isaac owned and would be the master of Isaac's land and servants. Another name for this situation is birthright. Because Jacob was born second, he would get nothing. He would be at his brother's mercy.

Jacob was cooking some lentil stew one day when his brother came wandering in from a long hunting adventure. Esau was very tired and hadn't eaten in quite a long time. He was starving! Nearly fainting from his hunger, Esau stumbled towards Jacob and said, "Give me some of your stew! I am starving."

"I will only give you some of my food," replied Jacob, "if you promise me your birthright."

"What good will my birthright do me if I die from starvation?" Esau laughed out bitterly. Esau reached for a bowl of stew but Jacob pulled it away.

"No," he said, "you must swear to the Lord that I may have your birthright."

"I swear! I swear!" shouted Esau desperately. Jacob finally gave his brother some of his food.

Years later, Isaac was nearing death. He was very old and had become completely blind. He called to his favorite son, "Esau, go kill me a deer so I may have one last feast before I bless you." A father's blessing was very important in those times, and would be treated as strongly as a will would be today.

Rebekah overheard Isaac promising his blessing to Esau. She rushed to Jacob. "Quickly! Go kill two goats so I might prepare them. Then take the feast to your father pretending to be Esau and he will bless you in your brother's place."

"But if he touches me," Jacob replied, "he will know I am not Esau and will probably curse me because of my lie."

"Don't worry about that," Rebekah told her son. "Leave it to me."

So Jacob did as his mother told and brought her back two freshly killed goats. When the feast was ready, Rebekah gave Jacob Esau's clothes to wear, and tied goat skins to his neck and hands. Jacob then went to see his dying father.

"Father," Jacob said softly while entering the tent, "here is your final meal."

"You made a kill so quickly? Which son of mine are you?" asked Isaac.

"I am your elder son, Esau," Jacob lied. "God blessed me with a quick kill."

Isaac was suspicious. "Your voice, it sounds like Jacob's. Come near me so I might touch you." Jacob obeyed his father and moved closer. Isaac reached out and felt the goat skins on Jacob's hands and neck, and felt the rough cloth he knew to be Esau's. "These are the hands of Esau." With that, Isaac blessed Jacob, believing he was Esau, and gave him all his wealth and property.

Just as the blessing was finished, Esau returned home with a deer. He prepared the deer and made a nice venison steak for his father. "Here is your meal, Father."

"Who are you?" asked Isaac.

"It is Esau."

"If you are Esau," stuttered Isaac, "then whom did I just bless before God?"

When Esau heard what his father said he cried out angrily. He begged his father to bless him as well so he could inherit all that Isaac owned.

"I will bless you, son. But I cannot give to you what I have already promised your brother before God."

Isaac died shortly after. Esau vowed that he would kill Jacob once the traditional mourning period for his father was over. Esau had told a few people about his plan and Rebekah overheard.

"Your brother is going to kill you," she told Jacob at once, "go to my brother Laban in Haran and stay there until it is safe here. I will send for you once everything is okay."

Jacob did as his mother told him. The trip was long, and Jacob was forced to stop along the way. He decided to spend the night in the wilderness.

He lay down on the ground and rested his head on a rock. While asleep he dreamed of an enormous stairway. The steps started on the ground right in front of him and reached up all the way into heaven. Hundreds of angels, all dressed in white, were climbing up and down the steps. At the top of the steps Jacob could see God.

"I am the Lord," a powerful voice said. "I am the God of Abraham, and the God of your father, Isaac. You and your descendants will be many, and I will give you the land on which you are lying."

When Jacob awoke he realized God had spoken to him! With wonder, Jacob propped up the stone he had rested his head against. It stood up like a small pillar. Jacob poured a portion of his oil on the stone and prayed. He named the place "Bethel," which means "the house of God."

15. Jacob, Rachel, and Leah

Genesis 29–31

After fleeing from his brother's fury, Jacob arrived at a large open field. He saw a large, round rock in the center of the field with three flocks of sheep around it. Jacob watched as several shepherds worked together to roll the rock. Under the rock was a pool of water. It was a hidden well! The sheep immediately began drinking from the well.

Jacob walked up to the shepherds. "May I ask where you all are from?"

"We are from Haran," one of the shepherds responded.

"Do you know Laban?"

"Yes, everyone in Haran knows Laban."

"How is he?" asked Jacob. "Is he well?"

"Yes," the first shepherd answered. "And look, there is his daughter, Rachel, with the sheep."

Jacob saw Rachel and walked up to her. He told her who he was and how he got there. He kissed and hugged her because he was so happy.

Rachel ran back to tell her father that his sister's son was there. Laban remembered running out to meet Isaac's servant so many years ago, and he ran out again just as joyously. Laban welcomed Jacob into his home.

Jacob worked for Laban for a month and refused any pay. "Just because you are family," Laban said to Jacob, "does not mean I should not have to pay you. Tell me what your pay should be."

Laban had two daughters—Leah and Rachel. Rachel was the younger and she was very beautiful and sweet. Leah was the older and had beautiful eyes. But, Jacob had fallen in love with Rachel during the month he had spent there.

"I will work for you for seven years if you will give me Rachel to be my wife," Jacob decided.

Laban agreed. The seven years seemed to fly by. Jacob was so in love with Rachel that he did not care how long he had to spend in order to marry her. When the wedding day came, Laban took his daughter Leah, the older one, and put a dark veil over her face. Jacob married her without realizing it wasn't Rachel!

When the next morning came Jacob woke up and saw Leah sleeping next to him! "What have you done?" Jacob asked as he ran to Laban. "Why have you tricked me? I worked for you for Rachel, didn't I?"

"In my country, the older daughter must be married first," Laban replied. "In one week you may marry Rachel as well, in return for another seven years' work after that."

Jacob agreed to this and married Rachel a week later. Jacob loved Rachel, but did not love Leah. However, over the years Leah had seven sons and one daughter. Rachel had not yet had any children.

"Why won't you give me children?" she asked her husband.

"Am I God?" Jacob replied.

Eventually, Rachel did have a son. She named him Joseph and was very happy. Her sadness disappeared.

After Joseph was born, Jacob went to Laban. "Let me be on my way to my homeland. Let me take my wives and children and be off," he said to his uncle.

Laban replied, "You are blessed by God, and while you have been here I have also been blessed. Please stay, you only need to name your wages."

Jacob thought for a while and then came up with a plan. He told Laban that for as long as he stayed, all the sheep that were born speckled in color would become his. All the other sheep that were a solid color would remain with his father-in-law. Laban agreed to this. The deal was to start the next day.

That night Laban took all of the speckled sheep from his flocks and gave them to his son. He was trying to trick Jacob. He had noticed that only speckled sheep had speckled-colored lambs.

Over the years, Jacob learned to breed the sheep very carefully so that the strongest sheep of Laban's flocks would mate with speckled sheep from his flocks. The weakest sheep in Laban's flocks were allowed to mate with each other. As a result, all the strongest newborn sheep were speckled, and therefore belonged to Jacob. The weakest sheep stayed with Laban. Soon, Jacob had a huge flock of strong, speckled sheep. Jacob became very wealthy.

Laban's sons were jealous of Jacob's success. Laban was becoming angry and irritable. Jacob noticed what was going on and was getting a bit worried about the whole situation. So one day, while Laban and his sons were out shearing sheep, Jacob gathered together his family, his servants, and all his flocks and property. They fled westward toward Jacob's birthplace. He sent messengers to his brother, Esau, to let him know he was on his way home and that he hoped that everything was good between them. Jacob's last memory of his brother, Esau, was when their mother told him that Esau was planning on killing him out of revenge. That was the day Jacob had fled his homeland and ended up at Laban's house.

16. Jacob's Return to Bethel

Genesis 32–35

acob had sent messengers to tell his brother he was arriving. The messengers returned with news that Esau was on his way with a huge army.

"I am afraid he means to attack us," Jacob said. He knelt down and prayed to God to save him. He divided his entire group into two parts, so that if Esau did attack them, at least half would have a chance of escaping. He also took from his flocks and herds several animals to give to his brother as a gift.

As the sun set, Jacob sent all of the people in his group across the Jabbok river. He stayed behind so he could be alone for a while. Then, appearing sud-

denly from the shadows, a man came at Jacob and grabbed him by the shoulders, trying to throw him to the ground. Jacob was able to grab a hold of the stranger as well, and the two men remained locked together like this all night, wrestling to try and overpower each other. Neither one of them made a sound.

As morning came the stranger said to Jacob, "Let go of me. It is almost day-time and I must be off."

"I will not let go of you," replied Jacob, "unless you bless me."

"What is your name?"

"Jacob."

"You are no longer to be called Jacob. You shall now be known as Israel, for you have wrestled with both God and man, and you have overcome all."

The stranger then blessed Jacob and disappeared. Jacob realized that he had been face to face with God.

Jacob crossed the river to be with his family and everyone else in his party. Not too far away he could see a large dust cloud rising. It was Esau and his army. Jacob told everyone to stay where they were. He walked forward to meet his brother face to face. When he approached Esau he bowed to the ground.

Rather than showing any anger, Esau wept with joy and hugged Jacob. "Welcome home, Brother!" The two brothers were together again and were happy. Esau looked behind Jacob at the women and children. "Who are these?" he asked.

"This is the family that the Lord has blessed me with."

"And what about all the animals you have sent me?"

"A gift, Brother," Jacob answered, "as a token of my desire for your acceptance."

Esau then said, "But I already have all I need, and you are certainly welcome here. You should keep what is yours for yourself."

"No, please!" begged Jacob. "Accept my gifts because this is one of the happiest days of my life. Please, accept my gifts because God has been kind to me and has given me all I have ever needed." Esau then accepted the gifts because Jacob was so insistent.

Esau and his army returned home to Bethel. Jacob decided to go to Bethel slowly with his flocks and family. They were all tired from the long journey and to rush would hurt many of the people and animals needlessly.

Eventually Jacob arrived in Bethel. He built an altar to the Lord out of stones and prayed and gave thanks. Jacob and his family continued to move about from place to place always returning to Bethel from time to time. They were now able to stay closer to their homeland, Canaan. Jacob never had to live in fear again, because of his faith in God. 📖

17. The Coat of Many Colors

Genesis 37

acob lived in Canaan with his large family. In all, he had twelve sons. One of the youngest was named Joseph. Joseph was Jacob's favorite son because he was his and his beloved wife Rachel's oldest son.

When Joseph was in his teens he would go out in the fields with his brothers to help take care of the sheep. When they all returned Joseph would tell his father about any misbehaving that his brothers may have done. His brothers hated him for this, and were also jealous of the way their father treated Joseph.

One day Jacob gave Joseph a fantastic coat. It was more colorful than any rainbow, and had long sleeves. It was a symbol that Jacob considered Joseph his true heir, which made his brothers very angry, because they were all older than Joseph and the tradition was that the eldest son would be the heir of the family.

One morning Joseph woke up and immediately rushed to his brothers. He'd had a very strange dream and wanted to share it with them.

"Last night I dreamed that we were working together in the fields. We were harvesting the wheat. We each made a sheaf of wheat. When we put the sheaves down mine stood upright and all of yours bowed down to it."

44

Needless to say, this upset Joseph's brothers. They were already angry enough about the coat. They began talking to one another about Joseph and how much they hated him and wished he wasn't always around.

Joseph's brothers all went out to the fields earlier than usual one day. They also went farther out than they normally would. Jacob woke up and sent Joseph out to go check up on them and make sure everything was okay.

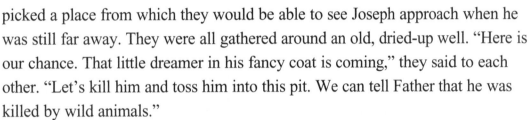

Joseph set out in the direction the servants said the brothers went. The eleven brothers had picked a place from which they would be able to see Joseph approach when he was still far away. They were all gathered around an old, dried-up well. "Here is our chance. That little dreamer in his fancy coat is coming," they said to each other. "Let's kill him and toss him into this pit. We can tell Father that he was killed by wild animals."

"We shouldn't kill him ourselves," said Rueben. He had a kind heart and although he was angry with Joseph, he still loved his brother and knew it would hurt his father a lot if anything were to happen to him. "Instead, let's just throw him into the pit unharmed. Let fate decide his death."

The brothers all thought this made sense and agreed. They didn't know that Rueben was planning on rescuing Joseph later to bring him back to their father.

The brothers all hid near the pit, behind some rocks. When Joseph finally reached them, they attacked him immediately. Once Joseph's brothers got a hold of him, they tore off his coat and threw him into the pit. They then walked away to eat lunch where they wouldn't have to listen to Joseph yelling for help. Reuben went off to tend the sheep while the others ate.

As they were eating, a caravan of Ishmaelites passed by on their way to Egypt. They had many camels loaded with spices and other valuables to sell in Egypt. Judah, one of Joseph's brothers, suggested that they sell Joseph to the caravan to become a slave in Egypt. "Then we would be rid of him forever, and not have to feel guilty about leaving him to die!" he said.

The brothers all thought this was a fantastic idea. They got Joseph out of the pit, tied him up, and gagged him. Then they sold him to the Ishmaelites for twenty pieces of silver.

When Reuben saw that his brother was gone, he realized that the Ishmaelites must have taken him. "Oh no!" he exclaimed. He ran to the rest of his brothers. "Joseph is gone! What should we do?"

They took Joseph's coat and dragged it around on the ground. They also ripped it in a few places. Then they killed a goat and spilled blood all over it.

That evening they returned home. "Father!" Judah said to Jacob. "Look what we found on our way back from the fields! Is Joseph around?" Judah then handed Jacob the coat all bundled up.

When Jacob held up the coat it spread out. Jacob saw the rips and filth and blood all over the coat and was filled with horror. He ripped his shirt and cried. "He must have been attacked and killed by a wild animal."

For days and weeks and months and years, Jacob mourned. No one could comfort him. Jacob loved his son Joseph that much. "I will mourn for my son until the day I die," he said to anyone who tried to comfort him.

18. Joseph the Prisoner
Genesis 39–40

After his brothers sold him to the Ishmaelites, Joseph was taken to Egypt. When they arrived, the Ishmaelites sold Joseph into slavery. A powerful man named Potiphar bought Joseph. Potiphar was the captain of the Pharaoh's guards and one of the Pharaoh's top officials. The Pharaoh was the most powerful person in all of Egypt. A "Pharaoh" was what Egypt had for a king.

God was with Joseph this whole time. Joseph had a lot of faith in the Lord and would pray often and obey the wishes of God as his father had taught him. Joseph did very well as a servant of Potiphar. Everything he did for Potiphar, he excelled at. Joseph always credited God for all his successes.

Potiphar quickly became impressed with Joseph's successes. Joseph was soon made head of the household, a position of high honor among servants. Joseph took care of everything for Potiphar, who now had no worries at all.

Joseph was a very handsome young man, and Potiphar's wife noticed him. One day when Joseph was working alone, she went up to him and said, "Come with me to my room." She was trying to charm him.

Joseph refused. "Your husband, who is my master, has treated me very well. He has put me in charge of everything in this household and has withheld nothing from me, except for you because you are his wife. How could I do such a wicked thing to my master and sin against God?"

She would not take no for an answer and was constantly after Joseph. Joseph refused her every time and would try to avoid her as best he could.

"Would you dare refuse your master's wife?" she asked him one day out of desperation.

"Better to refuse my master's wife than to wrong my master, and, more importantly, to sin against the Lord," answered Joseph.

One day Joseph was attending to his duties. Potiphar's wife had sent all the servants out so she could be alone with Joseph. She cornered him and grabbed him by the sleeve of the coat. But Joseph was quick thinking and clever. In a flash he slipped out of his coat and moved off quickly to work elsewhere.

She was furious! When Potiphar returned home she said to him, "Look at what that Hebrew did! He forced his way into my bedroom and only when I screamed out did he run away, leaving his coat behind." Potiphar immediately had the Pharaoh's guards arrest Joseph and throw him into the prison where all the Pharaoh's prisoners were kept.

While Joseph was in the prison, he continued to excel at any duties that he was given. Soon, the warden of the prison put Joseph in charge of all the prisoners. The warden soon didn't pay any attention to what Joseph did, because Joseph was very trustworthy, always honest, and did his work perfectly.

Because of his position Joseph was able to meet all of the other prisoners. Two of these prisoners had served the Pharaoh as his chief baker and his chief cup bearer. But, the Pharaoh had gotten angry with both of them and had them thrown in the prison as punishment. Joseph became friends with both men.

One night both the cup bearer and the baker had strange dreams. Joseph had already mentioned the strange dreams he had had long ago about his brothers. Both the cup bearer and the baker went to Joseph to tell him about their dreams.

"Joseph, I had this dream that I saw a vine with three large bunches of ripe grapes," the cup bearer told Joseph. "I took the grapes and squeezed the juice out of them into a cup. I then gave this cup to the Pharaoh to drink"

"Your dream means that in three days you will be freed," said Joseph. "The Pharaoh will forgive you and return you to your former position in the palace. Now that I have told you this, please remember me and do me a favor. Please tell the Pharaoh about me and get me out of this prison. I am being kept here for no reason. I committed no crime."

The baker then said, "In my dream, I was carrying three large baskets of bread to the Pharaoh, but then a large flock of birds came down and ate all of it."

"I am very sorry," Joseph said, "but your dream means that in three days you will be hanged."

It happened exactly as Joseph had said. Three days later it was the Pharaoh's birthday. He let his former cup bearer and baker out of the prison. He had the baker hanged. He looked at his former cup bearer and remembered how good a servant he had been before, so he forgave him and gave him his old job back. Unfortunately for Joseph, the cup bearer was so happy that he had his job back that he forgot about his promise to help Joseph. He forgot about Joseph entirely.

19. Joseph Finds the Pharaoh's Favor

Genesis 41

oseph remained in the Pharaoh's prison for another two years after his friend, the cup bearer, had been freed. During those two years, the cup bearer had not thought about Joseph even once.

Then one night, the Pharaoh had a strange dream. He was standing in a field by the great Nile River. Out of the river came seven cows that walked by the Pharaoh one by one and began to graze on the reeds by the river bank. Each of the cows was very big, healthy, and sleek. After the seventh fat cow, seven more cows walked out of the river. These cows were scrawny and ugly. They looked sick and worthless. After these cows walked by the Pharaoh, again one by one, they attacked and ate the seven healthy cows. The Pharaoh then woke up. He felt strange after such a vivid and weird dream, but he decided to forget about it and went about his day.

The next night when the Pharaoh went to sleep he had another dream. There were seven heads of wheat, all on a single stalk. Each of the heads of grain was very plump and healthy. Out of the same stalk, seven more heads of wheat sprouted, but these were thin, dry, and sickly.

Then the seven sickly grains swallowed the healthy ones. The Pharaoh then woke up, startled.

That whole day the Pharaoh was very troubled and his mind kept wandering back to his dreams. He knew they meant something so he called for the palace magicians, wise men, and most trusted advisors. He told them about his dreams, but none of them could figure out what they meant.

Just then, the cup bearer came in with some wine for the Pharaoh. As the Pharaoh took his cup he muttered, "Will no one be able to interpret my dream?"

The cup bearer's jaw dropped open and he fell to his knees. "What have I done? What a fool I have been!" he shouted out. "My lord, two years ago your former chief baker and I were in your prison because we had disobeyed you. One night we both had very strange dreams. There was a Hebrew man in there who interpreted both of our dreams. He said my dream meant I would soon be forgiven by you and have my job back and that the baker would be hanged. He even knew when it would happen. Everything he said turned out to be exactly right!"

The Pharaoh sent for Joseph. The warden gave Joseph clean clothes and a bucket of water so he could wash up. Once Joseph was clean and presentable, he went before the Pharaoh.

"I have had two dreams," the Pharaoh said to Joseph, "but none of my magicians or wise men can interpret them. My cup bearer told me that when you hear about a dream you are able to tell what it means."

"I cannot do that," replied Joseph, "but God can give the Pharaoh any answers he desires. I am merely the voice God will use."

The Pharaoh then told Joseph about his dreams, exactly how they happened. "Your two dreams mean exactly the same thing," Joseph said. "The seven healthy cows and the seven healthy heads of grain both represent the next seven years in Egypt. It will be a time of prosperity. The crops will be immense and food will be plentiful. But, after those seven years will come a famine like none you have ever seen. That is what the seven ugly cows and seven sickly heads of grain represent. The abundance that once showered the land will be forgotten quickly, because the famine will be so severe. The reason you have seen this same dream twice is that your destiny has been firmly decided by God, and will begin to happen soon.

"The only wise thing to do is for the Pharaoh to choose an intelligent and capable person to be in charge of all the harvesting in Egypt. Have one-fifth of all the crops be taken each year and stored away for the future. If this is done carefully, your people will be able to survive the famine that is on its way."

The Pharaoh was impressed. Not only with the interpretation of his dreams, but with Joseph's plan to keep Egypt from suffering too much. Pleased with Joseph, the Pharaoh said to him, "Since God has made this known to you, and since there is no one around who is as wise as you are, I will put you in charge of this task. You will be in charge of my palace, and will oversee the storage of the food. Everyone in all of Egypt shall obey your orders. Only I will have greater authority than you."

Because of Joseph's faith in God and because Joseph followed God's guidance, he was given a great reward! He had become one of the most powerful people in all of Egypt.

20. Joseph in Charge of Egypt
Genesis 42

oseph was now one of the most powerful people in all of Egypt. Only the Pharaoh had more authority than he. When the Pharaoh elevated Joseph from the position of an imprisoned slave to the governor of Egypt, he took a gold ring from his finger and put it on Joseph's. He also had Joseph dressed in nice clothes and gave him a chariot to ride around Egypt in order to do his work. Joseph was thirty years old.

Joseph traveled throughout the land of Egypt. During the seven years of abundance Joseph collected all the extra food and had it stored in the cities of the kingdom. There was so much food that Joseph stopped measuring it. There was too much to keep track of!

The Pharaoh had made a proclamation, or announcement of a law, that said, "I am your Pharaoh, but no one will lift a hand or do anything without consulting Joseph first." Because of this statement, everyone treated Joseph with as much respect as they did the Pharaoh himself. Joseph worked very hard and Egypt had stored more food than anyone would have thought possible. During these plentiful years, Joseph married an Egyptian woman and they had two sons together.

After the seven years of abundance, the famine began. Barely any of the crops that were planted grew. The people who worked the fields produced very little food, barely enough for themselves. No food was going into the city. Because of Joseph, the cities all had plenty of food in storage.

The famine covered an area much greater than Egypt. The entire world was feeling it. In Egypt, even the people who worked the fields and normally grew the crops were going into the cities to get food. The food warehouses in the cities of Egypt still had plenty for everyone.

Soon, people from all over the world were going to the cities of Egypt to buy grain. Joseph kept a watchful eye on how much food they had left to make sure that he wasn't selling off too much too fast. Because of his caution, Egypt would come out of the famine wealthier than when it started!

Meanwhile, the land of Canaan was also suffering from the drought and famine. Joseph's brothers and father still lived in Canaan. Years before, Joseph's brothers had sold him to members of a caravan who in turn had sold him into slavery when they reached Egypt.

When Jacob, Joseph's father, learned that a large amount of food was stored in Egypt, he told his sons that they must go there and buy some grain. If they failed, the entire family would starve to death.

Only ten of Joseph's eleven brothers went. The youngest of them, Benjamin, stayed at home. Benjamin was the other child Jacob had with Rachel, and after Joseph disappeared, Jacob began to love Benjamin most out of all his sons. Jacob didn't even know Joseph was still alive. Joseph's brothers had tricked their father into thinking Joseph had been killed by a wild animal, when they sold him to a caravan on its way to Egypt.

When the brothers arrived in Egypt, they approached the place where Joseph was selling grain to foreigners. Because Joseph was the

governor of the land, the brothers approached him and bowed down before him. Because it had been so many years and Joseph was dressed as an Egyptian, none of his brothers recognized him.

Joseph immediately recognized his brothers, but he pretended that he didn't know them. He acted mean to them and asked, "Where did you come from?"

"From the land of Canaan," they replied. "We are here to buy food for our family."

Joseph still acted as if he had never seen the men before. "You lie!" he shouted. "You are spies who have come here to find out where our land is unprotected."

"No, lord," they answered desperately. "We are all brothers. Our family is starving from the famine. We are your servants and have come to buy food."

"No!" Joseph said again, "You are definitely spies here to find our weaknesses."

The ten brothers were on their knees. "Please, lord, we are of twelve brothers. The youngest is back at home, and one other is gone."

"I do not believe you, but I will give you a chance. You will send back one brother to your homeland to fetch this brother of yours. If they return, then I will know you are telling the truth. If he does not come, you will all die." After Joseph said this, he locked all the men up.

The ten brothers were locked up for three days. During that time they talked among themselves. "This must be punishment from God for how we treated poor Joseph. Remember how he begged us for mercy and we showed him none. Now we are begging for mercy and will get none. We were all fools!"

After three days, Joseph let them out. "Do as I say and you will all live. Because I fear God and wish to cause no one unnecessary harm, I will send all but one of you back home, with plenty of food to feed your family. You must bring your youngest brother back with you, or the one who remains here will be hanged."

Reuben said to his brothers, "Didn't I tell you not to harm Joseph? But you wouldn't listen! This is our punishment for what we've done."

Joseph, who overheard this, turned away and began to weep. He then returned to the brothers and led them out to their donkeys. Before they left the prison, he had Simeon, one of the older brothers, tied up and thrown back into the prison cell while his brothers watched.

Joseph gave orders to his men to load the ten brothers' donkeys with grain and some food for the journey back to Canaan. The brothers paid for the grain and food with silver coins. However, when the brothers weren't looking, Joseph had his men also load the silver on the donkeys with the grain.

After their first day of travel ended, the nine remaining brothers set up a camp site for the night. One of them opened one of the grain sacks to give the donkeys some food and found the silver.

"Oh no!" he exclaimed. "What has happened? Our silver is still with us. They will surely think we stole it and come after us."

When the brothers got back home they explained everything to their father. Reuben said to his father, "We must take Benjamin back with us and then all will be well. I promise you on my children's lives that I will bring Benjamin back safely."

"No!" replied Jacob. "I have now lost two sons. I cannot risk losing another."

21. Benjamin Goes to Egypt
Genesis 43–46

he famine lasted and lasted. When all the food was gone, Jacob told his sons to go to Egypt again to get more food.

"We cannot," replied Judah. "The governor made it clear that we must bring Benjamin back with us. If we show up again without him, he would believe that we were spies and have us all killed. If that happens no food will come back here and everyone will starve." Judah promised to return Benjamin safely.

"Very well," replied Jacob. "But I will give you all many treasures to take with you, and twice the silver as before, so we can return what was supposed to be paid for the first grain we got."

So, this time, all the brothers including Benjamin went to Egypt to get more grain, and to hopefully get their brother, Simeon, back as well. When they arrived, they saw Joseph again. When Joseph saw Benjamin, he summoned a servant and instructed him to get a feast prepared for them all.

The brothers were afraid. They remembered the silver that they used to pay for the grain the first time that somehow had ended up back in their possession. They thought that the feast was a trick to get them inside where they would be overpowered and arrested. When they approached Joseph's door they immediately said to Joseph, who was waiting at the door, "Please sir, when we bought the grain last time somehow the silver ended up back in our packs. Here is your payment for the grain again."

"It is okay," replied Joseph. "Your God has given you that treasure; I have already received your payment. Come inside, I must attend to something, but will be with you shortly." Joseph instructed a servant to take care of them as he left.

The servant took them to the dining area, where their brother Simeon was waiting for them. They all rejoiced when reunited. Joseph was watching them and at the sight of all his brothers he was overcome with emotion. Once he regained his composure he went out and began the feast.

After they ate, the brothers were given a place to stay the night. In the morning they would be heading home again, all together. Joseph took his most trusted servant aside. "Fill the men's sacks with as much food as they can carry," he said to the servant. "Also, put their silver in their sacks. In the youngest man's sack, put my silver cup." Then as the men leave run up behind them and ask them, 'Why have you repaid my lord's good will by stealing from him? Where is my lord's favorite silver cup?'"

The servant did exactly as Joseph instructed. When he confronted the brothers about the cup, they were all shocked and confused. "None of us has taken anything from your master," they all said. "We even brought back extra silver for your master so why would we steal something like a cup? If anyone here is found to have it, you may put them to death!"

The servant, along with the palace guards, searched through the brothers' belongings. Sure enough, they found the cup in Benjamin's sack, just where the servant had placed it. They were all arrested and taken back to Joseph's house. "How stupid are you?" shouted Joseph. "Don't you think I would notice my favorite cup missing?"

The brothers all threw themselves to the ground begging for mercy. They all said how they had no idea how the cup got into the sack and that it must be a mistake.

"I am not unmerciful," said Joseph. "Everyone may go except for the one who was found to have my cup. He will become my slave."

"Please, my lord," said Judah sheepishly. "I have made an oath to my aging father that I would bring my brother Benjamin back home safely. Please, I beg of you, take me as your slave instead."

Joseph could not bear to keep his secret any longer. "I am Joseph, your brother!" he yelled out with joy. "Is Father still alive?"

The brothers all went pale and could not speak. They were all terrified.

"Brothers, come here," Joseph said. They did as he said, and he hugged them all. "Do not be afraid or angry with yourselves for what happened so long ago. God had guided you. Because I was sent here so long ago, many lives are being saved. And because I am here, I can give the entire family a place to stay. The famine will last for five more years and if you all don't come I fear that by the end of it you will be very poor."

The Pharaoh heard about Joseph's reunion with his brothers and he was pleased. The Pharaoh knew that Joseph had saved Egypt from what could have been a horrible fate. He was glad to see Joseph so happy. He gave Joseph's brothers carts to take back to Canaan to use to bring their families back to Egypt.

Jacob was overjoyed to hear that his son, Joseph, was still alive. He agreed that it would be best for everyone to move to Egypt where they could live comfortably.

22. The Birth of Moses

Exodus 1–2

oseph, his brothers, and their father settled in Egypt, along with their families and all of their servants. Each of the twelve brothers had many children, and those children had many children of their own. Soon the Israelites were so numerous that the land was filled with them. For a long while the Israelites and Egyptians lived together peacefully.

Years after Joseph died, a new Pharaoh began to rule over Egypt. He had never heard of Joseph or what he had done for the land so long ago during the great famine. All he saw were the many, many Israelites that populated the land he ruled over.

"They are so numerous," he said to his advisors one day. "We must do something soon to slow down their growth. What if we end up in a war? They could end up taking sides with our enemy and we would be in trouble."

So the Pharaoh appointed slave masters to rule over the Israelites. The slave masters were ordered to treat the Israelites harshly and make them work very hard. The Israelites were forced to build walls and buildings using large stones, and they had to work in the fields. In return they got very little, and always needed food.

However, it seemed that the more the Pharaoh made the Israelites suffer, the more children they had. The Pharaoh was even more worried. He then told the Hebrew midwives that any baby boys born to an Israelite woman should be killed immediately. A midwife is a woman who helps other women give birth.

The midwives were horrified. They couldn't kill their own people, and they knew that God would not approve. They had faith in God and chose to ignore the Pharaoh's command and let all the baby boys live.

When the Pharaoh realized that the Israelites' baby boys were still alive, he became angry. He summoned the midwives to stand before him.

"Why have you disobeyed my orders and let the Hebrew boys live?"

One of the midwives collected all her courage. "Hebrew women are different from Egyptian women," she replied. "They usually give birth before they have time to call for us."

The Pharaoh was disgusted. Furious, he gave an order to all his people that anyone who finds a Hebrew baby boy must immediately throw him into the Nile. The Nile is a very large river that flows through Egypt.

When the Pharaoh had made this proclamation, a young Hebrew couple who lived nearby had a newborn baby boy. They loved their son with all their hearts and decided to do whatever it took to save him from the Pharaoh's cruel order. For a while the mother was able to hide the baby in the house, but soon he became too big. The Israelites were all very poor and they did not have much space to begin with.

The boy's mother knew she would not be able to keep him. She made a basket and coated it with tar. She put the baby in it, covered the basket, and let it float in the tall grass that grew on the Nile's bank. She then left, praying that he could somehow be saved.

The baby's sister watched everything the mother did. She hid behind some bushes to see what would happen.

It was not long before the Pharaoh's daughter and her maids went down to the river bank right where the baby was floating. Seeing the basket floating among the reeds, she sent one of the maids out to bring it back to her. The princess opened the basket and saw the baby boy inside. The baby began to cry and the princess felt sorry for him.

"This is a Hebrew baby," she said.

Just then, the baby's sister came up to the princess.

"I can go get one of the Hebrew women to nurse the baby for you if you like."

"Yes, go," the princess said. So the girl went and got her mother.

"If you will nurse this baby for me I will pay you," the princess said to the woman, not knowing that she was the baby's mother. So, the baby's mother was then able to take him home and care for him a while longer. When the boy got a little older, she brought him back to the princess. The Pharaoh's daughter then adopted the baby and named him Moses. "Moses" means "to draw out," because the princess had drawn the baby out of the water.

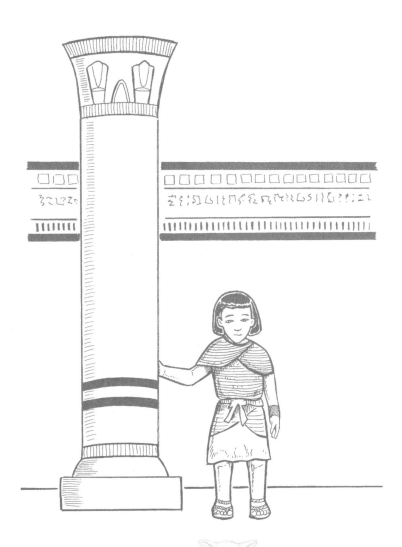

23. The Stranger in a Strange Land
Exodus 2

oses grew up with the Pharaoh's daughter as his adoptive mother. He lived with the Egyptians, but he knew that the Hebrews were his true people. He would often go out and watch the Hebrews, also known as the Israelites because they were the descendents of Israel, working in their harsh conditions. It made Moses sad to see his people treated so poorly.

One day, while he was watching his people hard at work, he saw one of the Egyptian slave masters beating a Hebrew man. The man was too ill to work hard. The slave master was beating the poor man to death. Outraged at seeing this cruelty, Moses grabbed a large stone and hit the slave master in the head, killing the Egyptian and saving the life of the sick Hebrew man. Moses then dragged the slave master's body away and buried it in the desert sand.

The next day, Moses saw a Hebrew man beating up another Hebrew man. Moses ran up to the man who was hitting the other and asked him, "Why are you hitting this man? He is of the same blood as you. You should stick together."

"What business is this of yours?" the man asked Moses. "Are you going to kill me now like you did that Egyptian?"

Moses turned pale. So, everyone must know what I have done, he thought to himself. He decided to run away, which turned out to be a smart thing to do. Just as Moses was leaving, the Pharaoh had heard what Moses had done and was furious. The Pharaoh had sent some soldiers out to kill Moses. Luckily, Moses had escaped soon enough and got out of Egypt.

Moses ended up in a land called Midian. When he got there, he sat down by a well to think about what he was going to do. Just then, the seven daughters of the priest of Midian arrived at the well to get some water and to let their flocks of sheep drink. When they tried to do this, some shepherds came along and, wanting the well for themselves, chased the girls off. Moses saw what they were doing and came to the girls' rescue.

Moses was young and strong. Growing up he had played a lot of sports and learned to fight well. He was also well fed. The shepherds were a scraggly bunch. When Moses easily knocked down the first shepherd, the other two

were scared and ran off, taking their sheep with them. Moses let the shepherd he knocked down run off without any further harm.

Moses gathered the seven girls' sheep, which had scattered when the girls ran off. He gave them all water and kept them together until the girls returned. They all thanked him profusely and returned home to their father.

When they arrived home, their father, Reuel, asked why they were back so quickly. Usually the girls had to wait and wait until the other shepherds were gone and wouldn't finally get back until very late. The daughters explained what had happened.

"Well!" the father exclaimed, "Why did you just leave him out there and not invite him here for something to eat?" The seven girls did as their father said.

Moses went to Reuel's house and had dinner with the family. When the priest learned Moses' story, he invited him to stay and help tend the flocks. He was offering Moses a new life. Moses agreed, and a short while later married a woman named Zipporah, one of the seven sisters. Although Moses had a good life, he was sad. He felt as if he had no home of his own. He felt like a stranger in a strange land.

Years had past since Moses had fled Egypt. In that time the Pharaoh had died from illness. A new Pharaoh took charge, but the suffering of the Israelites continued. If anything, it got worse. In their suffering, the Hebrew people cried out to the Lord for help.

God heard the cries of his people. He remembered his promise to Abraham about making his people a great nation. He looked down on the Israelites and became worried about them. God decided then that he would help them.

24. Moses Returns to Egypt

Exodus 3–6

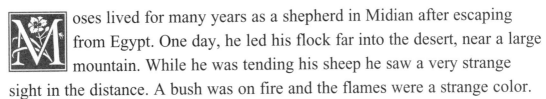

oses lived for many years as a shepherd in Midian after escaping from Egypt. One day, he led his flock far into the desert, near a large mountain. While he was tending his sheep he saw a very strange sight in the distance. A bush was on fire and the flames were a strange color.

Moses looked at the bush for a little while and noticed something remarkable. Although the flames were bright and strong, the fire was not actually burning the bush up—it just kept burning and burning. Moses walked to the bush for a closer look.

"Moses!" the voice of God shouted from within the flames.

"Yes?" Moses replied cautiously. He wasn't sure where the voice was coming from.

"Do not come any closer!" God said. "You are standing on holy ground. Take off your sandals. I am the God of your father and the God of your people." Moses took off his sandals and hid his face because he was afraid to look into the face of God.

"I have seen the misery of my people and have heard their cries for help," God said. "I am sending you to the Pharaoh of Egypt to bring my people out of Egypt."

Moses was stunned. "But who am I to go to the Pharaoh and bring the Israelites out of Egypt? I am just one simple man."

"I will be with you. When you get your people, bring them to this mountain and I will show them a sign."

"But, if I go to the Israelites and say that their God has sent me to rescue them, and they ask me, 'What is his name?' What should I tell them?" Moses asked.

"I am who I am," God answered in a powerful voice. "I am forever and everlasting. You tell them that 'I am' has sent you and they will come. Tell their elders why you have come and that if they follow you I will give them a wonderful place to live. I will give them a land flowing with milk and honey. I know the Pharaoh will resist, but do as I tell you and I will strike the Egyptians with a power they have never seen before."

"What if they do not believe me?" asked Moses. "What if they say I am lying?"

Then God said, "Throw your staff onto the ground." Moses did this. Once the staff hit the ground it became a large snake. Moses got scared and began to run away.

"Stop!" shouted God. "Pick up the snake by the tail." As soon as Moses did this it became a staff again. "This sign will be proof that you are who you say you are."

Moses was still hesitant. "Lord, I am no speaker. Perhaps you should send someone else."

"Who gives men the power to speak?" God's voice boomed angrily. "Your brother, Aaron, is on his way. He shall be your voice."

Aaron did arrive a short time later. Then the two brothers traveled to Egypt. They spoke with the Israelite elders and told them everything that had happened. The elders rejoiced and soon all the Israelites were celebrating. Moses and Aaron gathered their courage and went before the Pharaoh.

"Our God, the God of the Israelites, has spoken to us and wants us to go into the desert for three days to worship him and make sacrifices."

"No!" shouted the Pharaoh. "The Israelites must work. You are causing problems. I have noticed that lately the slaves have not been working as hard."

The Pharaoh spoke to the slave masters the next day. "The Israelites have been causing problems. They must have too much time on their hands. Until now we have been giving them straw for making bricks. From now on, let them get their own straw for brick making, but require them to make the same number of bricks each day."

Bricks were made then by mixing mud from the Nile's bank with straw and baking it. Made this way the bricks were hard and strong and not nearly as heavy as a stone the same size.

The Israelites were miserable. Now it took nearly twice as long to gather the straw and make the same number of bricks. Those who couldn't make enough bricks were beaten. "Look what you've done!" they shouted to Moses and Aaron. "We are now more miserable than before."

Moses prayed. "Look at your people, Lord. Their misery is greater than ever before. What should I do?"

"Go back to the Pharaoh again," replied God. "He will not listen to you at first. When this happens he will see my fury and wish he had listened to you the first time."

25. Moses Wields God's Power against Egypt
Exodus 7–12

Note to reader: *This story is a bit longer, so save it for a time when you are feeling up to reading for a while!*

The Pharaoh of Egypt was treating the Israelites more harshly than ever. So God sent Moses and Aaron to confront the Pharaoh again. They said the same thing to the Pharaoh as before: "Let the Israelites go." But the Pharaoh still refused.

"Throw down your staff," Moses told Aaron. When the staff hit the floor it turned into a snake.

"You think that is such a powerful trick?" the Pharaoh laughed. He gestured to his magicians. Three magicians stepped forward and threw down their walking sticks or staffs. Each staff became a snake as well. They all laughed until the snake that formed from Aaron's staff ate the other three snakes! Everyone was silent then. But the Pharaoh did not change his mind and sent the two men away.

The Plague of Blood

"The Pharaoh is stubborn and strong willed," God said to Moses. "You must return to him tomorrow morning when he goes out to the river." God continued to tell Moses everything he needed to do.

The next morning Aaron and Moses went out to the Nile, where the Pharaoh was approaching with some of his men. "Pharaoh! The Lord has sent me to tell

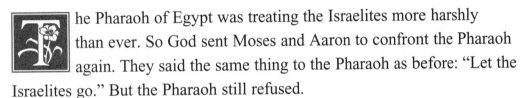

you to let his people go! Until now you have refused to listen. I will now show you the power of the Lord." Aaron then did as Moses had instructed. He raised his staff and waved it over all the waters of Egypt. As he did this the Nile turned red with blood! All the water in Egypt—in the wells, in the stone water jugs within the houses, even any water collected in small ditches—all turned into blood. The Nile smelled terrible and no one could drink from it. All the fish in the river died and floated to the top, with their white bellies showing in the dark red water.

Before the Pharaoh could react, his magicians showed him the same trick, by turning one last bit of fresh water red, just like the Nile. The Pharaoh then believed that Moses and Aaron were just trying to trick him. So he ignored them.

The Plague of Frogs

Seven days later Moses and Aaron returned to the Pharaoh. God had already instructed Moses what to do. The blood in the Nile had cleared away by this time, but there was still a bad smell in the air.

Aaron and Moses approached the Pharaoh. "The Lord has told us to tell you to let his people go. If you refuse to let them go, he will plague your whole country with frogs." Moses then gave Aaron the signal to raise his staff. Aaron raised his staff and waved it over the Nile. Suddenly, out of the Nile, thousands upon thousands of frogs hopped out of the water and began roaming all throughout Egypt. Frogs were everywhere! When an Egyptian lifted a bucket out of the well, it had more frogs in it than water! Wherever the Egyptians went, they found frogs, frogs, and more frogs! Even as the Pharaoh went to bed, under his sheets were dozens of frogs, making everything slimy and smelly!

It didn't take long for the Pharaoh to summon Moses and Aaron. "Pray to your God to get rid of all the frogs in Egypt, except for those that are already in the rivers. If you do this I will let your people go."

Moses and Aaron agreed. The next morning they prayed for all the frogs to leave Egypt except for the ones living in the waters. God caused all the frogs that were on dry land away from the waters to die instantly. Millions of frogs littered the streets and everything stunk horribly of dead, rotting frog.

The Pharaoh then changed his mind! Now that the frog problem was settled he said that the Israelites could not go anywhere.

The Plague of Gnats

Aaron and Moses stepped out onto the streets in front of the Pharaoh's palace. Aaron banged the ground hard with his staff. As the staff hit the ground, a large thud boomed, the ground vibrated, and dust rose into the hot dry air. Suddenly, all the dust that rose from the ground turned into tiny, biting gnats! The gnats swarmed throughout Egypt, engulfing the entire land. There were so many gnats, people were going crazy! They could not hide from them. The gnats were so tiny they could fly through even the smallest crack in a door.

The Pharaoh's magicians tried to use their powers to turn dust into gnats, but they couldn't. "This is truly the work of the Hebrew God!" they told the Pharaoh. By this time, the Pharaoh's mind had become fixed on not giving in. He would not let the Israelites leave, just as the Lord had predicted.

The Plague of Flies

The gnats dispersed soon enough, and things seemed almost back to normal. Then one morning, Moses and Aaron met the Pharaoh on his usual trip to the Nile to wash up and get some water.

"Pharaoh!" shouted Aaron because the Pharaoh was far away. "The Lord has told us to tell you to let his people go so they can pray in the desert and offer sacrifices. If you refuse, your country will be plagued with swarms of flies. You will know that this is the work of our Lord because the flies will swarm everywhere in Egypt, except where the Israelites live in Goshen."

Then Aaron raised his staff and a massive swarm of flies descended on Egypt. There were so many flies the sky was pitch black! Everywhere, the Egyptians were running. Flies got into their eyes, into their noses, and into their ears. Everywhere except in Goshen that is; just as Aaron had said.

The Pharaoh summoned Aaron and Moses to him. As the two representatives of the Hebrew people approached the Pharaoh, the swarm of flies parted around them. "Tell you what," started the Pharaoh. "I will give your people three days off to pray to God and make sacrifices, but they must do it here."

"We are sorry, Pharaoh, but that would anger our Lord. He has ordered us to go into the desert to make our sacrifices. To do otherwise would count for nothing."

"Very well, get rid of these flies and I will let your people go!"

The next morning Moses and Aaron prayed. When they did so, all the flies went away. However, once the flies were gone the Pharaoh again changed his mind and wouldn't let the Israelites go.

"What more could they possibly do?" wondered the Pharaoh.

The Plague of Livestock

Again the Pharaoh refused their request and again Moses and Aaron approached him. "The Lord has told us to tell you to let his people go so they can pray in the desert and offer sacrifices. If you refuse, all your livestock in the fields—your sheep, cattle, horses, camels, goats, and donkeys—will be killed. But the Lord will not harm any of the livestock belonging to the Israelites. When this happens you will know it is the Lord of the Israelites that has plagued you for your refusal."

The Pharaoh did not agree, but sent his soldiers to help protect all the livestock of his people and to prevent any tricks. It did no good. The next morning all the livestock belonging to Egyptians dropped dead. The Pharaoh sent people to check on the livestock of the Israelites. Not a single chicken belonging to an Israelite was even sick.

The Plague of Disease

Remarkably, the Pharaoh still did nothing. Aaron and Moses obeyed God's next set of instructions. Moses took two handfuls of black soot from a furnace and they both went before the Pharaoh. "Disobey the Lord's will and this is what happens!" shouted Aaron. Moses threw the black soot into the air. The black dust rose up in the air and became a big black cloud. The black cloud spread throughout Egypt. Whenever the cloud touched somebody's skin, that person's skin would immediately erupt in painful boils. Soon all of Egypt was engulfed in the soot and everyone was ill and in pain. Goshen, the area where the Israelites lived, went untouched.

Even the Pharaoh's magicians got sick. They were so uncomfortable that they couldn't think straight. They ran around as if they had gone crazy. They could do nothing to try to stop the plague. Even after all of this, the Pharaoh still wouldn't let the Israelites go.

The Plague of Hail

A few days later, Moses and Aaron went to the Pharaoh again. This time Moses spoke, "The Lord has told us to tell you to let his people go so they may pray in the desert and offer sacrifices. You still refuse to let them go, so tomorrow morning your land will feel the full force of his power. A destructive hail storm with rain down upon the land. If you fear the power of the Lord, order your people to stay inside and give their slaves shelter."

The Pharaoh ignored this threat, thinking it impossible. But some of his elder counselors were afraid of what Moses had said and immediately went home and prepared. Others ignored the warning and left their slaves and remaining livestock out in the fields.

Sure enough, that next morning thunder and lightning filled the sky! Large hail stones began falling on the ground. They fell with such intensity that anything caught in their shower was beaten down to the ground. All of the crops were crushed. The trees had no leaves, and only a few branches remained on the trees. Everything that remained outside was killed. The only place that went untouched was the land of Goshen, where the Israelites lived.

Again, the Pharaoh promised to let the Israelites go if Moses and Aaron would make the plague stop. And again, once Moses and Aaron stopped the plague the Pharaoh changed his mind. He was so stubborn and foolish in not wanting to lose, yet all he was accomplishing was increasing his people's suffering.

The Plague of Locusts

Moses and Aaron went to the Pharaoh again and said to him, "Our Lord, the God of the Hebrews, has told us to say, 'how long will you refuse to let the Israelites go? If you continue to refuse, tomorrow the entire land of Egypt will become covered in locusts. Every bit of grain, and every living plant that remains will be destroyed.'" After delivering their message, Moses and Aaron left without waiting for the Pharaoh's reply.

The Pharaoh's officials muttered to each other. One of them said to the Pharaoh, "How long will we be subjected to the powers of these two men? Egypt is in ruins! Maybe we should give them what they want."

The Pharaoh sighed. "Bring the two men before me," he said quietly. When Moses and Aaron returned the Pharaoh said to them, "Go and worship your God. But tell me one thing. Who of your people will be going?"

"Everyone," replied Moses. "All of the women, children, and men, and all of the livestock will go, because it is to be a great celebration."

"This I cannot allow!" the Pharaoh yelled. "Obviously, if all of you—the men, women, and children, with all of your most valuable property—are going, then you must have some evil deed planned! I will allow only the men to go, and they may take only enough animals for your sacrifices. They may take no weapons larger than a knife. I suggest you accept this bargain, because I am losing my patience with you!" After the Pharaoh spoke, Moses and Aaron were driven away by the Pharaoh's guards.

The next morning, Moses raised his staff and waved it across the land of Egypt. The ground everywhere became covered with fat locusts that began eating everything. The locusts devoured the grain the Egyptians were storing in huge warehouses in a matter of hours. All the trees in the field, and the crops that survived the hail were eaten so that nothing but bare ground remained. As the locusts flew from place to place their wings brought up big yellow clouds of dust.

With Egypt in a state of panic, the Pharaoh quickly summoned Moses and Aaron. "Truly I have sinned against your Lord," he said. "Please pray to your God to get rid of the locusts, then I will let your people go."

Moses and Aaron prayed. Immediately a powerful wind blew in from the west. The locusts were all blown away and fell into the Red Sea. When the Pharaoh saw what was left of Egypt tears came to his eyes. He then got angry with Moses and Aaron, blaming them for the wasteland his country had become. He decided there was nothing left in Egypt to destroy, so he had his guards make sure the Israelites didn't leave Egypt.

The Plague of Darkness

The next day was very sunny with clear skies. Moses raised his hands to the sky and it became dark. Everywhere, the entire land of Egypt was covered in darkness. When the Egyptians tried to light a lamp or start a fire, they couldn't even make a spark. However, all of the lamps in Goshen, the place where the Hebrews lived, worked.

The Egyptians were forced to stumble around in darkness for three days. After three days the Pharaoh summoned Moses and Aaron. "Your people may go worship your Lord. Your women, children, and men may all go, but you must leave your livestock behind."

"We cannot do this Pharaoh," replied Moses. "We must make sacrifices from our livestock to the Lord, and we won't know which to use until we have arrived in the desert."

The Pharaoh was furious. "Get out of my sight!" he shouted. "If I see you again, I will have you hanged."

The Plague on the Firstborn

God again spoke to Moses. "I will bring one last plague on the land of Egypt. This time it will be so devastating the Pharaoh will allow the Israelites to leave. At midnight tonight, every firstborn male will die—both people and animals."

God gave Moses very specific instructions on how to make sure none of the firstborn of the Israelites were killed in the plague. Everyone had to streak lamb's blood on the outside of their doors so God would know which house to pass over when he spread the plague across all of Egypt.

Moses and Aaron quickly summoned the Hebrew elders and instructed them in what all the Israelites had to do to save their firstborn sons. The elders passed the information along to all the people.

That night at midnight, a terrible mix of screams could be heard. Every firstborn male died, except for those of the Israelites. Because God passed over the homes of the Israelites, the day became known as Passover. The Pharaoh woke up and found out his oldest son had died. He was mortified. Dejectedly, he called for Moses and Aaron. "Go," he sighed. "Take your people and leave my land."

26. The Parting of the Red Sea

Exodus 13–15

fter the plague of the firstborn, where every firstborn male in Egypt died, the Pharaoh allowed the Israelites to leave Egypt. God's plan was for the Israelites to return to the land of Canaan—a land that he had promised to them years and years ago.

However, God did not lead them through the shortest path. He knew that if the Israelites were to face too much hardship—such as starvation or the threat of war—they would run back to Egypt and accept their position as slaves rather than die. The Israelites had been in Egypt for over 400 years. None of them knew any other place.

Moses led the Israelites with God's guidance. During the day, they headed toward a great big tornado—a dust cloud that reached high into the sky. At night, in the distance was a tall inferno, blazing high and bright in the sky.

One night, God spoke to Moses and said, "Lead your people back for a ways, then turn east and make camp by the sea. When you do this the Pharaoh will think the Israelites are wandering confused in the desert. He will send soldiers after you and, for once and for all, I will prove to the Egyptians that I am the Lord."

Moses obeyed and soon the Israelites were camped near the Red Sea. The Pharaoh had sent spies to follow the Israelites so he would know exactly what they were up to. When he heard about their confused wandering in the desert he became angry for giving in to such pathetic people.

"What have I done?" the Pharaoh asked his advisors. "We have let the Israelites leave Egypt and now we have lost their service!" Since the Pharaoh had agreed to let the Israelites leave for only three days, he sent out an army to go get them and bring them back to Egypt. The Pharaoh himself led this army of six hundred of Egypt's best chariots and many foot soldiers and officers. The Egyptian army set off and moved quickly in pursuit of the Israelites. They soon arrived at the Red Sea.

When the Israelites saw the Egyptian army approaching in an immense cloud of dust, they all became afraid. "What have you done to us?" they shouted to Moses. "We will all be killed!"

"Do not be afraid," replied Moses. "Stand here and witness the power of our Lord."

Moses raised his staff above his head. He waved the staff over the sea. A great wind began to blow from the east. The large whirling dust cloud that had guided the Israelites moved between them and the Egyptian army, blocking the Israelites from the Pharaoh's sight.

Moses then plunged his staff at the edge of the sea. The great wind from the east roared and the sea parted! In the middle of the sea, a wide path of dry ground was formed. The ocean formed a wall on both sides of the path.

Moses led his people on the path in the Red Sea. The Egyptians managed to work their way through the dust cloud and without hesitation chased after the Israelites. The Lord watched the Egyptians get closer and closer to his people. He made things difficult for the Egyptians. The wheels of every chariot broke off, so the horses were forced to drag them in the mud. Horses fell in ditches, and the foot soldiers feet sank in the mud.

"Let's get out of here!" an Egyptian soldier yelled. "The Lord of the Hebrews is fighting for them."

God instructed Moses what to do next. Moses turned to face the Egyptian army and raised his staff. As Moses waved his staff from the left ocean wall to the right, the walls came crashing down. In a violent splash the entire Egyptian army—the Pharaoh and all the chariots—was gone. None of the Egyptians made it out.

The Israelites continued to cross the sea with a wall of water on both sides and another behind them.

When all the Israelites had crossed the sea, the waters were flat again and the path was gone. Aaron's sister, Miriam, and several other Hebrew women took tambourines and began singing and dancing. Everyone rejoiced that the Lord had kept his word and delivered them from the Egyptians.

27. The Ten Commandments
Exodus 16–20

After the Israelites crossed the Red Sea, escaping the Egyptians who were swallowed into the water, they ended up in the Sinai Desert. They wandered the desert for weeks and were tired, hungry, thirsty, and miserable. Moses prayed to the Lord.

That evening, flocks of fat quail flew by. The birds were very tired from a long journey and could barely stay off the ground. It was easy for the Israelites to catch them. In the morning, the ground was covered with white flakes that tasted like honey.

The food God provided took away the Israelites' hunger. However, as they continued on their journey through the desert water became scarce, and the people were suffering again. Again, Moses sought the help of God. God told him to strike a stone with his staff. When Moses did, a fountain of water gushed out of it.

They traveled through the desert for three hard months. At the end of the third month they reached Mount Sinai. The made a camp at the base of the mountain. On the third day the Israelites were camped, black clouds covered the sky. Thunder boomed and lightning flashed across the sky. The earth shook, and fire and smoke blasted out of the mountain. God had descended from heaven to the top of the mountain.

"I am the one God. You shall worship no other gods before me.

"You shall not worship false idols. You will not bow down to any statue in the form of anything on earth or in heaven.

"You shall not misuse the Lord's name.

"You shall follow and respect the Sabbath, the seventh day, as a holy day—no one shall work. For on the seventh day of creation, I rested.

"You shall honor and obey your mother and father.

"You shall not commit murder.

"You shall not commit adultery.

"You shall not steal.

"You shall not lie or make false statements.

"You shall not be jealous of your neighbor's property or envy his or her life."

When the Israelites had seen the thunder, lightning, smoke, and fire, they were afraid and kept a far distance away. They thought they would die if they heard the voice of God. They asked Moses to go up to the mountain to listen to God's words.

Moses heard God's laws and returned to tell the Israelite elders, who in turn told all of the people. The people saw Moses return to the top of the mountain. The top of the mountain appeared to be on fire and Moses walked right into the smoke and flames. While there God gave him two stone tablets that had God's ten commandments carved on them.

God also told Moses how to build the Ark of the Covenant—a special chest in which to keep God's commandments or laws.

Moses was on top of the mountain for forty days. The Israelites got nervous because Moses was gone so long. They went to Aaron begging him to make a statue for them to worship. So Aaron collected all the gold jewelry that the Israelites had—earrings, bracelets, rings—anything anyone had made of gold. He melted the gold down and pounded it into the shape of a giant calf.

While the Israelites were breaking the commandment against worshipping idols or statues, Moses was still on top of the mountain. God sent him down to his people. When Moses returned, he saw the golden calf. The Israelites had built an altar in front of the calf and had made a sacrifice to it. They were all chanting and dancing wildly around a large bonfire they had built.

When Moses saw his people sinning against the Lord, he became very angry. He threw the two stone tablets onto the ground, breaking them into hundreds of pieces. He ran to the giant golden statue and pushed it into the fire. Everyone was shocked to see such an old man use so much strength.

The next morning Moses awoke. "You have all committed a great sin," he said to the Israelites. "I will now return to the Lord and ask him to forgive you for your sin."

28. The Journey to the Promised Land

Exodus 32–34, 37; Numbers 13–14

oses destroyed the golden calf that the Israelites built and worshipped. He was full of distress. It seemed that his people could not follow God's commands. The next day he climbed Mount Sinai again to pray for their forgiveness.

While Moses was praying, the Lord said to him, "Leave this place and head for the land of Canaan, which I promised to the descendents of Moses. I will send an angel ahead of you to chase away the people who are already there. However, I will not go with you."

"You keep telling me to 'lead the people' but I am just a simple man, replied Moses. If I have proved to be so special, please teach me your ways so I might be a better leader and continue to do as you wish if you are not going with us. How will the other people know the Lord is with us if your presence is not shown?"

"I will as you ask, because you have pleased me," answered the Lord. "I will stand before you and speak my name, but you must not look into my face, because any human who sees my face cannot survive." God's presence passed over Moses. The Lord covered Moses' face while he passed so that Moses would not be harmed.

The Lord then said to Moses, "Use a chisel to make two stone tablets like the first ones I gave you, which you broke. In the morning, climb up to the mountain again. You must be sure to be alone."

Moses did as he was told. In the morning he carved two stone tablets exactly like the ones he had broken before in anger when he saw his people worshiping the golden calf. He took the tablets up the mountain. God then descended from heaven and the two stone tablets became engraved with the commandments, just as they had been before. Moses took the tablets back to the Israelites. His face was glowing! The Israelites were afraid to get near him. Once Moses spoke to them, they were no longer afraid and all went up to him. Moses then told the Israelites the commandments of God.

The Israelites built an ark—a large chest—to carry the stone tablets containing God's ten commandments. The ark was covered with gold. At the four bottom corners of the ark were gold rings, so the Israelites could put two poles through the rings and carry the ark with them wherever they went.

So the Israelites set for to the land of Canaan. After traveling for many days, they arrived at the Desert of Paran, near Canaan. Moses sent out twelve men to have a look around Canaan. The twelve men set off for Canaan and explored the area for forty days.

When the men returned, two of them were holding onto a large pole that had large bunches of grapes fastened to it. The men reported to Moses. "The land truly is flowing with milk and honey!" they exclaimed. "Here is some fruit we picked. However, the cities are very well fortified, and the Canaanites are large and strong."

One of the twelve men, Caleb, said, "We should go and take the land. With the Lord we can do it."

"We cannot attack those people!" exclaimed the other men. "They are stronger than us. We will be defeated quickly. The people are the size of giants, and have better weapons. We are no more than grasshoppers compared to them." As the other explorers said this, the Israelite people became afraid and did not want to go into the promised land. They remembered only the better things about life in Egypt—always having enough food, not needing to struggle from day to day, and having a permanent home.

The Lord became angry that the Israelites did not have faith in his power to bring them into the promised land. As punishment, all the Israelites were forced to wander the desert. Because Caleb had faith in the Lord, he was allowed to enter Canaan and begin a new life of happiness. 📖

29. The Prophet and His Donkey

Numbers 21–24

The Israelites wandered throughout the desert. From time to time they stayed in places where other people lived and ended up in many battles with those people. They battled one group of people known as the Amorites and completely destroyed both the people and their cities. The Israelites decided to settle in that area.

The kingdom of Moab was near where the Israelites settled. The King of Moab, Balak, looked at the Israelites with some fear. They were becoming numerous in population and were becoming powerful. Balak knew the Israelites had destroyed the Amorites and he wanted to make sure that did not happen to his people. Everyone in land of Moab knew about the Israelites and they were afraid of them.

Balak sent messengers to a man named Balaam. Balaam was a powerful prophet known for his abilities to curse and bless. The messengers arrived at Balaam's houses and said, "Our king asks that you go to the place where the Israelites have settled and curse them so the kingdom of Moab may defeat them in battle." The messengers paid Balaam a large amount of gold and silver to curse the Israelites.

That night God spoke to Balaam. "You must not put a curse on the Israelites, for I have blessed them."

The next morning Balaam told the messengers he would not perform Balak's request. Some time later, Balak sent a large group of people, including many princes, to Balaam again. They asked again and said the reward for this service would be great.

"Go with them," God told Balaam, "but do only as I tell you."

The next morning, Balaam saddled his donkey and headed off with the messengers of Moab. During the journey, an angel appeared on the road with a sword drawn. The donkey could see the angel, but Balaam could not. When the angel pointed a sword at the donkey, the donkey walked off the road and into a field. Balaam got angry and hit the donkey.

Then the angel appeared before Balaam's donkey in a vineyard. The donkey was forced to walk tightly up against a rocky cliff, accidentally crushing Balaam's foot. Balaam, in pain, beat the poor donkey again.

Later on, Balaam and his donkey approached a narrow path, with large rocks on both edges. Again the angel appeared before the donkey. But again, Balaam could not see anything unusual. The donkey could not avoid the angel, so it sat down on the ground. Balaam was furious! He got off the donkey and began kicking it and hitting it with his fists.

God then gave the donkey the power of speech. "What have I done? Why have you beaten me these past three times?" asked the donkey.

Without thinking how unusual it is for a donkey to talk, Balaam answered, "You are making me look like a fool! If I had a sword I would kill you!"

"Am I not your trusted donkey you have had for so many years? Have I ever behaved this way before?"

"No," began Balaam. Just then, the Lord made the angel appear before Balaam.

"If not for your donkey, I would have killed you had you come any closer to me," the angel said.

Balaam fell on his knees. "I have sinned!" cried out the prophet. "If you wish me to return, only say so and I will obey."

"No," replied the angel, "go with the men, but do only as the Lord commands."

Balaam and the messengers arrived in Moab. Once there Balak led Balaam to a mountain that overlooked the place where the Israelites had settled. "I can only do as the Lord commands," Balaam told Balak. Balaam climbed to the top of the mountain alone.

When Balaam could see all of the Israelites' settlements he opened his mouth. As he did so God told him to say a blessing over the Israelites, which Balaam did.

Balak was angry when Balaam returned to him! "I asked you to curse these people! I promised you riches if you did! Now you shall get nothing."

"I can only do the Lord's will," Balaam replied. He then returned home on his donkey.

30. The Death of Moses and a New Leader of the Israelites

Deuteronomy 32–34; Joshua 1–3

Many years had passed since the Israelites escaped Egypt. Aaron had died. Moses was very old and did not have long to live. The Israelites had been wandering from place to place for forty years. They were not allowed to enter the promised land yet. They were being punished because they did not have enough faith in the Lord.

When Moses was 120 years old, God said, "Go climb Mount Nebo and view the land of Canaan, which I have promised to the Israelites. You shall see the promised land before you die, but you will never enter it."

Moses did as the Lord told him. He saw the promised land and was happy to know that his people would soon be there. Then, there on the mountain, Moses died. Moses was one of the greatest of God's prophets.

The Israelites took Moses' body and buried it. They all grieved for many days, because they loved their leader very much. Everyone was wondering who would become the next leader. There was a man among the Israelites named Joshua. When Moses died, Joshua became filled with wisdom because Moses had blessed him before he climbed the mountain his final time.

"Joshua, do not be afraid, for the Lord will be with you now wherever you go," God said to Joshua.

Joshua spoke to his people. He said, "In a few days we shall cross the Jordan River. Get everything ready to move!" The people immediately went to work. Everyone knew by this time that the Lord was with them and that they would soon be in the promised land.

That night Joshua sent two spies across the river to scout out the city of Jericho. Jericho was an immense city with a large wall all around it.

The two spies came upon a woman named Rahab, whose house was built into the wall of the city, and spent the night at her house. When they entered the city, one of the guards realized they were spies and alerted the king.

The king sent some of his officers out to find the spies. They found out that two men were seen entering Rahab's house. When they arrived at Rahab's door, she had hidden the two Israelites up on the roof, under the flax that was drying. Flax is a kind of plant used to make cloth. Putting it up on flat roofs was the best way for drying it out.

"We know the two spies of Israel are in here," an officer said to Rahab. "Tell us where they are."

"They were here," replied Rahab, "but they left a while ago and headed back to the Jordan to their people."

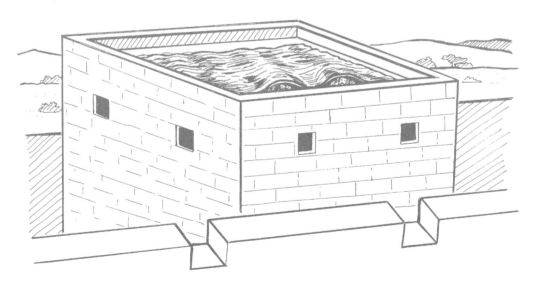

The officers didn't believe her at first and thoroughly searched through her house. They did not find the two spies, who were still up on the roof hiding. When they did not find the spies, the officers headed to the Jordan, closing the gate behind them.

Once they had left, Rahab told the spies it was safe to come back down. "Because I have saved your life," she said to them, "please show kindness toward me and my family. Everyone in the city knows about your people and how God is with you. When your people come to the city, please spare my family's lives."

"Very well," they replied. "As long as you don't tell anyone about our plans, we will treat you kindly once we have taken the land."

Rahab explained to them that the officers were looking for them at the Jordan River, so they couldn't return to their people just yet. She told them to head for the hills and hide for three days. Afterwards, they would be able to get back to their people safely and report on everything they discovered about Jericho.

Because the gate was closed, Rahab let out a scarlet rope from her window, which faced the outside of the city wall. "Leave this rope hanging from your window," the spies told her. "This way we shall know not to harm anyone in this house." With that, the two spies left, hid in the hills for three days, and then made their way back across the Jordan.

31. The Israelites Take the Promised Land

Joshua 3–24; Judges 4–5

oshua led the Israelites to the edge of the Jordan River. Once there, they made camp. "Tomorrow morning," Joshua told his people, "the priests will carry the Ark of the Covenant—the Ark containing God's laws—in the direction we will go. Everyone is to follow the Ark and we will soon be victorious."

Four priests carried the Ark of the Covenant to the Jordan River. As they walked into the river, the water stopped flowing and large path formed to the other side. All the Israelites crossed the river without even getting wet! Once they had all crossed the river, the water began to flow again as if nothing had happened. The Israelites were full of courage at this point. They knew that the Lord was with them.

Joshua led the Israelites to Jericho. The city closed its gates and no one could get in or out. The Israelites had an army of over 40,000 men surrounding the city. God spoke to Joshua and gave him instructions, which Joshua shared with the people.

The next day, the entire army walked around the walls of Jericho once.

No one made a sound. Behind the army seven priests followed, blowing on trumpets made from ram horns. The four priests carrying the Ark followed the priests with the trumpets. After they circled once, the Israelites made camp. On the second, third, fourth, fifth, and sixth days they repeated their actions exactly.

On the seventh day, the entire Israelite army circled the city seven times, again with the priests and the Ark following. Once they had all circled the city for the seventh time, Joshua halted the army. He signaled to the priests, who sounded their trumpets.

"Now, shout for the glory of the Lord!" yelled out Joshua. All the Israelites yelled out and the walls of the city collapsed! The Israelite army charged into the city. Soon they had completely taken control of the entire city.

As the army invaded Jericho, the two spies who had been to Jericho earlier went to the house of Rahab to keep their promise to her. Rahab had hidden the two spies when the king's officers were after them. Although Rahab's house was built into the city's wall, it was not destroyed. That was the only part of the wall that had not collapsed.

"Come! Quickly, the city is under attack. Gather your family and come with us." Rahab and her family followed the spies out of Jericho to a place near where the Israelites had camped. They were the only people living in

Jericho at the time to survive. After Jericho was destroyed, they were allowed to live among the Israelites.

Once they controlled the city of Jericho, the Israelites burned everything in it, including all the buildings and everything inside them. They gathered all the silver, gold, and bronze and put it in a special treasury of the Lord.

The rest of Joshua's life was spent fighting the other cities in the land of Canaan. Some were more difficult to defeat than others, but after seven years, most of Canaan was under the Israelites control. At last, the promised land had been delivered to the Israelites—God's chosen people.

When Joshua was an old man, the Israelites were a great nation—as God had promised Abraham so long before. Joshua addressed his people one last time to remind them about the long journey their people had made to achieve what they had, and that they must obey the Lord and stay in his favor if they are to keep it.

After Joshua died, the Israelites did their best to obey his wishes. However, after everyone who had originally came across the Jordan River into Canaan had died, and all of their children were now the population of Israel, the memories of what they had gone through began to fade.

The Israelites continued to fight the Canaanites and were often victorious in battle. But the Canaanites never went away completely. After a time, the Israelites began to forget about God's commands, and Jabin, the King of the Canaanites conquered them. He had a general named Sisera who treated the Israelites cruelly.

The prophetess Deborah, who was the leader of Israel at the time, sent Barak to lead an army of 10,000 to defeat Sisera and give the Israelites their freedom again.

Barak agreed to go only if Deborah went with him. She agreed and they set out for Sisera's army, which included 900 chariots.

When Sisera heard that the army was approaching he gathered his chariots and soldiers. His forces were much stronger so he decided to meet the Israelites to destroy them. Barak hid with his men in a forest near a marshy plain. When Sisera's forces were at the plain, Barak's led his army to attack. Because it had rained, the plains were muddy and the chariots could not move. The Israelites defeated Sisera and his army, but Sisera managed to escape.

Sisera fled and found the wife of one of King Jabin's friends. The woman let Sisera hide in her tent, but she betrayed and killed him. She found Barak and led him to her tent, to show him what she did.

Once Sisera was dead, the Israelite army attacked and attacked Jabin's forces, and eventually took back all of the land. Afterwards the Israelites remained free in Canaan for forty years.

32. The Story of Gideon
Judges 6–8

Again, the Israelites forgot the lessons they had learned. Again, they were disobedient to God's will. Because of their sins, the Israelites were conquered by the Midianites. The people of Midian attacked the Israelites relentlessly, stealing their crops and killing their livestock. To protect themselves, the Israelites began living in the mountains.

God heard the cries of the Israelites. Although they sinned often, the Lord still loved his people and sent an angel down to help them.

A young man named Gideon was threshing wheat inside his father's house, where the Midianites would not see him. The angel came up behind Gideon and said, "The Lord is with you, mighty warrior."

The angel just looked like any man to Gideon. "If the Lord is with us," replied Gideon sadly, "why is everything like this? Where are all the miracles that the elders told us about? The Lord has abandoned us into the hands of the Midianites."

"You will be sent to save Israel and destroy the Midianites," the angel responded.

"Me?" Gideon asked in disbelief. "How can I do this? I am a member of the weakest clan in the tribe. All my brothers have been killed by the Midianites, and I am the least in my family."

The angel responded, "I will be with you, and we will defeat the Midianites together." The angel then disappeared! Gideon realized that he had been talking with a divine being and he knelt down and prayed.

That night, obeying God's wishes, Gideon tore down a statue of Baal, a Midianite god. In the place of the statue, Gideon built an altar to the Lord.

In the morning, when the people of the town awoke, they saw the statue destroyed, and the altar built. When the people inspected the area they realized it must have been Gideon. "Why did he do this?" they all asked each other.

Some of them went to the house of Joash, Gideon's father. "Bring out your son!" they commanded. "He has destroyed the temple built to Baal and now must die."

Joash came out of his house to stand among the crowd of angry people. "Are you really now fighting for Baal? Whoever stands with him shall be dead by morning. If Baal truly is a god, let Baal take his own revenge!"

The Midianites heard about the trouble being caused in the mountains. They gathered a huge army and were on their way. The spirit of the Lord was with Gideon. Gideon blew his trumpet, summoning all the people of his town and the areas around him to come to him and arm themselves with weapons. Gideon was now in command of a large army!

That night Gideon prayed to the Lord, "If you plan on using me to save Israel from the Midianites, as you have said, please give me a sign. I will leave this fleece on the ground. If in the morning the fleece is covered with dew but the rest of the ground is dry, then I will know you are with us."

That next morning the fleece was covered with dew, but the rest of the ground was dry. Gideon's courage grew. "Lord, please forgive me," Gideon said. "Just to be sure this wasn't a coincidence, tonight I will leave the fleece in the same place. If this time, all the ground is wet with dew, but the fleece is dry, then I shall know you are truly with us."

Again, it happened exactly as Gideon had requested in his prayer. Gideon knew the Lord was with him. Gideon gathered the army of 32,000 men and made camp. They were preparing for war.

"There are too many men," God said to Gideon. "If an Israelite army of this size defeats the Midianites, they will not think I had anything to do with it. Send home anyone who is afraid." Gideon did this and 22,000 men left. Now the army had 10,000 men.

"There are still too many," the Lord said. "Take them down to the water and have them all drink."

Gideon took the 10,000 men to the river and told them all to drink. God told Gideon that any man who kneels down and drinks by bringing his hands to his face shall remain in the army. Any man who puts his face down to the water must go home. When all the men had drunk, Gideon found 300 who drank by kneeling and bringing the water to their mouths with their hands. Everyone else was told to go home.

God was still with Gideon. That night the Lord told Gideon what to do to defeat the

Midianites. During the night, while the Midianites were sleeping, Gideon's men sneaked into their camp. Each man with Gideon carried a trumpet and an empty jar. When Gideon gave the signal, the men blew on their trumpets and broke the jars. It made a loud noise. The noise woke up the Midianites. They thought they were being attacked by a great army and began fighting in every direction frantically. They ended up fighting with each other and many of the Midianites were killed by their own countrymen. They eventually all started fleeing.

The Israelites pursued the Midianites. Other people of Israel also joined in, recapturing the land that the Midianites had taken from them.

Israel won the battle and was free from their enemies. They remained free for the rest of Gideon's lifetime.

33. The Strength of Samson

Judges 13–15

he Israelites again began to disobey the will of God. This time, God handed the Israelites over to the Philistines. Of all the nations to rule over the Israelites, the Philistines were the most powerful yet. They came from the sea and invaded Canaan.

An angel of God appeared before an Israelite couple. The two had long been childless, but always did their best to obey the wishes of God. "You will have a son who will one day defeat the Philistines," the angel said to the couple. "You must make sure you never cut his hair, for he will become a Nazarite." Nazarites were completely dedicated to God. They promised never to cut their hair as a symbol of their dedication to God.

The couple did have a son, and they named him Samson. He grew up to be big and strong. He never cut his hair.

One day, Samson went to the city of Timnah. While there, he met a Philistine woman whom he liked. He returned to his parents and told them about her and said he wished to marry her.

Samson and his parents set off for Timnah. As they walked through some vineyards, Samson was attacked by a lion. Samson raised his hand and swatted the lion down as if it were nothing. The lion was dead by the time it hit the ground.

Samson met with the Philistine woman again and they agreed to get married. Weeks later, while returning to Timnah from his home, he saw the carcass of the very lion he had killed. Inside the carcass was a bees' nest. Samson broke it open and scooped out the honey as the bees swarmed around him.

Just before the wedding, Samson invited thirty friends of the bride to a great feast that was to last seven days, according to Philistine custom. On the first day, he told a riddle. If anyone could solve the riddle by the end of the seventh day of the feast, the friends would all get a great reward; if they could not solve the riddle, they would have to give him riches.

"Out of the eater—something to eat. Out of the strong—something sweet," Samson said. For three days no one guessed correctly.

On the fourth day the guests went to Samson's future wife. "Are you trying to rob us? Tell us the answer to the riddle!"

Samson's future wife begged him to tell the answer to the riddle, but he would not. On the seventh day, after constant appeals, he finally told her.

When, on the seventh day Samson asked the guests the riddle, one responded: "What is sweeter than honey? What is stronger than a lion?"

Samson was furious! He knew that he was tricked. In his anger he killed the thirty Philistines.

Later, Samson returned to his future wife's house. However, when he arrived, her father told Samson that he had her married to another man because he thought Samson was so angry he would call off the wedding. Samson really was furious this time. He did not realize that God was setting him up so he would destroy the Philistines.

Samson ran into the forests. With his great speed he caught 300 foxes. He tied the foxes' tails together in pairs. In the middle of each string used to tie the foxes' tails together, Samson fastened a lit torch.

The foxes were then set loose throughout the fields and houses of the Philistines. Everything that belonged to the Philistines started to burn—their fields of grain, their vineyards, and their orchards.

When the Philistines found out what Samson had done, they sent an army out to get him where he lived. They told the people living there that they had better hand Samson over or they would all die.

The Israelites went to Samson, who was hiding in a cave. "What have you done?" they asked him. "Don't you know that the Philistines are our rulers? They have said we will all be killed if you are not handed over to them."

"I have only done to them what they have done to me," replied Samson. "But, I will go with you, so long as you promise to hand me over to the Philistine alive."

They agreed and tied Samson's hands together. When they handed Samson over to the Philistines, Samson felt the strength of the Lord inside him. He snapped the ropes around his wrist as if they were strings and grabbed a jaw-bone off the ground to use as a weapon.

The Philistines all attacked him, but Samson quickly defeated them all, killing 1,000 Philistine soldiers all by himself!

Samson continued to fight the Philistines for the next twenty years. During those twenty years he was the leader of the Israelites.

34. Samson and Delilah

Judges 16

Samson was the leader of the Israelites. The Philistines were still very strong and many lived in Canaan. One day, Samson went to Gaza and was going to spend the night there. Gaza was populated by Philistines, and they recognized Samson. Samson had become their biggest enemy.

The Philistine people at Gaza surrounded the place where Samson was staying. The city's gate was closed for the night so they decided to wait until dawn to attack him. But Samson heard their rustling outside. In the middle of the night, Samson got up and escaped. When he approached the gate he grabbed hold of it and ripped it from the ground. He carried the heavy gate off with him. The Philistines who watched him from behind became frozen in fear.

More time passed, and Samson fell in love with a woman named Delilah. Delilah was extraordinarily beautiful. Samson and Delilah got married. The leaders of the Philistines approached Delilah in secret. "Tell us the secret of your husband's strength and we will each reward you with eleven hundred pieces of silver."

So that night Delilah asked Samson, "Tell me the secret of your strength."

"If anyone was to tie me up with seven fresh bowstrings, I would have the strength of any normal man."

So Delilah got seven fresh bowstrings and tied Samson's hands together with them. Several Philistine soldiers were hiding in their house. Once he was tied, Delilah cried out, "Samson! The Philistine's are here!" Samson pulled his hands apart and the bowstrings snapped like a string held close to a candle. He chased the Philistine soldiers off.

"You lied to me," Delilah sobbed that night. "I feel so stupid. What is the real secret to your strength?"

"The truth is I can be held only by ropes that have never been used," Samson replied.

Acting playful, Delilah got a brand new rope and tied Samson up. Once she was done, more Philistine soldiers burst into their house. Samson was able to snap the ropes without any effort and chased the soldiers away.

"You continue to lie to me, why? Tell me the secret of your strength."

"If you weave my long hair into the fabric on your loom, I would become as weak as any person," Samson replied.

While Samson was sleeping, Delilah wove his hair into her loom. When the Philistine soldiers came in, Samson awoke easily, broke free, and chased off the soldiers.

"How can you say you love me?" Delilah sobbed. "If you really loved me you would tell me the truth." She continued to nag him day and night until Samson could take no more.

"No hair on my head has ever been cut. I am a Nazarite and my hair separates me as a man dedicated to God. If my hair were to be cut I would lose my strength."

Delilah went to the leaders of the Philistines and told them to return that night with her reward, because she now knew how to take away Samson's strength. That night, Samson rested his head on her lap and fell asleep. Once asleep, the Philistines entered and Delilah cut off his hair. They then tied him with ropes. Again, she called out, "Wake up, Samson! The Philistines are here!"

Samson awoke and realized he was tied up. However, when he struggled to free himself the ropes did not break. He then realized his hair had been cut and he had lost his strength. The Philistine then cut Samson's eyes so that he was blinded. Laughing, they led him away to Gaza. From the moment his hair was cut, it began to grow again. It grew too slowly for someone to notice, but much faster than normal.

When the people of Gaza saw Samson being led into the city, they cheered, "Praise be to Dagon, he has handed us our enemy!"

The rulers of the Philistines got together to offer a sacrifice to Dagon, their god. The sacrifice became a great celebration in the city's temple. Everyone was dancing and singing. "Bring out Samson so we can see him!" they shouted.

The blind Samson was brought out before the Philistines. They had him stand between the two main pillars at the doorway, where everyone could see him. "Move me to where I can feel the pillars, so I can balance myself," Samson said to the servant who had led him into the temple.

"O Lord, remember your servant. Give me the strength for one final victory over the Philistines." Samson then braced his hands against the pillars of the temple, one hand against each. "Let me die with the Philistines!" he shouted as he pushed against the pillars with all of his might. The entire temple came crashing down, killing everyone inside, including Samson and the leaders of the Philistines. With God's help, Samson was able to achieve one final victory over his enemies. 📖

35. Ruth—the Dedicated Daughter

The Book of Ruth

Around the same time Samson was ruling the Israelites, a famine hit the land of Judah. The famine drove Elimelech from Bethlehem to the country of Moab with his wife Naomi and two sons. Moab was not suffering from the famine.

On the way to Moab, Elimelech died. Naomi and her two sons arrived in Moab and settled in. Soon, both the sons married Moabite women, Ruth and Orpah.

The five of them lived together for about ten years, but then both the sons got ill and died around the same time. Naomi heard that her homeland had recovered from the famine and was producing crops again. She decided to return to the place where she had been born.

When Naomi set off, her two daughters-in-law followed her. Naomi stopped and turned to the two young women. "Go back to your home," she pleaded with them. "I am an old woman and neither of you have any use for me. Go back to Moab. You are both young enough to find new husbands."

They both wept, "We want to go with you." Orpah and Ruth had both grown to love Naomi as much as they did their own mother.

"No," Naomi begged. "I am old. I am returning to my home. There won't be anything special there for you. You should stay here."

Orpah and Ruth cried some more. Orpah then hugged Naomi and wandered back toward Moab. Ruth, however, clung to her mother-in-law. "I will not leave you," she said. "Wherever you go, I will follow. Your people will become my people and your God my God." Naomi realized Ruth was determined to come with her, so she stopped trying to convince her to return to Moab.

The two women traveled until they reached Bethlehem. Naomi was very sad because she was returning alone to the place she had left with her husband and two sons. Ruth comforted Naomi. The two women arrived at the beginning of the barley harvest.

Naomi had a relative from her husband's side named Boaz. Boaz was a rather wealthy man. Ruth asked Naomi to allow her to go to the fields and glean the grain behind the harvesters of the barley. Gleaners would follow behind the harvesters and gather any grain that was missed. It was a job only the very poor did.

Boaz went out to his field to greet his harvesters. He noticed Ruth in the distance, very hard at work. "Who is that girl?" Boaz asked one of the harvesters.

"She is the Moabite woman, who came here with Naomi," the harvester replied. "She asked if she could glean behind the harvesters. She has been at work all day, with only one short rest."

Boaz approached Ruth and said, "Do not glean from any other field, it is dangerous. Stay here with my servant girls and you can glean from my fields. Also, if you get thirsty, come and drink from the water my men bring out here every day."

Ruth bowed down. "Thank you, sir. May I ask why I deserve such kindness?"

"Because I have heard about how you showed such kindness to my cousin, Naomi," Boaz replied. "May the Lord reward you for your dedication."

As Boaz was leaving his fields, he told his harvesters that Ruth should always be welcome to glean from the fields. He also told them to be sure to leave extra grain for her to gather.

Because the harvesters left extra grain behind, Ruth was able to glean a large amount. When Naomi saw how much grain Ruth had gathered one day, she asked her, "Whose fields are you gleaning so much grain from?" Ruth explained everything that had happened.

"God bless him!" Naomi exclaimed. "Boaz is a relative of ours. Yes, you should stay close to him, it will be safer for you. He is very kind."

After the harvests were over, Naomi went up to her daughter-in-law. "My daughter, I should find a home for you. Boaz is a close relative of your husband. Go to him and seek out his protection. Tonight he will be working on the threshing floor. Go there and wait until he has finished eating. Then, when he lies down to sleep, uncover his feet and lie down. He will tell you what to do then."

Ruth did what her mother-in-law said. Boaz woke up in the middle of the night to find someone sleeping at his feet. "Who is that?" he asked.

"It is Ruth," she answered. "I have come to you for protection because you are the kinsman of my husband."

Boaz was touched. He gave Ruth a large amount of grain and told her to return to Naomi. He also said he would come for her once he made sure with the town that no one who had a closer relation to her husband. Boaz returned that same day and soon, he and Ruth were married. They had a son whom they named Obed.

36. The Birth and Call of Samuel

1 Samuel 1–3

In the land of Ramathain, there was an Israelite named Elkanah. Elkanah had two wives—Hannah and Peninnah. Peninnah bore children, but Hannah was unable to. Even so, Elkanah loved Hannah very much and always tried to comfort her. Hannah was sad because she had no children.

Every year, the entire family of Elkanah would go to Shiloh to pray at the temple and make sacrifices. Whenever they went Peninnah would tease and insult Hannah for not having any children. Peninnah was jealous of the extra love and kindness Elkanah showed toward Hannah.

Hannah would always get very upset from Peninnah's teasing. Every time Hannah would burst into tears. "Why are you crying?" Elkanah would ask her. "Am I not worth ten sons to you?"

While at Shiloh, Hannah remained at the temple while the rest of her family left. "O Lord," she prayed silently. "Please look down on me with kindness and give me a son. If you give me a son I will make sure his life is dedicated to your service."

Hannah continued to pray for a long time. She was so caught up in her silent prayer that her lips were moving without her making a sound. The High Priest of the temple, a man named Eli, saw her praying and moving her lips strangely. Eli thought the woman was drunk.

"How long will you stay there, woman? Why don't you quit drinking and go home to your family."

"I am not drunk, my lord," replied Hannah. "I am very sad and have been praying to the Lord for a very special wish."

Eli saw that Hannah was indeed very sad and not drunk at all. "Go in peace, and may God grant your wish."

God did listen to Hannah's prayer, and she had a son. She named him Samuel, which means "God hears."

Hannah and Elkanah raised Samuel until he was about three or four years old. Once Samuel was old enough, Hannah took him back to the temple where she had prayed to God for a son. She also took some livestock, a sack of flour, and some wine. When she reached the temple at Shiloh, she took Samuel in and went to the High Priest.

"I am the woman who stood here a few years ago and prayed silently to the Lord," Hannah said to Eli. "You blessed me and said, 'May God grant your wish.' God has granted me my wish for a son, and now I wish to return him to the Lord."

Eli took young Samuel in and began training him in the ways of the Lord. Samuel grew up to be honest and good. Eli's own children were very bad and deceitful.

One evening Eli said goodnight to Samuel. Eli had become nearly blind. Samuel went to lie down in the temple in his usual place. Just as he closed his eyes he heard his name called.

"Here I am," Samuel called out. He got up and went to Eli's bed. "Here I am. You called me?"

"I did not call for you," Eli replied. "Go back to sleep."

Samuel returned to his mat and lay down again. "Samuel! Samuel!" a voice called out. Samuel clearly heard the voice and immediately got up.

"What do you need, lord?" Samuel asked Eli.

"My son, I did not call for you," Eli replied. "Go back and lie down."

Samuel did not realize that it was God speaking to him! The Lord had never spoken to Samuel before. God called out to Samuel a third time. Samuel got up again, and went to Eli.

This time, Eli realized that it must be the Lord speaking to Samuel. "Samuel, next time the voice calls out your name, reply: 'Speak, Lord, your servant is listening.'"

Samuel lay down. "Samuel! Samuel!" the voice of the Lord called out.

"Speak, Lord, your servant is listening," Samuel said, just as Eli had instructed him.

The whole night God spoke to Samuel, telling him about what the future held for him. God also told Samuel about the curse that was placed on Eli and his sons. Eli's sons were full of sin, and because he did nothing to stop them, Eli was to be punished as well.

In the morning, Eli went to Samuel to find out what God had said to him. "Tell me everything my son, do not leave anything out."

Samuel told Eli everything about his future and how God would not forgive Eli or his sons for the sins they committed. Samuel was afraid because he was telling Eli bad news about him and his sons.

"So be it," Eli replied. "It is the will of the Lord."

37. The Philistines Capture the Ark of the Covenant

Samuel 3–6

The Lord continued to speak to Samuel, and soon Samuel was known as a great prophet among the Israelites.

Now the Israelites were still struggling with the Philistines at that time. One day, the Philistine army attacked the Israelites and won a big victory. Many of the Israelite soldiers were killed.

The Israelite elders spoke among themselves. "Why did the Lord give us this defeat?" they asked one another. The elders continued to mutter about what happened when one came up with the idea of getting the Ark of the Covenant and taking it into battle with them.

The Ark was taken to the battlefield. When the Israelite soldiers saw it, they gave a great shout, shaking the ground all around them. The Philistines heard their shout and became afraid. Eli's two sons were among the men who had brought the Ark to the battlefield.

"The Israelites have brought their God with them onto the battlefield!" The Philistines knew the tales of what God did to the Egyptians many years before. "We must all fight with all our bravery and strength to defeat the Israelites."

The Philistine and Israelite armies fought again. The Philistines defeated the Israelites again. The Philistines also captured the Ark. Among the Israelite dead were both of Eli's sons.

After the battle, a man from the Israelite army ran to Shiloh to report what had happened. Covered with dust, and his clothes torn to shreds, the man ran into the city. When he told everyone what had happened the Israelites all became afraid and cried out.

"What is the uproar?" asked Eli. Eli was very old and blind. He was standing by the road waiting for news. He was worried about the Ark.

The man went up to the High Priest and told him about the defeat of the Israelite army, his sons' deaths, and how the Ark had been captured. When Eli heard all this news, he fell and died, because when he learned that the Ark of the Lord had been captured, his heart stopped beating.

The Philistines took the Ark back to their land called Ashdod. They took the Ark into their temple and set it beside a large gold statue of Dagon, the god of the Philistines. Early the next morning, the statue of Dagon was found lying on its side in front of the Ark. The Priests of Ashdod picked the statue up and returned it to its correct position.

The next morning, the priests of Ashdod entered the temple. They saw the statue of Dagon fallen on the ground again! This time its hands and head had been broken off. Throughout Ashdod, everyone began to get sick. The people of the city demanded that the Ark be sent away.

The Philistines tried moving the Ark from place to place within their territory. No matter where they went, disease and disaster followed them. The rulers of the Philistines gathered together to decide what to do. "Let us return the Ark of the God of Israel to its rightful place," said one of the elders. "If we do not, we will all be destroyed."

The Philistines put the Ark on a cart pulled by two cows. They also put five gold rats and five gold lumps in the shape of the sores all the Philistine had gotten from the diseases spreading throughout their land. The Philistines hoped that this peace offering would make the Lord heal their illness.

When the Philistines released the cows pulling the cart that carried the Ark, the cows immediately headed along the road toward the Israelites. Without anyone leading them, the cows took the Ark back to the Israelites.

Some Israelites were harvesting wheat in the fields when the cart approached. They looked up at the strange sight and saw the two unattended cows pulling the cart. Once they recognized the Ark, they were overjoyed! The Ark was again with the people of Israel.

38. The Israelites Get a King
1 Samuel 8–10

amuel grew old. The Israelites grew to love him after years of wise leadership. He also became known as a powerful prophet of the Lord. Because he was getting older, Samuel appointed both of his sons to be judges over the Israelites. Instead of kings, the Israelites had judges to guide them in legal and moral difficulties. Unfortunately, both of Samuel's sons were not very much like their father—they accepted bribes and were poor leaders.

The elders of Israel gathered one day and decided to ask Samuel to appoint Israel its first king. When Samuel heard this request he was upset. Israel had never had a king before. Samuel warned them that a king would rule over them and they would be like his slaves. The Israelites did not care, they wanted a king.

"So be it," Samuel said. "Go back to your homes, I will appoint a king to rule over Israel."

A few days later, a tall young man came up to Samuel at the gateway to the city. "Are you the seer of this town?" he asked.

"Yes, I am a seer," answered Samuel. A seer is another word for prophet.

"I have lost three donkeys and was wondering if you could tell me where to find them."

"Come with me to the top of the hills," Samuel said to the young man. "We will eat there, and in the morning I will tell you all that is in your heart. Do not worry about the donkeys. They have all ready been found. You are to be a great man among your people."

"But I am just a Benjamite," replied Saul. "We are the smallest of the tribes, and I am from the weakest of its clans. Why would you say such a thing to me?"

The next day Samuel led Saul to the edge of the town. "Tell your servant to return home. I have a message from the Lord to give to you."

After the servant left, Samuel got out a ram's horn full of oil and poured some on Saul's head. "With this oil I anoint you King of Israel!" Samuel announced. "Now return home. One your way you will meet two men who will tell you that the donkeys have been found and that your father is now worried about you. Then you will meet three men on their way to Bethel. One will have three young goats, another three loaves of bread, and the third a skin full of wine. They will give you two of their loaves of bread. Lastly, you will meet a group of prophets. You will join with the prophets and be one of them for a while. Once these signs have been fulfilled, you should do as your heart tells you, because the Lord will be with you then.

It happened exactly as Samuel said. Samuel then summoned the people of Israel to announce the new king. But when he announced that Saul was to be the first king of Israel, Saul was no where to be found. The Lord told Samuel that Saul was hiding among some baggage of the Israelites who had to travel to the city for the announcement. Saul was feeling overwhelmed by everything that was happening.

When Saul was brought out he was a full head taller than everyone else. "Here is your new king!" Samuel shouted to the people, "See how the Lord has made him unlike all other men."

"Long live the king!" everyone shouted.

Saul became the first King of Israel. He proclaimed laws in the name of the Lord and organized the Israelite army to fight against the Philistines.

39. Saul the King
1 Samuel 11–14

hortly after Saul became the King of Israel, the Ammonites attacked the city of Jabesh Gilead. The Ammonites were an ancient enemy of the Israelites. The Ammonite army was so large, and the city of Jabesh Gilead was rather small, so the people in the city offered to surrender. They thought it was the only way they could survive.

Nahash, the cruel general of the Ammonite army, said that he would accept surrender only if he could gouge out the right eye of everyone in the city. The people panicked. They asked if they could have seven days to think it over.

They immediately sent out messengers from Jabesh Gilead to all the Israelite tribes pleading for help. Soon word reached Saul about the cruelty of the Ammonites. Saul was filled with rage that God's chosen people would be treated this way. He quickly sent word to everyone in Israel and gathered the largest army Israel had ever seen—over 300,000 soldiers!

Saul led the army to Jabesh Gilead. He divided the army into three groups to surround the Ammonites and attack them from all sides. The Ammonite army was completely wiped out. The people of Israel rejoiced.

Years later, Saul and his son Jonathan were battling with the Philistines. One day, he led 2,000 men to the hills near Bethel, and had his son lead 1,000 men to the land of Benjamin. Both armies attacked outposts belonging to the Philistines. They caused so much damage that the Philistines decided to amass an enormous army and destroy the Israelites once and for all.

The Philistines gathered a large army near Israel's border. Saul sent word out that every Israelite man able to fight was to come. Many of the men hid in caves and the thick forests of the hills. As the Philistine army approached, Samuel told Saul to wait seven days. After seven days Samuel said he would come and make a sacrifice to the Lord and pray for victory.

Seven days came and went. The Philistine army was nearly upon Saul and his dwindling army. The Israelites were running away in great numbers. Saul decided that he had to do something so he prepared the sacrifice himself.

"Why have you disobeyed me?" Samuel asked, as he suddenly appeared, almost out of no where.

"You did not come," replied Saul. "My men were scattering so I made the sacrifice to God in your place so we would not be defeated in the coming battle."

"You have wronged the Lord," Samuel said to Saul. "Because of your sin, Israel will not be ruled by your family. When you die, someone else's son will become king." Samuel, full of anger, left Saul's presence.

Saul had only 600 men with him, and none of them had swords. All they had were axes and other tools used for farming. Only Saul and Jonathan had swords.

One night, Jonathan and his armor bearer left the small army and headed for the Philistine forces. Armor bearers were used by high-ranking soldiers to carry their extra weapons, shields, and other armor they didn't need when not fighting (this way the soldier didn't need to lug all that heavy metal around himself). They came to a deep ravine that separated them from the Philistines' camps. Tall cliffs were on both sides of the ravine. Jonathan and his servant

walked around the ravine, but could not find an easy way to cross it without being seen by the enemy. "We will let God decide for us. Let's make ourselves seen," Jonathan told his armor bearer. "If the Philistines tell us to wait where we are and they come and attack us, we shall wait. But, if they tell us to go over there, that is what we shall do."

"Do as you will, I am with you," Jonathan's trusting servant replied.

Jonathan and the armor bearer stood up and walked into the open. When the Philistines saw them they shouted across the ravine, "Come over here. We want to give you something!" The Philistines shouted and laughed at them.

Jonathan took their response as a sign from God that he was to cross the ravine. Once he and the armor bearer made it to the other side of the ravine, they attacked the large group of Philistines with intense ferocity!

God was with Jonathan. The fighting shook the ground and caused the Philistines to become afraid. Confusion spread throughout their camp like a wildfire. Soon the Philistines were running in every direction and frantically flailing their swords about.

Saul and his small army saw the Philistines in disarray across the ravine. Saul also saw the two Israelite soldiers fighting among them. Saul searched through his camp and discovered that it was his son fighting.

Saul and his army set out to help Jonathan. Among the Philistines were soldiers who were Hebrews. They had just agreed to be a part of the Philistine army because they lived in Philistine territory. When they saw Jonathan fighting the Philistines their eyes were opened and they changed sides!

The commotion of the battle shook the earth. The Israelites who had fled to the caves in the mountains when the Philistines first invaded came out and joined with their fellow countrymen. Soon the Israelites had the Philistines completely scattered throughout the land.

40. David the Shepherd Boy, the Next Chosen King of Israel
1 Samuel 16–17

"Go to Bethlehem," God said to Samuel. "There you will find a man named Jesse. I have chosen one of his sons to be the next king."

Samuel went to Bethlehem. The leaders of Bethlehem trembled when Samuel approached them. Samuel was a very powerful prophet, and well known among all the Israelites. "Have you come in peace?" they asked Samuel.

"Yes," Samuel replied. "I have come to make a sacrifice to the Lord. Go and prepare yourselves and come with me." Jesse happened to be there as well when Samuel arrived. Samuel told Jesse to attend to the sacrifice as well, and to take his sons with him.

Samuel stood at the site of the sacrifice. Soon Jesse approached with seven of his sons. Samuel looked at each of the sons, but none of them was the one God had chosen. "Are these all of your sons?" Samuel asked Jesse.

"There is one more, my youngest," answered Jesse. "He is out in the fields tending my flocks."

"Send for him," Samuel said. "We shall not begin until he arrives."

Jesse sent a servant out to get his youngest son, a boy named David. When David approached, Samuel looked at the boy and heard the voice of God: "He is the one," it said.

Samuel took out a ram's horn full of oil and poured it over David's head and blessed him. When Samuel blessed him, the spirit and power of the Lord entered David's body.

Saul was still the king of Israel at this time. Like David, Saul also had been anointed by Samuel. However, Saul had been disobedient to God and as a result, God left him. After God's spirit left Saul, an evil spirit would torment him from time to time.

Saul's servants and advisors were worried. The king's fits would put him in a rage and he became dangerous to everyone around him. One day, while Saul was behaving normally, one of his most trusted servants said, "My lord, we have sought the advice of wise men and they say that the music of a harp played very well by someone pure of heart and spirit will chase away the evil spirit that has been plaguing you."

"Go then," replied Saul, "and find someone who plays the harp well and has a pure heart and spirit."

It just so happened that David was very good at playing the harp, so good that he was well known throughout Israel. David would play his harp out in the fields while tending his father's sheep. Saul's servants asked David's father, Jesse, to send David to Saul.

David left immediately and went to Saul. Saul liked David right away, and gave him a job as one of his personal armor bearers. Whenever Saul became possessed by the evil spirit, David would play his harp. Once the soft music began to hum, the evil spirit would leave Saul immediately.

After David had served Saul for a short time, trouble began brewing. The Philistines had gathered a large army on a hill near a valley. Saul led an army of Israelites to a hill on the opposite side of the valley. Three of David's

 brothers were soldiers in the Israelite army, so David's father needed him to help tend the flocks of sheep.

Among the Philistine soldiers was one man who was a lot bigger than anyone else! He was nine feet tall, and wore heavy bronze armor covering his entire body. In one hand he had a giant sword, in the other a javelin. His name was Goliath, and he was the champion soldier of the Philistines.

Goliath and his armor bearer walked toward the Israelites, leaving the Philistines standing in their ranks at their camp. "I make a challenge!" Goliath's voice boomed as he yelled across the valley. "Let any man among you come forward and fight me. If he strikes me down, then the Philistines shall become the servants of the Israelites! But, if I strike him down, you shall become our servants! Are you not the men of the great King Saul?"

No one stepped forward because they knew they could not defeat such a powerful soldier. Every day for forty days Goliath made the same challenge, and each time he taunted them more. Every time, the Israelite soldiers cowered in fear.

Jesse gave David some food to take to his brothers. He also wanted David to return with news about how things were going on the battlefield. When David arrived, he went to greet his brothers. As he did so Goliath appeared to make his challenge again. When the Israelites saw Goliath they all ran.

"Who is this man who defies the people of the Lord?" asked David. The Israelite soldiers explained Goliath's challenge.

Saul heard that David had arrived at the camp and sent for him. "Fear not my lord," David said to Saul. "I will fight this Philistine."

"You cannot fight Goliath!" answered Saul. "You are just a boy."

"While tending my father's flocks, if a lion or a bear killed a sheep and ran off with it, I chased after it and killed it. Goliath will be no different from them. I will have God on my side."

"So be it," replied Saul. "May the Lord be with you." Saul gave David his own armor and his own sword. When David put Saul's armor on and tried to walk, it felt heavy. David was not a soldier and had never worn armor before.

"I cannot wear this because I am not used to it. God will be my armor." David took the armor off and went to the stream that ran at the bottom of the valley. All he took with him was his shepherd's staff and his sling. He chose five smooth stones from near the stream.

Goliath came out from the Philistines camp. He saw David approaching him. "What is this?" he laughed loudly. "Are you going to beat me with that stick like a wild dog, little boy? I will tear you to pieces and scatter your parts all over the valley for the birds to eat!"

"You come ready to fight with a sword and javelin, but I come with the power of the Lord." Goliath took long strides toward David, his sword drawn and ready to strike. David ran toward Goliath and took a stone from his pouch and put it in his sling. David then slung the stone at Goliath. The small stone struck Goliath right on the forehead and he fell over! David grabbed Goliath's enormous sword and killed him with it.

When the Philistine saw their champion—the mightiest soldier—fall, they all panicked and ran. The Israelites cheered and chased the Philistines down and defeated them. David was a hero!

41. David the Hero

1 Samuel 18–20

After David had defeated the Philistine champion, Goliath, Saul rewarded him with a high command in the Israelite army and let him live in his house. Jonathan, Saul's only son, and David became the greatest of friends. They were like brothers.

"You are like a brother to me," Jonathan said to David. "And from this day forth I shall love you like a brother." He gave David his robe, his best sword, his favorite bow, and his royal belt as a symbol of his devotion to David.

As Saul's highest leader in the army, David was sent off to many battles against the Philistines. David was enormously successful, defeating the Philistines wherever he went. David was already heralded as a great hero by all of Israel for his victory over Goliath. After his many victories over the Philistines, David became an even greater hero in the eyes of the Israelites, and especially among the other leaders in the army.

One day as Saul was outside waiting for David to return from a great victory, he saw the people of Israel all celebrating and waiting for

David as well. Some women were dancing and began chanting a song: "Saul has slain thousands, but David has slain tens of thousands!"

Saul was angry. He thought They credit David with killing tens of thousands, but me, only thousands. I have already rewarded him greatly. If I give him any more, he will have the whole kingdom. Saul's jealousy grew and he began keeping an eye on David.

Saul became afraid of David, because the Lord was with David and had left Saul many years before. To get David away for a while, Saul put him in charge of 1,000 men and sent him on a long and dangerous attack against the Philistines far away. Saul hoped David would not come back. However, God was with David always, and David had enormous success in his battles against the Philistines. The people's love for David only grew.

When David returned, Saul was even more jealous than before. He began thinking of ways to kill him. Saul's youngest daughter, Michal, fell in love with David. Saul was pleased. He told David he should marry Michal and become his son-in-law. Saul thought that if David married Michal he'd be easier to get to.

David did get married to Michal, and Saul's jealousy only intensified. Saul told his son Jonathan and his servants to kill David. But Jonathan remembered his oath to David and instead warned David about Saul's plot. Jonathan told David to hide out for a while and he would speak to his father.

"What wrong has David ever done to you?" Jonathan asked his father. "He has won us great victories and has never disobeyed you. He also risked his life when he faced Goliath, and because of this we all live free. The Lord is with David and we have all been rewarded."

Saul seemed moved. "You are right, son. David shall not be harmed."

All was okay for a while. But one day while David was playing his harp in Saul's house, Saul was overcome with hatred and jealousy. He flung his spear at David. David was able to dodge the spear, and he ran home.

Saul told his officers to go to David's house and surround it in the night. When David left his house in the morning, they were to kill him. Michal was in her father's house at the time and heard what Saul planned to do.

"You must leave tonight!" she pleaded with her husband. "My father plans on having you killed in the morning." So David escaped in the middle of the night. Michal put a statue in David's bed and put some goat hair on the statue's head and covered the rest. When the soldiers came to her house in the morning asking for David, she said David was very ill and could not come out. The soldiers looked in the bedroom and saw the statue with the goat hair on its head and thought it must be David. They returned to Saul to tell him what happened. Saul originally didn't want them killing David in his house because Michal, Saul's daughter, would be there and Saul loved his daughter and didn't want to see her harmed.

By the time Saul sent the soldiers back and the statue was discovered, David had made his escape and was safe. He went to see Jonathan. "What have I done that Saul wants me killed?" he asked Jonathan. What wrong have I done that I must die?"

"This is impossible!" Jonathan replied. "My father promised me that you wouldn't be harmed."

"He must know that you would warn me if he told you, the way you did the last time. I have an idea. Tomorrow is the Moon Festival. Go, and if your father misses me tell him I had to go home to Bethlehem to pray with my family. If he says 'very well' and does not seem angry then you know I am safe. But, if he gets angry you know that he wishes to kill me. If I am guilty of any wrong, you may kill me yourself."

"Never!" answered Jonathan. "If my father wishes to harm you, I will warn you. Hide on the far side of town behind the large stone that stands alone in the field there. I will shoot three arrows near the stone. I will send a servant boy to fetch the arrows, and if everything is safe I will shout to him, 'The arrows are just to your side.' But if you are in danger I will shout, 'The arrows are still further beyond you'."

The next day at the festival Saul noticed David's seat was empty. He had a plan in place to have him killed that night. "Where is David?" he asked Jonathan, who was seated beside him.

"He told me to tell you he is sorry, but he had to go and pray with his family, a relative of theirs has recently died."

Saul was furious. He stood up violently and flung the dishes and cup in front of him. "I know you are on his side!" he shouted at Jonathan.

"Why are you so angry, Father? What has David ever done?" asked Jonathan. Just then, Saul flung his spear at Jonathan. Jonathan dodged the spear, stood up, and left in anger. He went to the far side of town where David was hiding and gave the signal that told David that Saul wanted to kill him. Saddened, David left.

42. David the Outcast
1 Samuel 21–24

King Saul was trying to have David killed. Saul's son Jonathan, who also happened to be a devoted friend of David, tipped David off that Saul was plotting the murder. David was able to escape with only the clothes he was wearing. He was alone in the world.

David headed to the city of Nob, where he knew a man named Ahimelech. Ahimelech was the high priest of the city, and all his many sons were priests as well. "Why have you come here? Why are you alone?" Ahimelech asked David. He hadn't heard yet that David was wanted by Saul.

"The king has given me a mission that I must keep secret. I left my men behind and told them to meet me later. I'm sorry but I am in a rush and had no time to collect supplies. I need five loaves of bread and a weapon. Can you help me?"

"I usually don't have any bread. But, I happen to have five loaves. There are no weapons anywhere in the holy city of Nob, except for the sword you took from the Philistine champion, Goliath."

David got what he had come for and headed to the land of Gath, which was not under the Saul's rule.

After David left Gath he headed to the Caves of Adullam. The caves interconnected throughout the mountains and hills near the desert. It was a

good place to hide. The cave was not far from where his father and brothers lived. Soon, David's family and their neighbors got word of where David was hiding out. A group of about 400 went to David. These people were loyal to David. Many had been treated poorly under Saul's rule over Israel. They all decided to stay with David in the caves and have David be their leader.

One day, one of David's men went up to him. "The city of Keilah is under attack by the Philistines! They are looting their food stores." Keilah was a small city near the caves.

"Should I go and save Keilah?" David asked the Lord.

"Yes, go attack the Philistines and save Keilah," God told David. David obeyed and attacked the Philistines with his men. Although greatly outnumbered, David and his 400 men defeated the Philistines and saved the city.

Saul found out that David was in Keilah. He immediately gathered a strong force of soldiers and led them toward the city. Within Saul's forces were men still loyal to David. They sent word ahead to David telling him that Saul's troops were on their way. David fled with his men, now numbering just over 600. (Many of the men of Keilah decided to join with David's forces.)

Saul pursued David, only a day or two behind. God was watching over David, and always kept Saul just one step behind, whether by calling up a wind storm or confusing Saul's mind. Through deserts and mountains and plains and caves, Saul chased David. During the chase, David's group passed through many towns and cities, and in each place more and more men joined David's group.

Saul heard that David was in the Desert of En Gedi, so he led his forces there. The desert was hot. Saul decided to spend the hottest part of the day in a cave. It just so happened that the cave he went into was the same one David was hiding in. David was deep inside the cave and Saul could not see him. But David saw Saul enter through the sunny entrance of the cave.

David's men whispered to him, "This is the day the Lord said he would deliver your enemy into your hands! Now is your chance to kill the king and end our constant running." David slowly crept up behind Saul and pulled out a dagger. Creeping very close, David grabbed onto a corner of Saul's robe and cut it off. David then returned to his men.

"The Lord forbids that I harm my master, no matter what his sin!" David said to his men. He forbade them from taking any action against Saul. They all watched as Saul got up and left the cave.

As Saul was walking away from the cave, David stepped out. "My king and master!" David shouted. He was holding up the cloth. "Why do you think I wish you harm? Look, I cut off the corner of your robe and did not touch you! Please understand that I have not wronged you."

Saul blinked as if waking up from a dream. "David? Is that you, my son?"

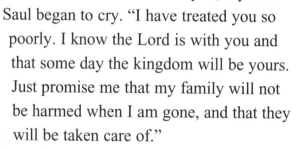

Saul began to cry. "I have treated you so poorly. I know the Lord is with you and that some day the kingdom will be yours. Just promise me that my family will not be harmed when I am gone, and that they will be taken care of."

David promised Saul that his family would never be in need. Saul then returned to his home, but David stayed at his desert stronghold. ✑

43. The Death of Saul

1 Samuel 28–31; 2 Samuel 1–2, 5

amuel had died. After Samuel died, Saul expelled all the witches and fortune tellers from the land of Israel. Although Saul had promised not to hurt David, there was still trouble between the two.

David decided to head to land controlled by the Philistines and ask the king there to give him and his men some land to settle on. The king of the Philistines, Achish, agreed and gave David some land in the country of Gath.

The Philistines and Israelites were still warring. King Achish gathered one of the largest Philistine forces ever and began heading into the Israelites' territory. Saul gathered all the Israelite soldiers he could. When Saul saw the Philistine army approaching from the distance his heart sank. He became terrified. Saul asked the Lord for guidance, but got no response.

"Find me a witch that I can consult with, quickly!" Saul said.

"There is a witch still in Endor," one of his servants replied.

Saul disguised himself in ragged clothes and headed to Endor. "I need you to talk to a spirit for me," Saul asked the witch when she arrived.

"Who from the land of the dead would you like to speak with?"

"Bring up the prophet Samuel," Saul said. "Tell me what you see."

"I see the spirit of a man. He is old and wearing the robe of a high prophet."

Saul bowed to the ground. Even though he couldn't see Samuel, he knew he was in his presence.

"Why have you called for me?" the voice of Samuel asked.

"I am in trouble," Saul said. "The Lord has left me and there is a powerful Philistine army preparing to attack Israel. I came to ask you for guidance."

"Why do you come to me?" asked Samuel. "You have disobeyed the Lord, which is why he has left you. The Lord is going to take away your kingdom and give it to David. The Lord will hand over Israel to the Philistines and both you and your sons will be with me soon."

Saul collapsed. He hadn't eaten all day and had been traveling hard. The witch and Saul's men urged him to eat something before returning to the Israelite army. At first Saul refused. He felt unworthy of food or rest. Eventually they convinced Saul to eat and they all rested a while before returning to the battlefield.

Saul returned to the Israelite army, and they prepared for a great battle. When the Philistines attacked, they swarmed over the Israelites because the Philistines outnumbered them. The Israelites had no chance, and almost immediately they all began running.

Jonathan and Saul's other sons were killed. Saul and his armor bearer were fleeing, but the Philistines were too many. They overcame Saul and one archer shot an arrow into Saul's leg.

"You must kill me!" Saul pleaded with his armor bearer. "Soon, those heathens will be upon us and I will die a horrible death."

"I . . . I cannot, my lord!" the armor bearer cried.

Saul stood up as best he could. He dug the handle of his sword into the ground and held the point to his body. He fell on his sword and killed himself, rather than allow the Philistines the glory of killing the great king of Israel.

Some time later God told David to return to Israel—to the land of Hebron. The men of Judah came to David and anointed him king. David learned that it was the people of Jabesh Gilead—the city Saul once saved from the Philistines—who retrieved Saul's body and gave it a proper burial. David sent word to Jabesh Gilead thanking them for their service and informing them that he had been anointed the new king.

However, Abner, the commander of Saul's army, was loyal to Saul's family. He saved Ish-Bosheth, the only remaining son of Saul, and had him named as king of Israel. David became king over the land of Judah in the south. Ish-Bosheth ruled as king of the land of Israel in the north.

The House of Saul and the House of David were at war. They fought for over seven years. The Lord was with David and he eventually won, and Ish-Bosheth was killed. David then became the King of all of Israel and Judah—the land of the Israelites.

44. David, the King of Israel

2 Samuel 5–13

fter David became king over all the Israelites, he decided that Jerusalem would be the new capital of the united Israel. Jerusalem was a great city under the control of the Jebusites.

When David and his people arrived at Jerusalem, the Jebusites closed the city's gates and would not let them in. David sent some of his men to climb into a water shaft that led them deep inside the city. Once in, David's men were able to open the gates. Once the gates were open, David and his army were able to take control of the city easily.

Jerusalem became known as the City of David. David lived in an enormous palace in Jerusalem and began at once to have the city built into the greatest on earth.

David was a great ruler. He led the Israelite army to victory over the Philistines and finally gave control of the entire land to the Israelites. David decided that the Ark of the Covenant—the Ark containing God's laws—should be brought to Jerusalem.

The Ark of the Covenant was brought to Jerusalem by a crowd of 30,000—all singing and dancing. As they entered the gates, David removed his royal robes and began singing and dancing along with his people. Trumpets blasted, the sounds of tambourines and pipes filled the air, and everyone was cheering and singing and shouting. It was a day of great rejoicing. David was very happy. He made a sacrifice to the Lord, thanking him for everything they had achieved. David then had a feast brought out for all the people to eat.

However, David's wife Michal watched from the palace window and saw David singing and dancing with the common people. Michal was the daughter of Saul, and had been raised as a princess. She thought it disgusting that anyone of royalty would be rejoicing with his subjects.

David had the Ark of the Covenant placed in a special tent he had prepared for its keeping. He blessed all those who helped bring the Ark to its new resting place. David then returned to the palace to rejoice with his family and bless them as well.

"How royal and majestic the King of Israel has shown himself to be today," Michal said to David mockingly. "Singing and dancing with common people as if he were a commoner himself!"

"I was singing and dancing before our Lord," David replied calmly. "The Lord who chose me over your father and any of his descendents to rule over the Israelites. Nothing that I do in the name of the Lord is shameful. It is you, who despise my service to God, who is full of shame!"

David ruled Israel for forty years and had many sons. He resolved to have a great temple built in Jerusalem. He had the plans laid out but did not have time to have it built before he died. During his rule, David won many victories over the enemies of Israel, and the people prospered.

Before dying, David named his son, Solomon, as the next king of Israel.

45. King Solomon, the Wise Ruler

1 Kings 1–4

When King David was older, and did not have long left to live, he summoned one of his wives, Bathsheba, the mother of Solomon. "I have asked you here today to make an oath to you. In the name of the Lord I swear that Solomon, our son, will be king after I am gone and will sit on the throne in Jerusalem."

Word of David's promise to Bathsheba spread quickly through the kingdom. David had many sons, and many of them were angry that they were not chosen to be the next king. Traditionally, the oldest son inherited his father's wealth and status as head of the family. However, Solomon was one of David's youngest sons.

In order to prevent too much squabbling over the throne, David had Solomon anointed king while he was still alive. Being anointed was serious business. Once anointed, Solomon had God's blessing as the king. So for a while Solomon was king with David still around to guide him.

But David was old. "I have reached the time of the end of my life, my son," David said. "You will no longer have my guidance. Just remember always to be strong, true, and honest, and always listen to and obey the Lord. If you remember to do this, you will be fine."

Shortly after saying this to his son, David died. After forty years of ruling as king of Israel, David was buried in Jerusalem, the City of David. Because

Solomon had sat on the throne with his father, his rule was already firm and well accepted by the people.

Solomon went to work quickly, taking revenge against his father's enemies. He also met with the Pharaoh of Egypt and made a treaty. Solomon married the Pharaoh's daughter and the two rulers agreed their kingdoms would exist in peace with each other. He decided to build the temple his father had planned, as well as a royal palace. While the temple was being built, Solomon was forced to travel from temple to temple throughout the land to pray and make sacrifices to the Lord.

One day, Solomon traveled to Gibeon, which was the site of the most important temples in the land. When there, Solomon made a large sacrifice and prayed to the Lord.

That night when Solomon went to sleep he had a dream. In his dream he heard the voice of God. "Solomon, make any wish and it will be granted," the Lord said.

"You have been very good to Israel and my father, David. You have already extended this kindness to David by giving him a son to succeed him. Now that I am the king of all of Israel, I would wish for the wisdom to rule Israel as it needs to be ruled," Solomon answered in his dream.

"You have made a good wish," God replied. *"Many men would have wished for long life or wealth or victory against enemies, but you have wished for the most precious thing of all—wisdom. Because you have made such a request, I shall grant you the greatest wisdom in a man that the earth has ever seen. I will also give you great wealth and a long life so long as you obey my laws as your father did."*

Solomon awoke. He realized he had dreamed, but he also realized that God had spoken to him in his dream. He rejoiced and thanked the Lord. He returned to Jerusalem and held a great celebration.

Just days later, Solomon's wisdom was put to the test. Two women came before the king. They both lived in the same house and had both had children at around the same time. One of the babies had died, and both mothers said that the living baby was hers.

"Her baby is the one that died!" the first woman shouted. "I think I would know my own baby!"

"No," the other woman cried. "I woke up this morning and found the dead baby lying near me. I was horrified but noticed that the dead baby was not my own. Then I saw this woman carrying my baby and letting on that he was hers! She must have switched the babies in the night . . . ."

"No! The dead baby is yours. This is my son," the other interrupted. The two women argued for some time.

"Give me the child," Solomon said. "Since there is no way to know who I lying, I will cut the child in two and both of you will get half."

"No! Do not hurt my baby!" the second woman cried, the woman who claimed the other must have switched the babies in the night. "She may keep the child, I will take back my claim."

At the same time the other woman said, laughing, "Yes, cut him in two my lord!" She then turned to the other woman, "Now neither of us will have him."

Solomon held the baby. "This child belongs to the woman who was willing to give up her child in order to save his life. That woman is the child's mother."

The news of Solomon's wisdom spread throughout Israel and all the people were happy to have such a king. God gave Solomon wisdom and a great ability to solve problems and settle quarrels. His understanding was as vast and measureless as the grains of sand on the seashore. He was the wisest man on earth.

As soon as he had the chance, Solomon began work on building a great temple to the Lord in Jerusalem. He sent messages to neighboring kingdoms asking for some of the supplies they would need. Eager to make friends with the Israelites, the neighboring kingdoms were quick to offer assistance.

The temple was to be like none other on earth. Solomon had all the stones cut and carved at the mining site, so no sound of a chisel would be heard where the temple was being built. When the stone structure was completed, Solomon had the entire inside lined with cedar boards, so that on the inside you couldn't tell that the temple was made of stone. The altar was coated in gold, and the Ark of the Covenant was put within its walls, deep in the inner sanctuary. That room was completely coated in gold! 📖

46. The Prophet Elijah
1 Kings 16–17

fter Solomon died Israel immediately began to fall apart. The land of the Israelites split in two. The split was the same as when David had first become king—Judah in the south with Jerusalem as its capital, and Israel in the north with Samaria as its capital.

After some time, Ahab became king of the northern kingdom of Israel. Ahab was an evil man. He worshipped Baal, the Canaanite god, and built statues and altars to him.

One day Elijah, a prophet, approached Ahab. Elijah wore a simple brown robe and had black curly hair. "As surely as the Lord exists, whom I serve, there will be no rain, except by my command!" Ahab was angry to hear this simple prophet threatening him. But before he could do anything, Elijah had slipped away.

After Elijah had left Ahab, the Lord spoke to him. "Elijah, you must go east and hide in the Kerith Ravine. At the bottom of the ravine flows a brook that you can drink from. I will send ravens to bring you food."

Elijah did what the Lord told him. He went into the Kerith Ravine and drank from the brook at its bottom, while all the rest of the land was dry. The Lord also sent ravens carrying bread and meat to Elijah every morning and evening.

Elijah stayed there for quite some time, until the brook dried up. The Lord instructed Elijah to head to the city of Sidon. When Elijah reached the city's walls he was very tired, thirsty, and hungry. A woman was gathering sticks by the gate. "Please," Elijah said to her, "can you get me something to drink?"

The woman nodded and headed to get some water for Elijah. As she turned, Elijah said, "and some food too."

"I am sorry, but I have only a handful of flour in a jar and a small bit of oil in a jug. I am gathering sticks so I may make one last meal for my son and me, before we die from this horrible drought."

"Go and do as you said, but first make a small loaf of bread and bring it to me, then make something for yourself and your son. This is what the Lord says, 'The jar of flour and jug of oil will not run out until rain returns to the land.'"

The woman did as Elijah said. She made a loaf of bread for Elijah and brought it to him with some water. She then returned home with Elijah and began making bread for herself and her son. As she made the bread she took pinches of flour from the clay jar and add a few drops of oil. However, neither the jar nor the jug became any emptier.

"You truly are a man of God," the woman said to Elijah. "The word of the Lord is spoken through you."

47. Elijah Faces 450 Prophets of Baal

1 Kings 18

 lijah's prophecy to Ahab continued. It did not rain for three full years anywhere in the kingdom of Israel. Ahab was very angry with Elijah and blamed him for the drought. Ahab had his men out searching for Elijah, but the Lord told Elijah where to go and hide.

After the three years of drought the Lord spoke to Elijah. "Go and stand before Ahab, and I will send rain." Even though Elijah knew Ahab was very angry with him, Elijah immediately obeyed the Lord without any hesitation. Elijah headed for Samaria, the capital city of Israel.

The city of Samaria was hit very hard by the drought. Ahab had a man named Obadiah working in the palace. Obadiah followed the Lord, unlike Ahab and most of Israel. Most of the Israelites had turned from God and now worshipped Baal. When Ahab had come to power, his wife sent out soldiers to kill all the prophets of the Lord. Obadiah was able to hide 100 of the prophets in a cave and snuck them out of Israel so that they might live.

While Obadiah was walking outside Ahab's palace, Elijah appeared before him. Obadiah recognized Elijah and bowed before him. "Is that really you, my lord Elijah?"

"Yes, my friend. I need you to go to your master, Ahab, and tell him that Elijah is here."

"What wrong have I done you that you would make me do something like that?" Obadiah asked Elijah. "You must know that Ahab has been searching high and low for you, asking everyone who passes through Samaria if they have seen you. Now if I go and tell him, 'The prophet you have been seeking is here' and you do not appear before him, I will be frowned upon!"

"I promise you," Elijah replied, "once you tell your master that I have arrived, I will appear before him."

So Obadiah went to Ahab and told him Elijah was near. Ahab immediately set out to see Elijah. "Is that you, the one who has caused all this trouble on Israel?"

"I have caused no harm to Israel," replied Elijah. "It was you, your fathers before you, and the people of Israel that have brought this trouble upon themselves! You have abandoned the Lord and now worship Baal. Now, summon the people of Israel to Mount Carmel. Also get the 450 prophets of Baal. Then we shall see just who is the true Lord."

Ahab summoned the 450 prophets of Baal, and sent out word to the people of Israel to be at Mount Carmel the next day. When the massive group was gathered around Elijah and the 450 prophets of Baal, Elijah shouted out to the crowd. "How long will you waver between two gods? You worship both the Lord and Baal. You must today choose between the Lord and Baal—you may not side with both!"

No one spoke up. Elijah turned to the 450 prophets of Baal. Prepare a sacrifice on the altar of Baal, but do not set fire to the wood. I will prepare a sacrifice to the Lord in the same way. The god that answers with fire will be the true God.

The crowd murmured in approval. "What Elijah proposes is a good idea," they said to one another.

"Since there are so many of you," Elijah said to the 450 prophets of Baal, "you should go first, but remember not to set fire to the wood. That is the job of Baal." The prophets of Baal prepared the sacrifice. Then they called on the name of Baal all morning, but nothing happened. The 450 prophets of Baal all began chanting and dancing around the altar.

"Maybe you need to shout louder," Elijah said mockingly. "Perhaps your god is asleep? Maybe he is just tired and can't be bothered."

Evening came and the altar of Baal remained cold. Elijah then spoke to some of the people gathered around. "Go fetch buckets of water and pour them over the altar of the Lord. As the people went out to get the water, Elijah dug a deep trench all around the altar. Several Israelites all dumped water all over the wood. Elijah then had them all do the same thing two more times. By the time they finished, the altar was soaking wet, and even the trench around it was full of water.

Elijah stepped forward and stood in front of the altar. "O Lord, God of Abraham, show these people that you are the God of Israel so that you might turn their hearts back to you." As Elijah said these words a streak of flame fell

from the sky onto the altar, igniting the wet wood and turning it into a powerful blaze. The water filling the trench quickly boiled away.

"The Lord! He is our God!" The people of Israel began shouting and cheering. While they did this, the sky turned dark with thick clouds. A strong wind began to blow and then a heavy rain fell. The three years of drought had finally ended! 📖

48. The Chariot of Fire

2 Kings 1–2

hab, the king of Israel, was killed in a battle so his son Ahaziah became the new king. Ahaziah was much like his father and did not follow the ways of the Lord, but instead worshipped Baal. One day Ahaziah fell through the floorboards of his palace and seriously injured himself. Bedridden, he sent messengers to the prophets of Baal to find out whether he would survive his injury.

As the messengers started out, Elijah, the prophet of the Lord, got in their way. "I know where you are going," Elijah said the messengers. "Return to your king. The Lord says, 'You will not leave the bed you are lying on alive!'"

The messengers returned to King Ahaziah and told him what Elijah had said. When Ahaziah realized Elijah, the longtime enemy of his father, was within the city of Samaria, he sent a captain of the Israelite army along with fifty soldiers to bring Elijah before him.

The captain led his men around the outskirts of Samaria. He came upon Elijah sitting on top of a hill. "Man of God, the king says for you to come down and stand before him," the captain said to Elijah.

"If I am a man of God," replied Elijah, "then may fire rain down from heaven and destroy you and your fifty

men!" Once he said this, fire poured down from the sky and killed all the king's soldiers.

The king heard what happened and sent another captain with fifty men. "Man of God," the captain said when he approached Elijah who was still sitting on the hill, "the king says to come at once!"

"If I am a man of God," replied Elijah, "then may fire rain down from heaven and destroy you and your fifty men!" Once he said this, fire poured down from the sky and killed all the king's soldiers, just as it had happened before.

The king heard what had happened, but was still set on having Elijah captured. He sent another captain with fifty men to Elijah. The third captain approached Elijah cautiously. When he was close to the hill he got down on his knees. "Man of God," he said shakily, "please do not harm me or my men. I have been ordered by my king to ask you to come before him."

Elijah got up and went to the king with the third captain. He was led to the king, who was still in bed. "This is what the Lord has told me," Elijah said to the king. "Because you sent messengers out to seek advice from the false god, Baal, you will never leave that bed alive."

King Ahaziah died in his bed as Elijah spoke.

Elijah was getting old. He chose a young prophet, Elisha, as his successor. The two prophets were walking when Elijah stopped in his tracks. "The Lord wishes for me to head to Bethel. You should stay here," he said to Elisha.

"My lord, I do not wish to leave you. Please let me follow." With that, the two men went to Bethel. Elisha, although young and inexperienced, was still a prophet and knew that Elijah was going to die soon.

When they arrived at Bethel a large group of prophets gathered and followed them. "The Lord is sending me to the Jordan River. Stay here," Elijah said to Elisha.

"I will not leave your side," the devoted Elisha said.

The group of prophets went and stood at a distance where they could see what was happening. When Elijah approached the edge of the Jordan he removed his cloak, rolled it up, and struck the river's edge. When the rolled-up cloak struck the water, the splash split the river, opening a path across it, like a zipper being undone. Elijah and Elisha walked across the dry path that went through the Jordan.

When they arrived on the other side, Elijah turned to face Elisha. "Before the Lord takes me, is there anything I can do for you?"

"Yes," replied Elisha. "Let me inherit twice the spirit and power God has given you."

"That is lot to ask and I am not sure you could handle that. If you can see me when I am taken, then your request will be granted. Otherwise, it will not."

Just then, a chariot made of fire pulled by horses of fire ran from the sky between them. The chariot left with Elijah. Elisha saw it happen and cried out, "My father! My father!" over and over again. Elisha then got up and picked up Elijah's cloak, which still lay rolled up on the ground by his feet.

"Now, is the God of Elijah with me?" he asked as he struck the water with the cloak, as Elijah had done earlier. The water separated and a dry path formed leading across the river, just as it had before.

The prophets all ran up to Elisha. "The spirit of Elijah is resting within you!" they all said to Elisha.

49. The Prophet Elisha
2 Kings 2–4

The prophet Elisha inherited all the power of Elijah. After Elijah was taken away by God, Elisha remained in the city of Jericho, which had been rebuilt long before—even though God had ordered the Israelites not to rebuild the city. The king who rebuilt the city did so at a great price. His oldest and youngest sons both died.

The people in Jericho went up to Elisha. "Although our city is in a good location, the water here makes us ill and is not good for crops."

"Get a new bowl, fill it with salt, and bring it to me," Elisha told them.

When Elisha was given the bowl of salt, he walked to the spring and flung the salt into the water. "The Lord has said to me, 'This water is healed. Never again will it make anyone ill or make crops die.'" From that day on the water remained pure.

Elisha left Jericho and headed toward Bethel. On his way a group of children ran out to where he was on the road and began yelling names at him. They were taunting Elisha because he was bald. Elisha stopped and looked at the boys. Suddenly a giant bear came out of the woods and attacked the boys, chasing them off.

154

Elisha performed many miracles and soon became well known among the Israelites. One woman pleaded with him, explaining that her husband had died with a lot of debts and now the creditors were going to take her children as slaves in payment for her husband's loans.

"What can I do?" asked Elisha. "What do you have in your house to sell?"

"Nothing," sobbed the woman, "except for a little bit of oil."

"Go with your sons to all your neighbors and ask for every empty jar and pot you can get hold of. Get as many as you possibly can. Then take the jars to your house and begin pouring the oil from your jars into each pot, just a little bit at a time."

The woman and her sons did as Elisha instructed. The woman poured a little bit of oil into each jar, then a little bit more, until all the jars were full. When she was done her entire house was full of jars of oil. She was able to sell the oil and get enough money to pay off her debts and had enough left over to pay for her family's needs for a good long while.

Elisha traveled throughout the land of the Israelites. He often found himself in the city of Shumen. A wealthy woman who lived there with her husband would invite Elisha to stay with them whenever he was around. She even made up a special room for him.

One night when Elisha was staying there he summoned one of the servants of the house. "How can I repay this woman for all the kindness and hospitality she has shown me?"

"I know that more than anything, she wants a child, but her husband is too old to have children."

"Ask her to come here," Elisha replied.

The woman went to Elisha's room. "I will be back here in about a year's time," Elisha told the woman. "When I arrive, you will have a son."

"That is impossible," the woman said sadly. However, shortly after Elisha left, she became pregnant and did have a son, just as Elisha had foretold.

When the boy was older he ran out to the fields one morning where his father was supervising his workers. "Help! Father, my head hurts!" the boy cried. The man was worried about his son and had one of his servants carry the boy to his mother. The boy sat on his mother's lap all morning until noon, but his sickness worsened and he died.

The woman cried and cried. "Go get me a donkey. I must go find the prophet Elisha." She got on the donkey and headed for Mount Carmel, where Elisha often went. When she arrived, she found Elisha and went up to him.

"Didn't I tell you not to get my hopes up about having a child?" she cried. "My son has died."

Elisha turned to his servant and said, "Take my staff and run to the boy's house. Do not greet anyone you come across or respond to any greeting you might receive. When you get to the boy, lay the staff over his face. I will be there as fast as my old legs will take me.

The servant ran all the way to the boy's house and laid the staff on his face. The boy was dead and the servant did not know what to do. Elisha arrived shortly after and told everyone to leave the boy's room. He shut the door and said a prayer to God. Elisha then put his hands on the boy's face and soon the boy's skin became warm. He sneezed seven times, then opened his eyes!

Elisha opened the door. "Go inside," he said to the woman, "and see your son."

50. Elisha Heals Naaman
2 Kings 5

he commander of the Syrian army, Naaman, was a brave soldier. He won many victories for his king. However great Naaman was, he had a painful skin disease that had tormented him for years.

Naaman's wife had a maid who was an Israelite. One day the Israelite girl said to her mistress, "My master should go to Samaria, where the prophet Elisha is. He could most certainly cure my master of his ailment."

Naaman's wife told him what the Israelite girl had said. So he went to the king and asked permission to go to Samaria and seek out the help of the prophet who lived there. "You absolutely must go!" the king said. "I will send a letter to the king of Israel asking for their help." Syria had previously warred with Israel and won, and now the two kingdoms were at peace.

Elisha knew about Naaman's being in Samaria and sent a messenger to the king. "The prophet Elisha requests that you send Naaman to his house," the messenger said to the king.

So Naaman and his horses and chariots rode up to Elisha's house. Elisha sent one of his servants out to greet Naaman when he arrived. "Go to the Jordan River and wash yourself seven times in it. Once you do this you will be cured."

Naaman stormed off away from Elisha's house angrily. "Why didn't the prophet come out to speak

to me himself?" he asked. "Shouldn't he be able to call upon the power of the Lord and cure me? Any why is the Jordan so special? We have rivers at home!"

Naaman began heading back to Syria. His servants caught up with him and one of them said, "Lord, if the prophet had asked you to do some great deed, would you not have done it? Why don't you at least try it?"

Naaman sighed. He turned his chariot and headed toward the Jordan River. Once there he dipped himself into its waters seven times. And, just as Elisha had said, Naaman's sores disappeared and he was healthy!

Naaman was so happy he rushed back to Elisha's house. "Now I know that there is only one true God. Please accept this gold."

"As long as I serve the Lord," replied Elisha, "I will accept no gifts."

Naaman tried to convince Elisha to take something, but Elisha refused. So, after saying thank you one last time, Naaman headed back home. However, on his way home, Elisha's servant, Gehazi, caught up with him.

"My master has changed his mind. Two new men have arrived at our place and Elisha has asked for some silver to give to them." Gehazi lied.

"Of course!" Naaman exclaimed. He was still very grateful and eager to show his thanks. He gave Gehazi all the silver he could carry.

"Where have you been, Gehazi?" Elisha asked when the servant returned.

"I haven't been anywhere," he answered.

"Am I not a prophet of the Lord?" Elisha asked. "My spirit watched over you as you took those gifts from the Syrian. Because of your disobedience, Naaman's affliction will now be with you for the rest of your life!"

Immediately Gehazi felt his skin burn and feel incredibly itchy. When he looked at his arms he saw a bright red rash appear. Ashamed, Gehazi ran from his master, never to be seen again.

51. King Hezekiah
2 Kings 17–20

he kingdom of Israel was falling apart. The kings and people continued to disobey God, and as a result their power weakened. Then one day, the king of Assyria invaded Israel and enslaved the Israelites. Sennacherib, the Assyrian king, decided to take the Israelites and move them to another land. He also brought in people from his land to resettle in Samaria and the other cities and towns of Israel.

The southern kingdom of Judah was still in the hand of the Israelites, but it was in constant conflict with the Assyrians. King Hezekiah ruled over Judah. He obeyed the Lord's commands. He destroyed the statues made to other gods and made the people follow God's ten commandments.

God was with King Hezekiah, and the king was successful in everything he did. He stood up against the Assyrians and fought to keep the Philistines out of Judah. However, after holding up well for many years, some of the large cities of Judah were attacked and captured by the Assyrians.

Hezekiah saw that his people would not stand a chance against the Assyrians in a full-fledged battle. He sent word to the King of Assyria saying that he would pay any price for the Assyrians to leave his country. The Assyrian king asked for a tremendous amount of

silver and gold. Hezekiah had to strip all the gold from the inside the temple Solomon had built in Jerusalem. He gave the gold to Sennacherib and the Assyrians.

Once Sennacherib had his treasure from Hezekiah, he immediately sent a vast army to Jerusalem. He did not care about promises, only wealth and power. When the Assyrian army reached the walls of Jerusalem, they shouted to the people of Israel, promising them a good life if they surrendered the city. "Where was your God when Samaria fell?" one of them shouted.

None of the people of the city said anything. Hezekiah, whom everyone loved and trusted, ordered all the people to not answer anything the Assyrians said. Hezekiah was in great distress. He knew that the promises the Assyrians gave meant nothing, and that a horrible fate awaited the Israelites if the city fell into the Assyrians' hands.

Hezekiah prayed to the Lord for deliverance. The Lord heard Hezekiah's prayer and during the night he sent an angel to Jerusalem. As the angel of death flew over the Assyrian camp, all that were under the angel's path died in their sleep. In the morning, King Sennacherib woke up to find that 185,000 of his men were dead! Terrified, he broke camp with his remaining men, and they all returned to their lands in the north, never to return.

Some time later, Hezekiah became ill. A prophet named Isaiah went to visit the king as he lay in bed.

"The Lord has spoken to me," Isaiah told Hezekiah. "He says to get your affairs in order because you will not leave your bed alive."

Hezekiah turned his head away and faced the wall. "O Lord, please remember your servant who has walked faithfully in your ways. Please do not take life from me now." Hezekiah prayed while tears ran down his face.

"The Lord has heard your prayer," Isaiah said. "In three days' time you will rise from this bed and live for another fifteen years."

Hezekiah sighed, somewhat relieved. "Please," he said to Isaiah, "can the Lord give me a sign to show that this will truly happen?"

Isaiah pointed to a sundial. "Watch the shadow of the sundial as it moves backwards!" The sundial did exactly as Isaiah said it would, and the king knew that God was with him.

It happened exactly as Isaiah had prophesized. The king got better three days later. Hezekiah was a courageous king who always turned to God for help.

52. The Ancient Scroll
2 Kings 21–23

When King Hezekiah died, his son became the new king of Judah. Manasseh was only twelve when he became king. He spent much of his life undoing everything his father had worked so hard for. He rebuilt the pagan temples, turned away from God, and was a very cruel and evil leader.

When Manasseh died, his son Amon became the new king. Amon continued in Manasseh's ways and the Israelites turned further away from the Lord. He was also a cruel and harsh leader, so much so that his own most trusted advisors betrayed and killed him. When Amon died, the people of Judah made Josiah, Amon's son, the new king. Josiah was only eight years old at the time.

Josiah grew up to be a good and honest man. When he was eighteen he decided to have the Temple of the Lord in Jerusalem—the temple Solomon had built—restored. The temple had been neglected for a long time and was in ruins.

Hilkiah, the high priest of the temple, was in charge of paying the men who worked on rebuilding the temple. While he was going through the temple's scrolls and papers, he found an ancient scroll. The scroll was the final copy of the Book of the Law, which contained all of God's laws as he had told them to Moses.

Hilkiah took the scroll to Josiah's secretary. Together they presented the scroll to the king. The king sat down while the secretary read from the scroll all of God's laws. As Josiah listened to the words he became full of despair. "We have turned away from God's laws!" he cried out.

Josiah sent his secretary to Huldah, a well-known prophetess in the land. When the secretary found her, he told her about the scroll and what it said.

"The Lord knows that the people have turned away from the law," the prophetess said. "They will be punished. Jerusalem will face many difficult times. However, because King Josiah follows in the ways of the Lord, this punishment will not happen while he lives."

The next day the King summoned all the people of Jerusalem to gather around the great temple. When they were all there, the Book of the Law was read to the people. They were told to follow the commandments with all their hearts and souls. When everyone heard the words from the scroll, they promised to follow in God's ways again. They went around destroying the altars to the false gods and began to pray to the Lord again.

53. Esther Saves Her People

Esther 1–10

The Persian empire stretched over most of the area the Israelites once controlled, and over a vast area from Asia to Africa. The Persian King, Xerxes, ruled over the entire land. In the third year of his reign he held a giant banquet for all of the nobles and great military leaders of his empire. For 180 days he displayed the wealth and power of his throne.

After the 180 days were over, the king set up a great banquet within the gardens of his palace. All the people of his kingdom were invited to attend. The gardens were unlike anything ever seen on earth. Large marble pillars with blue and white linen hanging from them circled the garden. Gold and silver decorations covered the walls. Everyone who went to the banquet drank wine from a gold goblet decorated differently from every other goblet. The king ordered his servants to serve everyone whatever they wanted.

Xerxes's wife, Queen Vashti, was also having a banquet at this time for the women of the palace. On the last day of the king's banquet, he decided he wanted his wife to appear with him before the people. Queen Vashti was very beautiful, and the people adored her. The king sent his servants to summon her. However, when the servants gave the king's order to the queen, she sent them back and refused to appear.

King Xerxes was furious. He consulted his wise men and counselors and decided to banish Queen Vashti from the kingdom and find a new queen.

"There should be a search for all of the beautiful young maidens in the empire," one of the king's counselors suggested. "Then the finest of them will be brought before you and you can then pick the queen you want."

The king thought this was a good idea. The king's messengers sent out word to the provinces of the empire that the search was on. The most beautiful young women in the empire went to Susa, the city from which Xerxes ruled, to be presented before Hegai. Hegai was in charge of teaching the girls how to behave before the king and how to act like a queen.

Within the walls of Susa was a Jewish man named Mordachai. Mordachai had a young cousin named Hadassah, whom everyone called Esther. Esther's parents had both died and Mordachai raised her as if she were his daughter. Esther was very beautiful, and when they learned about Xerxes search for a new queen she went to Hegai.

Because the Israelites had undergone so many hardships and crushing defeats, Mordachai told Esther from a very young age to never reveal to anyone that she was a Jew. Many people did not like the Jews.

Xerxes immediately fell in love with Esther and chose her as his new queen. He had a golden crown made for her and declared a holiday throughout the empire on that day.

During this same time, Mordachai was hanging out by the palace gates. He was out of sight of the guards who were at the gate. While there, Mordachai overheard the guards plotting to kill the king. Mordachai immediately sent word to Esther to have her warn the king. Esther immediately reported the plot to the king, giving full credit to her cousin as the one who discovered the plot. The two guards were hanged.

Some time later, King Xerxes promoted one of his best counselors, Haman. Haman was given a place of honor in the palace and became the most powerful man in the Persian empire, next to Xerxes. Due to his position, everyone in the kingdom would kneel down before Haman, except for Mordachai. When others asked Mordachai why he would not bow to Haman, he told them that he could not because he was Jewish.

When Haman found out about Mordachai he became very angry. He was so enraged he decided that killing Mordachai alone would not be enough. He wanted all the Jews who were scattered throughout the empire to be killed as well.

Haman approached the king. "There are a certain group of people scattered throughout the empire," Haman said to the king. "They are the Jews and they are not like your other subjects. They do not obey our laws and are a bad influence to others. It is not in the empire's best interest that these people are tolerated."

The king trusted Haman's judgment in almost all matters. He removed his ring and handed it to Haman. "Do what you think is necessary to these people," he said. The ring Xerxes gave him had the king's seal on it.

Haman immediately set to writing up the decree. The decree said that on the thirteenth day of the twelfth month, the people of the empire were to attack and kill every Jewish person living in their land. As a reward they could keep the property that once belonged to those they killed. Haman sealed the letters the decree was written on with wax, using the king's ring to leave the royal mark. The mark the king's ring made in the wax was a sign to the people that they dare not disobey the kings ruling.

The letters were sent by messenger to every province in the kingdom. The Jews became terrified and mourned. Mordachai mourned deeply. He tore his clothing and put on a sackcloth as a sign of his despair. A sackcloth is a piece of clothing made from camel hair or some other rough, scratchy material that is very uncomfortable. When someone wore a sackcloth it meant that he or she was very sad and was suffering. He approached the palace gate, but was not allowed to enter because of the way he was dressed. Esther saw him by the gate and sent out a servant with new clothes for him.

Mordachai refused the clothing. He gave the servant a message to send to Esther. The message explained Haman's decree and how her people were in great peril. Mordachai wanted Esther to approach the king and beg for mercy on behalf of the Jews.

"Doesn't Mordachai know that anyone who approaches the king without permission is put to death?" she asked her servant. "How can he ask me to do this?" She sent the servant back to Mordachai to explain her situation.

When Mordachai heard Esther's response he said, "Tell your mistress, 'Do not think that because you are in the king's palace that you alone among the Jews will survive. If you refuse to help, the Jews will survive some other way, but you and your father's family will perish.'"

Esther got Mordachai's new message and then had an idea. "Go," she said to her servant. "Tell Mordachai to have our people pray for me for the next three days. When this is done I will go to the king. My fate will be my fate."

After three days Esther dressed herself in her finest gowns and stood outside of the king's chamber. The king was discussing matters of the empire with his counselors when he saw Esther standing outside of the room. He held out his scepter to her as a request to approach him. "My queen," Xerxes said to Esther, "what is it that you want? Name anything and it will be yours."

"Only that you, with your counselor Haman, come to a banquet that I am holding tomorrow."

Xerxes agreed and sent for Haman. The next day they both arrived at a bountiful banquet Esther had prepared. "What may I do for you, Esther?" the king asked her again. "You only have to name it and it will be done."

"If I do please you and you truly wish to do something for me," Esther said to the king, "then please spare the lives of my people! They have been set to be murdered. I would not bother you if it was anything less dire."

"Who did this? Who has done such an evil thing?"

"This evil act has been set by your counselor, Haman!"

The king was in a rage. Unable to control himself he stormed out of the banquet hall to his gardens. Haman became terrified and clung to Esther's robe begging for mercy. Just then King Xerxes came back into the room. When he saw Haman hanging onto Esther he thought he was attacking her. Xerxes, still in a rage, had the palace guards arrest Haman and take him away.

Haman was hanged for his treachery and the Jewish people were saved! Esther was given all of Haman's wealth. Also, the king remembered that Mordachai had uncovered the plot to kill him. So, the king made Mordachai his highest counselor, the position Haman once had!

54. The Testing of Job
Job 1–4; 38–42

I n a land called Uz lived a man named Job (pronounced jobe). Job was a very good man who worshipped God regularly and always obeyed God's laws. He possessed a large amount of wealth and had a large family.

One day all the angels presented themselves before God. The angel of darkness and evil, Satan, also went before God. Satan had been banished from heaven and spent his time wandering the earth, causing trouble. He loved doing evil things.

"Where have you come from?" God asked Satan.

"I have been wandering all the land from the east to the west," Satan answered.

"Then you have seen my servant, Job," God said. "He is blameless among men. There is no one as good as he is."

"Sure, he loves you now that he has wealth and happiness. Look how you have shown him favor! But, take away all his wealth and comfort, and he will without a doubt curse you!"

"Very well," replied God. "To prove you wrong I put Job in your hands. But, you may not harm Job himself." With that, Satan left God's presence.

Job sat in his house a few evenings later. One of his servants entered who was covered with dirt and looked awful. His face was full of fear and sadness. "Master!" he cried. "I was out with your other servants tending to your oxen and donkeys when a band of raiders came and stole the animals! They killed your servants as well. I was the only one to escape!"

Before the servant finished speaking, another one of Job's men came rushing in. "The Chaldeans came down upon us with all your camels! They killed everyone but me and ran off with every animal worth taking!"

A third messenger ran in before the second had finished. "Master!" he cried out. "I was at your eldest son's home. He was holding a feast with all his brothers and his sister. All your children were there. Then suddenly a great wind blew in from the desert and tore the house down. It crashed almost instantly. I was the only one to escape alive!"

Job tore his robe and shaved his head, signs that he was in mourning. He knelt on the ground and prayed. "Naked I came into the world, and naked I will leave it. The Lord gives and the Lord takes. May the name of the Lord be praised."

Again, Satan stood before God. "See," said God. "You have taken all of Job's wealth and family away, yet he still loves God and shuns evil, even though you convinced me to ruin him without any reason."

"Ha!" scoffed the devil. "So long as his skin is still intact he will not dare speak out against you. Take away his comfort and he will surely reject you."

"Very well," replied God. "He is in your power, but you must not kill him."

Satan then left the Lord's presence and went to where Job was still mourning the death of his children and servants. Satan inflicted Job with a horrible disease.

Job's skin became red and hot. It itched and burned, and painful sores erupted all over his body. Job cried out in agony.

Job sat down on the ground and tended the sores on his body. His wife looked at him in horror. "Are you still holding onto your dignity?" she said to her husband. "Why not curse God and die in peace?"

"Watch what you say!" Job yelled back angrily. "Are we only to love God when things are going well for us?"

Job had three good friends that lived in the land of Uz—Eliphaz, Bildad, and Zophar. They all heard about the troubles Job had been going through and all got together to discuss them. "We should go to our friend and comfort him," they said to one another.

The three men traveled to what remained of Job's house. All his servants were gone so it was getting run down already. When the men approached, they saw Job sitting on the ground in the distance. They hardly recognized him, he looked so downtrodden. Job's three friends wept aloud. They walked up to their friend and sat beside him on the ground—they said nothing, because they knew there was nothing they could say that would ease Job's suffering. They all sat there for seven days and seven nights, not saying a word.

After the seven days and nights, Job stood up. "Curse the day I was born!" he cried out. "May God forget that day ever happened so I will be no more!"

Job's friends told him that God had done him wrong, that he should feel betrayed for the suffering he has endured after being such a good and noble man. Job would not curse God, but only himself and his fate.

A great dark storm hovered over the four men. Out of the storm the voice of God spoke to the Job's three friends. "You have not spoken of me what is right. You try to turn Job away from me in the time of his greatest need. However, because Job is righteous, he will pray for you, and I will hear his prayer. Now go back to your homes."

Job prayed for his three friends and the Lord heard his prayer. Afterwards, Job became even more successful than before. Job had more than twice the camels, sheep, donkeys, and cows that he had had before. And although he missed his children who had died very much, the Lord blessed him with more children and soon Job was surrounded by loved ones again. So Job lived the rest of his life in peace to a very old age. ✎

55. The Prophet Jeremiah
Jeremiah 1–20

eremiah was a shy, quiet, and gentle man. While Jeremiah was out walking, he heard the voice of God. "Before you were even born you had been chosen as a great prophet of the land!" God said.

"But Lord," Jeremiah replied, "I am young and inexperienced. I am not good with people either."

"Do not be afraid," the Lord said. "You will go where I tell you to go and say what I tell you to say. When you do this, I will protect you." Just then Jeremiah felt the Lord's hand touch his lips. "Now I will send you out to overthrow kingdoms and to rebuild the spirit of the people. Now, what do you see, Jeremiah?"

"I see the branch of an almond tree," Jeremiah replied.

"Yes, the bloom is a symbol that I am always watching out for you. What else do you see?"

"I see a boiling pot on a fire. The pot is tilted toward the north."

"Yes, I am about to pour disaster upon all the lands in the north—the land of Judah. The people have forgotten me. You must go to them and tell them the error of their ways. They will turn against you, but do not fear. I will protect you."

Jeremiah was then a prophet. He spoke to the people of Judah. "While wandering in the desert, the Lord spoke to me. He said, 'Go and buy a linen belt and tie it around your waist. Just be sure not to get it wet or soiled.' I did as the Lord commanded.

"A few days later the Lord spoke to me again. This time he said, 'Go to the hills ahead of you and bury the linen belt between the two largest stones.' Again, I did as I was told.

"A few weeks went by when I again heard the voice of the Lord. 'Go and retrieve the belt you have hidden,' He said. So I went to the place I buried the belt and dug it up. It had become rotten and useless.

"As I looked at the belt, God explained, 'This belt to you is like my people to me. When the belt is secure around your waist and protected, it remains it its best shape. But, when the belt is hidden away from me, it becomes rotten and useless!'

"So, people of Judah, I am telling you that you must mend your ways and not hide from God! For, if you do, you will become like the linen belt."

Later on Jeremiah walked by a potter's house. A potter makes things out of clay, such as jars. Jeremiah saw the potter spinning the wheel and shaping a jar out of clay. However, no matter how hard the potter tried, the jar kept drooping to one side or another. Then the potter stopped the wheel, smashed the clay down and reformed it into a block to use later to make something else.

"People of Judah!" Jeremiah shouted to a crowd. "The Lord is shaping you like the potter shapes the clay jar! You are his to shape and form as he pleases. However, if you continue to resist his direction he will crush you like the potter crushes the clay that won't form. If you continue to do evil, you will all be destroyed. But if you yield to the will of God, you shall become strong and will always be protected."

The people of Judah muttered to themselves. They did not like the way Jeremiah spoke to them. They taunted Jeremiah and did not listen to what he said. Jeremiah took some of the elders and priests with him to the potter's house. At the potter's house Jeremiah bought a clay jar and then led the group of people to a valley.

Jeremiah stood up on a rock and shouted to the people. "This is what the Lord says," Jeremiah shouted. "Disaster will fall on the people of Judah if they do not change their ways! This valley will be the beginning of the end for the people of Judah!" Then Jeremiah threw the clay jar on the ground. It shattered into hundreds of small pieces. "Just as this potter's jar is smashed, God will smash this city."

They did not listen. The people attacked Jeremiah, beat him, and locked him away. They let him go after a while and Jeremiah again told them that they were heading for disaster.

Jeremiah's prophecy came true. The Babylonians invaded Judah through the very valley where Jeremiah smashed the jar and took over the land. Many of the Israelites were locked up in chains and sent to Babylon, including the priests and elders who had Jeremiah beaten and locked away.

The city of Jerusalem was destroyed. Many Israelites surrendered or fled. The ones who stayed to defend the city were captured and sent to far away lands. Because the Judeans disobeyed the word of the Lord, the kingdom of Judah was no more.

56. The Young Israelites in Babylon

Daniel 1

he Israelites no longer had a land of their own. Most of the Israelites lived within areas controlled by the Babylonians. When Judah, the last land of the Israelites, fell, the king of Babylon was Nebuchadnezzar (pronounced NEB–ah–kud–NEEZ–ar).

King Nebuchadnezzar ordered his chief counselor to choose from the Israelites a group of young men. Only the most intelligent, quick witted, well-mannered, and handsome were to be chosen. The chief counselor would train the men selected to work in the king's palace.

Among those selected were Daniel, Hananiah, Mishael, and Azariah. These four were all from the kingdom of Judah before it fell to the Babylonians. All the Israelites who were in training to serve the king were treated very well. They were even served the same food and wine that the king ate.

Daniel asked that he and the other three Judeans be served only vegetables. Daniel felt that if they ate the food of the enemy of God's people, they would be committing a sin. The chief counselor liked Daniel, Hananiah, Mishael, and Azariah, so he was not too angry when they asked for only vegetables.

"I am afraid I cannot allow this," the chief said in response to Daniel's request. "The king has ordered that all the Israelites in training be fed the food from his very table. He would be insulted if he knew his generosity was being refused. And if you eat only vegetables, you will become weak and sickly."

"Tell you what," replied Daniel. "Let us eat only vegetables and drink only water for ten days. After that, if we appear less fit than all the other Israelites here, then we will do as you say and eat whatever food we are given."

To this the chief agreed. For ten days Daniel, Hananiah, Mishael, and Azariah were given nothing but vegetables and water. Daniel prayed to God often to watch over him. After ten days the chief summoned the four Israelites and saw that they looked even healthier and stronger than before!

Because Daniel, Hananiah, Mishael, and Azariah honored God with their sacrifice, the Lord looked on them favorably. The Lord kept the four young Israelites strong and healthy, and gave them great wisdom and understanding of everything around them. Because Daniel was the one who spoke up to the chief counselor, God gave him the ability to interpret dreams and visions.

Three years passed. Daniel, Hananiah, Mishael, and Azariah were among the quickest learners being trained to serve the king. After they completed their training for the king's service, all of the young Israelite men were brought before King Nebuchadnezzar.

The king questioned all of the Israelite men one by one. When he questioned Daniel, Hananiah, Mishael, and Azariah, he was astounded by their wisdom. The king chose Daniel, Hananiah, Mishael, and Azariah to serve him within the palace. He gave them all grand positions of honor. They became wise men and advisors to the king.

57. Nebuchadnezzar's Dream
Daniel 2–3

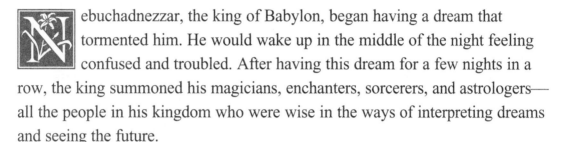ebuchadnezzar, the king of Babylon, began having a dream that tormented him. He would wake up in the middle of the night feeling confused and troubled. After having this dream for a few nights in a row, the king summoned his magicians, enchanters, sorcerers, and astrologers—all the people in his kingdom who were wise in the ways of interpreting dreams and seeing the future.

"I had a troubling dream," the king told his wise men. "It has been bothering me and I want it interpreted."

"O great king!" the wise men replied. "You only need to tell us your dream and we will interpret it for you."

"If I told you my dream, you could make up anything and pretend that it was the correct interpretation. I need to be sure that you will tell me the true meaning of this dream. So, you must prove your powers are for real."

The king paused and then continued, "I will not tell you my dream. Whoever of you can both tell me my dream and interpret it will receive reward beyond your imagination. However, if you are unable to tell me my dream correctly, you shall be put to death!" For some time the king had suspected that many of his wise men had been lying to him for their own personal gain.

"But you ask the impossible!" the wise men cried. "No one has the ability to know someone's dream! No king, no matter how great and powerful, has ever made such a demand!"

Hearing this defiance made King Nebuchadnezzar furious! In his rage, he summoned his chief counselor and told him to have all the wise men of Babylon executed.

Daniel, Hananiah, Mishael, and Azariah—four young Israelites—had been placed in high positions within the king's palace, and were among the wise men of Babylon. When Arioch, the chief of the king's guard, approached the four Israelites, he told them of the decree made by the king.

"Please," replied Daniel, "allow me to approach the king so I may interpret his dream and none of the wise men will have to be put to death."

Arioch agreed and took Daniel to the king. The king repeated his demand. "Give me until the morning," Daniel requested of the king, "then I will tell you your dream and what it means."

The king agreed and allowed Daniel to return to his quarters. Daniel spoke to Hananiah, Mishael, and Azariah and explained what was going on. "We must all pray to God that we can perform this nearly impossible feat."

That night Hananiah, Mishael, and Azariah prayed while Daniel went to sleep. In his sleep Daniel had a vision given to him from God. The vision showed Daniel exactly what the king's dream was and what it meant!

The next morning, Daniel, Hananiah, Mishael, and Azariah were summoned to stand before King Nebuchadnezzar. The king had his guards and executioners there as well.

"Are you able to tell me what I saw in my dream and interpret it?"

"No, my king," replied Daniel, "but the Lord has told me your dream and what it means. You saw an enormous statue. Its head was made of pure gold. Its chest and arms were solid silver. Its belly and thighs were bronze. Its lower legs were iron. Its feet were a mix of clay and iron.

"As you saw this, a stone cut itself out of the ground and struck the feet of the statue. The feet shattered and the statue fell over, smashing to bits. All that was left was the stone. Then the stone began to grow. It grew so big it became an enormous mountain that covered the entire world.

"And this is what your dream means. The gold head of the statue represents you and your kingdom, because you are the king of all kings. After you, another kingdom will rise, inferior to yours, and then another. These kingdoms are represented by the silver and bronze, because they are inferior to gold. Following these, a fourth will rise up, a kingdom with the strength of iron. And just as iron can smash anything to pieces, this fourth kingdom will smash the others and rule over the world. In your dream, the feet were part clay, part iron. The clay and iron represent a fifth kingdom, and just like the feet of the statue, this kingdom will be divided and will not remain together—just as iron and clay won't stay together.

"In the time of this fifth kingdom, God will set up his kingdom—a kingdom stronger and more enduring than any ever seen on earth. This kingdom will rise up and rule over the entire world. It will last forever. This kingdom is represented by the stone that destroyed the statue and then grew to become a mountain covering the entire world."

King Nebuchadnezzar dropped to his knees and thanked Daniel over and over again. "Surely your God is the true Lord to have given you this knowledge!" He gave Daniel the highest position among all the wise men and gave him great wealth. Daniel requested that the king make Hananiah, Mishael, and Azariah governors over different provinces of Babylon, which the king agreed to.

58. Three in the Fiery Furnace
Daniel 3

King Nebuchadnezzar, ruled over the most vast empire in the world at the time—Babylon. He appointed Daniel, a young Israelite who had shown great wisdom, as one of his highest ranking advisors. Three of Daniel's Israelite friends—Hananiah, Mishael, and Azariah—were appointed governors of different provinces in Babylon.

King Nebuchadnezzar had a gigantic statue erected that was almost 100 feet tall. It was a statue of a Babylonian god and was covered in gold. When the statue was finished being built, he invited all the governors, wise men, judges, and other officials of the empire and its provinces to the field where the statue stood to celebrate its completion.

It was to be a grand celebration! King Nebuchadnezzar had a feast set up and a large group of musicians. "Oh people of Babylon!" shouted one of the king's officials, "When you hear the musicians begin to play their instruments, everyone is to kneel down and pray to the great golden statue! Anyone who dares to defy the king's order shall be thrown into a blazing hot furnace!"

When the music started, the hundreds of people gathered in the field all knelt before the statue with their faces to the ground and their hands stretched out toward the statue's

feet, except for Daniel's three friends—Hananiah, Mishael, and Azariah—who remained standing. Daniel was away taking care of some business for the king.

King Nebuchadnezzar had many magicians, enchanters, astrologers, and similar wise men. They hated the Jewish people with all their hearts because years ago Daniel was able to know and interpret the king's troubling dream, which none of them had been able to do. They were jealous. The king had rewarded Daniel and as a result, all the other wise men of Babylon lost a lot of their influence, power, and stature in the empire.

When the other wise men of Babylon saw Hananiah, Mishael, and Azariah still standing when the music began playing, they quickly rushed up to the king. "Oh great king," they said, "see how the three Jews defy your orders and remain standing!"

The king had his guards bring the three Israelites before him. "Hananiah, Mishael, and Azariah, you have been loyal and capable governors within my empire. Why do you defy my orders? Because you have served me so well, I will give you one last chance. Kneel before the statue and worship it or else you shall be thrown into a fiery furnace and burned to death!"

"King Nebuchadnezzar," Hananiah, Mishael, and Azariah replied, "we mean no disrespect to you, but we also serve a higher power, our Lord in heaven. Even if you throw us into the hottest fire on earth, our Lord can protect us from it. And even if he chooses not to, we shall never worship your gods or bow before the statue you built in the field."

King Nebuchadnezzar was furious! He ordered his servants to make the fire of the furnace seven times hotter than it had ever been before. The entire furnace began to glow white it was blazing so hot! Nebuchadnezzar ordered his guards to tie up Hananiah, Mishael, and Azariah and throw them into the furnace. The guards did as ordered, and threw the three Israelites into the furnace.

But the fire in the furnace was so hot, that just by getting close to its opening, the guards were all overpowered by the heat and dropped dead.

King Nebuchadnezzar jumped to his feet. "Did we not just throw in three men with their hands and feet tied?" he asked his advisors.

"Certainly lord, we all saw it," they replied.

"Look!" the king shouted, "I see four people in there, walking around untied and not burned at all! And look! One of them is unlike any person I have ever seen!"

Nebuchadnezzar approached as close as he could get to the blazing furnace. "Hananiah, Mishael, and Azariah, servants of the Most High God, come out of the furnace!" he ordered.

Hananiah, Mishael, and Azariah stepped out of the furnace. Nebuchadnezzar and his advisors all crowded around the three Israelites and examined them. The Israelites were completely unharmed! Their clothes were not burnt. Not a hair on their heads was singed. They didn't even smell like smoke!

"Praise be to the God of Hananiah, Mishael, and Azariah, who sent down an angel to save them from death!" shouted Nebuchadnezzar.

"They put all of their faith in their Lord and defied me, the king of all Babylon, and were willing to die rather than serve or worship any other god." The king then decreed that no one was allowed to speak against the God of the Israelites. He also promoted Hananiah, Mishael, and Azariah to positions of even greater power within the empire.

59. Nebuchadnezzar in the Wilderness

Daniel 4

About ten years had passed since King Nebuchadnezzar had thrown Hananiah, Mishael, and Azariah into the fiery furnace and had seen the power of the Lord who saved the three Israelites. Nebuchadnezzar summoned the people of his kingdom to gather around his palace.

Thousands of people gathered around the palace, which stood high and majestic in the great city of Babylon. The people of Babylon looked up at a balcony of the palace. King Nebuchadnezzar appeared from behind a purple curtain and stood where everyone could see him.

"People of Babylon!" the king shouted to the crowd. "May you all live in peace and prosper! I have summoned you all here today to tell you about the miracles the Lord has performed for me.

"I was at home in my palace, happy and at peace, because my empire was strong and we had been at peace for some time. Then, while lying in bed, I saw a vision that astounded and terrified me! I saw a field. In the middle stood a tree all by itself. The tree was more massive and awe inspiring than any on earth. Its top nearly touched the sun, and its branches reached out to the ends of the earth. Its leaves were lush and golden hued. There wasn't a dead branch or a dead leaf to be seen. Underneath the tree, the beasts of the land found shelter. The birds of the air lived in its branches. And from this tree every creature in the land was fed.

"While looking at this tree, I was filled with great joy. Suddenly, a messenger descended from the heavens. He was robed in white and glowing!

In a powerful voice he yelled out, 'Cut down this tree and trim off its branches. Strip off its leaves and crush its fruits. Let the animals of the fields run away from its protection and the birds of the air find new homes. However, leave the tree's stump and roots unharmed.'

"The messenger from heaven then said, 'Let him be drenched in the dew and live among the animals and plants of the earth. Let his mind be changed from that of a man to one of a wild creature foraging in the wilderness for seven years. This will be done so that the living will know that the Most High is the true king over all that lives and that everyone's fate is in his hands.'

"After this I came to a sudden shock. I knew that there was only one man in all of Babylon who could tell me what my vision meant. So I summoned Daniel. I told him everything about my vision.

"Daniel stood before me silently for a good long while. After a time I noticed he was full of distress. I told him not to fear and to tell me whatever the meaning was.

"Daniel then sighed, 'If only the vision was about your enemies and not you, my king! The great and powerful tree you saw with its leaves touching the sky and visible from all the earth represents you. You have become great and strong and your empire stretches all across the earth. Then the messenger came down to you and ordered the tree torn down. You will be driven away from your people and will live like a wild animal in the wilderness. Seven years will pass before you realize that the Lord is the true king of all people and resign yourself to obey his will. The part of your vision in which the messenger orders the stump be left in place means that your kingdom will be restored to you when you realize God's power.

"Then Daniel finished with some advice for me. 'Please my king, may I advise you to renounce your sins now and obey the will of the Lord. If you do this God may show mercy upon you and your prosperity will continue.'

"For a year all things went well. Then exactly a year later I was strolling in the gardens of the palace and thought to myself, "Babylon, my kingdom, is by far the greatest power the earth has ever seen, and all because of my doing."

"When I hadn't even finished my thought, I heard a voice, the very voice of the messenger I had heard in my vision a year before, 'King Nebuchadnezzar, your authority has been removed. You will now be struck dumb and live like a wild animal until you learn to be humble before the Lord!'

"Just then, I felt myself lose control of my thoughts. I became wild and ran into the woods. For seven years I lived in the wilderness like an animal. I ate grass from the fields and became covered in their dew.

"After seven years, however, my eyes opened! I raised my eyes to heaven and prayed to the Lord. I realized that the Lord's kingdom is all lands, and his power is unending. I realized that we are all nothing compared to the Lord, because he is the creator of everything that we are and that we know.

"After I said this my mind became clear. At the same time, my advisors and nobles found me! They had been searching for me for the whole time I was missing. Since then I have been restored to my throne and have become greater than ever before. Now I, Nebuchadnezzar, praise the Lord most powerful. We are all to be humble before him."

Nebuchadnezzar lived out the rest of his life humble before God and was a great ruler. He kept Daniel close by his side as his most trusted advisor. In time, he had a son, whom he named Belshazzar.

60. The Writing on the Wall
Daniel 5

ebuchadnezzar, the king of Babylon, died. His son, Belshazzar, became the new king. Now in his lifetime Nebuchadnezzar had learned many lessons, but his son was born when Nebuchadnezzar was older. Belshazzar did not know much about the lessons his father had to learn.

After Belshazzar had been king for a short time, he wanted to hold a great feast. He invited 1,000 of his nobles to join him and his family. Eager to show off his wealth and power, he had the royal treasury opened. In the treasury were hundreds of gold and silver goblets that had belonged to the Israelites. The goblets were taken from the Lord's temple in Jerusalem by Nebuchadnezzar.

At the feast, Belshazzar, his family, and the nobles were drinking wine from the gold and silver goblets that came from the Lord's temple in Jerusalem. While drinking, they praised the gods of gold, silver, bronze, iron, wood, and stone.

Suddenly, a white, glowing hand appeared out of thin air! The hand floated in the air and began to write some words on the wall with its finger. After it had written a few words it vanished.

The king saw the hand appear and write the words. He stared at where the hand was writing on the wall and became pale. He was so frightened he shook uncontrollably. As he looked at the strange words written in an unfamiliar language his legs gave out on him and he fell to the ground.

Once he recovered from his shock, King Belshazzar summoned his wise men to the room to read the strange writing on the wall. It was a language that the king had never seen before. "Anyone who is able to understand and interpret this writing will be rewarded immensely," he said to the wise men. None of the wise men had any clue what the words meant, however. They didn't even know if they were really words or just scribbles.

The king became even more distraught. He had to sit because he was feeling so woozy. All the noblemen at the feast were completely baffled.

Just then the queen spoke up. "My king, there is a man in your kingdom who is known to be the wisest of all your wise men. His name is Daniel and he was the most trusted advisor of your father, King Nebuchadnezzar. Get Daniel and he will tell you what the writing means."

Daniel was brought before Belshazzar. "Are you Daniel, the Israelite my father brought here from Judah? I heard that the spirit of the gods is within you, giving you great wisdom and insight. I have had all my wise men come here to read and interpret the writing on this wall, but none has been able to explain it. I have heard you have a gift for interpretation and being able to solve difficult problems. If you can tell me what this writing means, I will reward you greatly and will promote you to the third highest-ranking ruler in all the kingdom!"

"I have no need for power or gifts," Daniel replied. "However, I will read the writing for the king and tell him what it means." Daniel studied the writing carefully for a while.

"Oh king, your father was a great and powerful ruler. However, he became too arrogant and the Lord humbled him. King Nebuchadnezzar was forced to live in the wilderness like a wild animal, until one day he realized the true power of the Lord. After that lesson was learned, The Lord restored your father to power.

"But you, my king, have never been humbled, even though you know what your father went through. Instead you oppose the Lord. You had the sacred goblets that came from the Lord's Temple in Jerusalem used in your banquet. You even toasted with the goblets to your gods of silver, gold, bronze, iron, wood, and stone, which are false gods that cannot hear anything you say. You all have refused to honor God, who holds your lives in his hands. Because of this, the Lord sent the hand that wrote the words on the wall."

Daniel looked at the wall one last time, then he faced the king. "This is what is written on the wall: *Mene, Mene, Tekel, Parsin.* And this is what they mean. *Mene* means number, for God has numbered your days. *Tekel* means weighed, for your spirit has been weighed and has been found lacking. *Parsin* means divided, for your kingdom will be divided between the Persians and the Medes."

Weak and tired, Belshazzar still realized that Daniel spoke the truth. He commanded that Daniel be given a royal robe made out of luxurious purple fabric. The king also gave Daniel a golden chain to wear around his neck and proclaimed that Daniel was now the third highest ruler in all of Babylon.

That same night, while everyone was sleeping, Belshazzar was killed. Darius, a Mede, became the new king.

61. Daniel and the Lions

Daniel 6

fter King Belshazzar, son of Nebuchadnezzar, was killed, Darius the Mede became the king of Babylon. Darius appointed 120 governors known as satraps to rule throughout the kingdom. Darius also had three administrators who were in charge of all the satraps. One of the three administrators was Daniel, an Israelite who had been brought to Babylon from Judah by Nebuchadnezzar's soldiers many years before.

Daniel did such a good job and pleased Darius so much that the king decided to put Daniel in charge of the whole kingdom. However, the satraps and other administrators all hated Daniel. They were jealous of Daniel's success and the way the king favored him.

The satraps and administrators conspired against Daniel. They tried to find something to accuse Daniel of. But no matter how hard they tried, they only found out how perfect and loyal Daniel had always been. This knowledge just made them angrier and more jealous of him.

"We will never find anything to charge Daniel with unless it has something to do with the laws of his God," one of the administrators said. They all murmured in agreement and discussed a plan.

"Oh great King Darius," a small group of the satraps said to the king the next day, "the royal administrators, satraps, and other officials and governors have all been discussing a way of honoring you. We thought it would be a good idea to issue a decree that everyone in Babylon must pray to no one but you for the next thirty days. Any person who prays to their own god shall be thrown into a pit of lions! We think you should issue this decree in writing, so that it cannot be changed or altered by anyone, according to our traditions."

King Darius thought this was an excellent idea. He announced the decree and put it in writing. His secretaries wrote up the decree in every language of the empire and Darius put his seal on each decree.

When Daniel heard about the decree, he went to his home. He climbed to the attic and knelt by the window which faced where Jerusalem used to be. He then prayed to God, as he did three times a day, every day. He prayed as he always did, but also prayed for help overcoming the new decree.

Some of the satraps had been following Daniel since the decree was written. When they saw Daniel praying to God, they quickly rushed to the king. "My lord, didn't you issue a decree that anyone who prayed to anything but you for the next thirty days was to be thrown in the lions' den?"

"Yes," replied the king, "I have issued the decree in writing. It now stands and cannot be altered by anyone, even me."

"Well," they said to the king smugly. "Your servant Daniel, one of the exiles from Judah, ignores you and continues to pray to his God three times a day!"

Darius was upset by this news. He greatly valued Daniel's wisdom and loyal service. However, according to Mede and Persian tradition, once a royal decree was put in writing it could not be altered, not even by the king! Darius would make the entire empire very upset if he made an exception for Daniel.

The king ordered his guards to get Daniel and take him to the lions' pit. The satraps had made a den that was a big hole in the ground. They had lions put into the den, which was so deep the lions could not get out. The hole at the mouth of the den was small enough so that it could be covered with a large stone.

The guards went to Daniel's house and took him to the lions' den. Darius was there, feeling greatly troubled. Many of the satraps and administrators were not far off, chuckling to each other and rubbing their hands together greedily. As Daniel was tossed into the pit the satraps cheered. Darius shouted into the pit, "May the God you serve so devotedly save you!" Darius glared at the satraps who quickly quieted down. He then went home. The guards put a large stone over the mouth of the pit so that Daniel could not climb out, and no one would be able to lower ropes down to save him.

That night, Darius could not sleep. He did not eat that night and did not request any entertainment be brought to him. He could think of nothing but poor Daniel. At the first light of day, Darius got out of bed and immediately set for the lions' den.

When he got there, he had his guards remove the stone. "Daniel! Daniel!" he called. "Has your God protected you?"

"My king! I am okay!" shouted Daniel from within the pit. "The Lord sent down an angel who sealed the mouths of the lions. They did not even scratch me! They did not harm me because I was found to have done no wrong in the eyes of God. I have also done no wrong to you, my king."

Darius ordered the guards to lower a rope for Daniel. When Daniel was out of the pit, Darius examined him. He was unharmed without a single rip in his clothing. The king was overjoyed and embraced Daniel.

The next day a new decree was issued. It said, "In all the lands of the kingdom, everyone must fear and honor the God of Daniel. He is the only true God and will endure forever. His kingdom is the biggest and he rules over us all. He has rescued Daniel, his most faithful servant, from the lions' jaws!"

From that point on Daniel continued to prosper. The satraps and administrators were arrested and removed from power. Daniel continued to serve the king of Babylon and lived out the rest of his life in peace.

62. The Story of Jonah and the Giant Fish
The Book of Jonah

 onah was one of the Lord's prophets. He was born in Galilee. God often sent him to various places to warn people of what would happen as a result of their sins. One day the Lord spoke to Jonah. "Go to the city of Ninevah and preach against it. Tell them I have become angry with their wickedness and I will destroy the city."

Jonah was disheartened. He did not like the city of Ninevah, and knew that if he went there and gave them the word of the Lord and warned them about their doom, they would repent. Jonah wanted the city to be destroyed.

Instead of doing what God told him to, Jonah ran away from the Lord. He decided to head for Tarnish, a land far away. He went to the ocean port city of Joppa, and found a ship heading for Tarnish. He paid his fare and went aboard.

Once the ship was at sea, the Lord caused a great powerful wind to blow. The wind filled the sea with giant waves, and the little cargo ship was tossed around in every direction. All the sailors aboard the ship were terrified. They threw as much cargo as they could overboard, to lighten the ship. The sailors, who were from all parts of the world, each prayed to their gods, but the storm seemed only to worsen.

The captain of the ship went below deck, to see if there was anything else that could be thrown overboard. There, he saw Jonah, sleeping! "How can you sleep at a time like this?" the captain asked Jonah. "There is a violent storm surrounding us! We are going to sink if it doesn't stop soon! Get up and pray to your God."

The other sailors came down. The walls of the ship creaked and cracking sounds could be heard. "Who is responsible for this?" they all asked, knowing that this storm was very unusual and must be someone's punishment. No one said anything; Jonah just kept quiet as well. "Let's draw straws, the person who draws the shortest one must be the one responsible."

When they all drew straws, Jonah had the shortest. All the sailors turned to him. "What country do you come from? Who is your God? What have you done?" Jonah had already mentioned to them that he was running away from his God when he entered the ship.

"I am a Hebrew and I worship the Lord, the One who created the earth and the seas," Jonah answered.

This terrified the sailors. The sea continued to toss the ship around. "What can we do to please your God and calm the seas?" they asked Jonah.

"You must pick me up and throw me into the sea," Jonah answered. "I know it is my fault that this storm has come upon you all. Once I am gone, the sea will become calm."

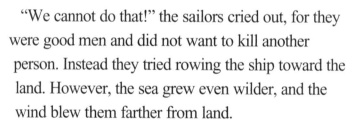

"We cannot do that!" the sailors cried out, for they were good men and did not want to kill another person. Instead they tried rowing the ship toward the land. However, the sea grew even wilder, and the wind blew them farther from land.

"O Lord, please do not judge us for taking this man's life!" cried out the captain. Then the sailors took hold of Jonah and threw him overboard. Once Jonah was off the ship, the skies cleared up, the sun shone, and the sea was calm.

The men on the ship got on their knees and praised the Lord. They all vowed to follow in the ways of the Lord.

Jonah was tossed into the sea. Before the sea calmed a great wave crashed down on him and forced him deep under water. When under, the Lord sent an enormous fish to Jonah that swallowed him whole! Jonah was still alive inside the fish.

Jonah was in shock. The last thing he remembered was sinking in the seas, with seaweed wrapping around his face, and water growing colder. He saw the enormous fish swim to him and open its enormous mouth, but somehow he was still alive. He realized he must be inside the belly of the fish. Yet he wasn't hurt! "They must be giving me another chance," Jonah thought. Jonah began to pray, and promised to do what the Lord commanded.

After three days inside the fish, Jonah was spit out on the shore near Ninevah. He was unharmed!

"Now go to Ninevah and tell the people I plan to destroy the city," God said to Jonah. This time Jonah obeyed the Lord without hesitation. Ninevah was a vast city. It would take three days just to walk across it! Jonah walked through the city, and each day continued to proclaim: "In forty days the Lord will cause Ninevah to fall!"

The people of Ninevah believed the word of the Lord that Jonah pro-claimed. Everyone, including the king, humbled themselves before God and prayed for forgiveness. When God saw how the people of Ninevah—from the beggars in the streets to the nobles in the palace—all repented, his heart soft-ened to the people and he did not cause them any harm.

Jonah was upset that the city did not fall. He was angry with how easily the Lord forgave these people, who had caused his homeland much harm in the past. "Oh Lord, this is why I fled in the first place," Jonah said out loud. "I knew you are compassionate, quick to forgive, and slow to anger. This is all too much for me. Come down and take my life!"

"What right do you have for being angry?" God asked Jonah. Jonah became confused. Now that he was on the far side of the city and away from the sea, he decided to set up a shelter on a hill that overlooked all the land. He hoped that the city might still fall.

Jonah's shelter was merely some sticks that provided just a little shade from the hot sun. God made a thick, leafy vine grow over the shelter to give Jonah lots of shade and keep him cool. The whole vine grew in only a single night! Jonah was very happy about the vine and remained sitting there, watching the city.

While Jonah was sleeping the next night, the Lord caused the vine to die and shrivel up. The following day the sun burned hotter than it had ever before. Jonah was miserable. His skin was burning and he felt faint. "I wish I would die," he cried out.

"Do not be angry Jonah," the Lord said to him. "You feel you are not being given compassion, yet you wish the people of Nineveh harm. The 120,000 people who live there are spiritually lost and need guidance. You are crying about a vine, which you neither planted nor cared for, without any concern for all those people down there begging for forgiveness."

The New Testament

The Books of the New Testament:

Matthew	Ephesians	Hebrews
Mark	Philippians	James
Luke	Colossians	1 Peter
John	1 Thessalonians	2 Peter
Acts	2 Thessalonians	1 John
Romans	1 Timothy	2 John
1 Corinthians	2 Timothy	3 John
2 Corinthians	Titus	Jude
Galatians	Philemon	Revelation

63. The Birth of John
Luke 1

undreds of years had passed since the empire of Babylon ruled the earth. The Roman Empire now controlled most of the land where the Israelites lived. The lands of the Empire were divided into several kingdoms. Herod was the king of Judea, the kingdom that had Jerusalem as its capital.

In the time of Herod's rule, there was a priest named Zechariah. Zechariah, along with his wife Elizabeth, was a good person, and always obeyed God's laws. Although they had good lives, Elizabeth and Zechariah were very sad. They were old already and did not have any children.

One day Zechariah was holding a prayer service outside of the temple. As was the custom, Zechariah then went inside the temple to burn incense. While he was inside, everyone else remained outside and prayed.

As Zechariah approached the altar, an angel of the Lord appeared before him. Zechariah had never seen an angel and was scared. "Do not be afraid Zechariah, the Lord is with you. Your prayer has been answered. Your wife will bear you a son and you will name him John. He will be filled with the Holy Spirit even at the time of his birth, and the people of Israel will follow him back to the ways of the Lord."

"How can this happen?" Zechariah asked. "I and my wife are too old for children."

"I am Gabriel," the angel replied. "I stand in the presence of the Lord, yet you question his plan? You will be unable to speak from now until the day this prophesy is fulfilled, which will occur in due time!" Zechariah fell to his knees.

While this was happening, the people outside the temple began to wonder what happened to their priest. Just as a few of
the people began murmuring to each other, Zechariah emerged from the temple. They realized he had seen a powerful vision because he was making wild gestures, yet was unable to say what he saw.

Zechariah returned to his wife Elizabeth. He had to write down for her what happened to him, because he still could not speak. Soon, Elizabeth became pregnant.

"This is the work of the Lord," Elizabeth said. "He has blessed us with a child."

Nine months later, Elizabeth gave birth to a son. Even though she was very old, Elizabeth was able to have her baby easily. All of Zechariah's and Elizabeth's neighbors and relatives celebrated the miracle that had happened.

As was the custom, eight days later the same friends and neighbors came to Zechariah's house for a special ceremony and to name the baby. They discussed among themselves that the child should be named after his father. Zechariah still could not speak.

"No," said Elizabeth, "My son is to be named John."

"But you don't have any relatives of that name," they said to her. They tried to consult Zechariah, to see what he wished. They were having difficulty, but then Zechariah grabbed a writing tablet and to everyone's shock, he wrote, "His name is John."

When he finished writing, Zechariah was suddenly able to speak again! The angel Gabriel's prophesy had come true. Zechariah immediately praised God.

The neighbors were all astonished. "What destiny does this child have?" they wondered to each other. They were all in awe because they knew the Lord was with John.

"Praise be to the Lord, the God of Israel, because he has come and has redeemed his people," Zechariah called out. "My child shall be one of the highest prophets the world has ever seen and prepare the way for the Lord on earth!"

John grew up and became strong in spirit. He lived in the desert during the first part of his life. He was waiting for the right time to present himself publicly to Israel.

64. An Angel Visits Mary
Luke 1

After the angel Gabriel visited Zechariah, his wife Elizabeth became pregnant. Before Elizabeth gave birth to John the angel went to Nazareth, a town in the kingdom of Galilee, north of Judea.

In Nazareth a young virgin named Mary was engaged to marry Joseph, who was a carpenter and a descendant of King David. "The Lord is with you!" the angel Gabriel said to Mary. "You are highly favored over all women!"

Mary felt uneasy about receiving such a strange greeting from a person whom she had never seen. She wondered what this meant. "Do not be afraid." the angel said. "You have been chosen by God. You will have a son whom you will name Jesus. He will be called the son of the Most High and will inherit the throne of David. He shall reign over God's people, and his kingdom will endure forever!"

"How will this happen?" Mary asked the angel. "I am just a girl, and not even married yet."

The angel faced her. "The Holy Spirit will come down upon you and you will then be with child. You will become the mother of the

son of God. Remember your cousin Elizabeth who is past child-bearing age and was barren, yet now she is pregnant. Nothing is impossible for God!"

"I am the Lord's servant," Mary said, realizing that she was in the presence of a messenger from heaven. "May what you have said come to happen." The angel then left Mary's presence.

The next day Mary got ready to travel and headed for Judea, to see her cousin, Elizabeth. Mary was welcomed into Zechariah's house and when Elizabeth went up to greet Mary, she felt the baby inside her leap in joy. Elizabeth felt the presence of the Holy Spirit all around her.

"Blessed are you among women, and blessed is the child that you will bear!" Elizabeth said to Mary in awe. "Why am I so honored that the mother of my Lord should come to me? As soon as I heard your greeting, the child within me leaped for joy. Blessed is the woman who believes what the Lord has said to her and will come to be!"

Elizabeth was the first person to realize that Mary would give birth to the son of God. Mary was overjoyed by her cousin's words. "My soul rejoices that God, my Savior, has blessed me with this honor," Mary said in prayer. "The Lord has looked on me with kindness, and because he has honored me, all future generations will remember my name. He is the most merciful to those who love and obey him, but he humbles those who turn their backs to him. He feeds and cares for the hungry and meek, but to the greedy he ignores and gives nothing."

Mary stayed with Elizabeth for about three months. At the end of the three months she said farewell to Elizabeth and returned to Nazareth. Mary never doubted the word of the Lord, and because of this she was blessed to become the mother of Jesus, the Savior of God's people. She was humble and loving—a good and courageous young woman.

65. The Birth of Jesus

Matthew 1–2; Luke 2

After visiting her relatives in Judea for three months, Mary returned to Nazareth in Galilee. Soon she was supposed to get married to Joseph, a carpenter who was a descendant of King David. When Mary returned to Nazareth, her pregnancy began to show. Word quickly spread in the town that she was carrying the son of the Holy Spirit.

Joseph was unsure what to do. He was a righteous and good man and did not want to cause Mary any disgrace. He decided that he would quietly release her from their engagement together.

After he considered this option, he decided to sleep on it before making the final decision. An angel of the Lord appeared to Joseph in a dream. "Joseph, descendant of David, do not be afraid to take Mary into your home as your

wife," the angel said to him. "She will have the son of the Holy Spirit and you are to name him Jesus, because he will save his followers from their sins." Jesus means "the Lord saves."

When Joseph woke up, he did what the angel of the Lord had commanded. Joseph and Mary were married. Soon after, Caesar Augustus, the emperor of Rome, issued a decree that a census of the entire empire be taken. Every head of the household had to return to the town of his birth with his family to be counted.

So Joseph and Mary headed for the small town of Bethlehem because he was a descendant of King David. When they reached Bethlehem, the time for Mary to have her child arrived. Bethlehem was a small town, and many people had arrived there to be counted. The streets were full. Joseph searched for a place to stay but could not find anything.

At one inn, the innkeeper told Joseph that they had no rooms available. When Joseph explained that his wife Mary was about to have a child and that they desperately needed shelter, the innkeeper said they could stay in the stables. That night Mary gave birth to Jesus.

Mary wrapped her son in some soft fabrics and placed him in a manger. A manger is a box that was used for feeding sheep.

That very night some shepherds were out in the fields, watching over their flocks. An angel of the Lord suddenly appeared before them, glowing with an intense white light. The shepherds trembled in terror.

"Do not be afraid!" called out the angel. "I bring you news of great joy for everyone. Today in the city of David, a Savior has been born. He is Christ the Lord. You will know it is he when you see this sign—you will find the baby wrapped in soft cloths and lying in a manger."

As the angel finished speaking, an enormous group of angels descended from heaven and sang out in joy, "Glory to God in the highest, and on earth peace to men on whom his favor rests!"

"We must go into town and find out what has happened," the shepherds said to one another. They then all hurried off and eventually found the inn's stables where Mary and Joseph had gone. When they saw the baby in the manger, they knew everything that they had been told was true. Joyously, they gave praise to the Lord and went out and told everyone what they had seen. Everyone in Nazareth was amazed at what the shepherds told them.

Mary was quiet. She thought about all the amazing things that happened, and how they all occurred exactly how the Lord had foretold.

66. The Three Magi

Luke 2; Matthew 2

 n the day the Son of God was born, three Magi—or wise men—saw a new star light up in the night sky over Judea. The wise men were from a land far to the east of Judea. They immediately set off for Jerusalem.

When they arrived in Jerusalem, they asked everyone they came upon, "Where is the one who has been born to become the king of the Jews? We saw his star from the east and have come to worship him."

No one knew what to say to these strange foreigners. Soon, word of what the Magi were saying reached Herod, the King who ruled over Judea. Hearing that the "King of the Jews" had been born upset him, and he felt that his power was threatened. He called for his chief priests and wise men, and consulted them. "Where would the Messiah be born?" he asked them. Messiah was the name people gave to the coming Savior and King of the Jews.

"In Bethlehem," one of the priests said. "For it is written, Bethlehem, in the Land of Judah, are by no means the least among the rulers of Judah; for out of you will come a ruler who will be the shepherd of all my people."

King Herod summoned the Magi to stand before him. Herod was pleasant to the wise men, acting as if he were as overjoyed about the birth of the new king as they were. Herod found out when the child had been born, and then told the Magi that the child would have been born somewhere in the town of Bethlehem.

"When you find the child," Herod said to the Magi, "please come back to me and tell me where he is, because I would like to worship him as well."

Herod was lying and wished to find out where the child was only so he'd be able to get rid of him.

The Magi bowed gratefully before Herod, not knowing his evil intentions. They headed for Bethlehem and again saw the star they had seen from the east shining in front of them. They followed the star until it stopped over the place where Mary, Joseph, and the baby were staying.

The three wise men from the east bowed down before the child with Mary and worshipped him. Each of the Magi presented the baby with a gift—one gave him myrrh, a valuable scented resin that comes from trees; another gave frankincense, another resin that is burned as incense in worship; and the third gave a gift of gold.

The Magi spent the night in Bethlehem. In their sleep they each had a dream that warned them not to return to Jerusalem, and to send no messages to Herod. So, in the morning, the Magi woke up and returned to their homeland by a different route from which they came.

Eight days after Mary gave birth to the son of the Holy Spirit, it was time for the special ceremony for boy babies. At this time he was given the name Jesus as the angel of the Lord had said. Another custom of the time was to present all newborn sons to the Lord. So Mary and Joseph traveled to Jerusalem with the baby Jesus to present him in the Temple of the Lord and offer a sacrifice so that the baby might be blessed.

In Jerusalem lived a man named Simeon who was a priest in the Temple of the Lord. Simeon was a righteous and good man, who obeyed God's laws. He was also a prophet of the Lord. The Lord had revealed to him that he would live to see the coming of the son of the Lord. Simeon stood by the temple's entrance when Mary and Joseph came with the baby Jesus to present him to the Lord.

Simeon took the baby into his arms and held him up. "O great Lord, you have fulfilled your promise!" Simeon said in great praise. "I may die in peace now that my eyes have seen your salvation."

Mary and Joseph were in awe of what Simeon said about their child. Simeon then blessed them both and said to Mary, "This child is destined to cause the falling and rising of many souls in Israel. He will be both a beacon to yearn for and a symbol to be spoken against. Because of this you will face many challenges yourself."

Just then, a very old woman came shuffling from another part of the temple. The woman, Anna, was a prophetess whose husband had died eighty-four years before the birth of Jesus. She never left the temple. Day and night she prayed. Anna approached Mary and Joseph with the baby Jesus and blessed them. "This is the child we have all been waiting for," Anna said. "He will be our Savior."

When Joseph and Mary had finished presenting Jesus and made their sacrifices they left the temple. They returned to Bethlehem.

67. Escaping the Enemies of Jesus

Matthew 2

The three wise men had visited the newborn baby Jesus, worshipped him, and returned home. King Herod, the King of Judea who served the Roman Empire, had told the Magi to return to him and tell him where he could find the baby—the one who was said to be the future King of the Jews and therefore a threat to his throne. Herod was devising an evil plan to get rid of the baby before he could grow up. Herod believed that once grown, Jesus would overthrow his rule.

After the wise men left, Joseph and Mary took the baby Jesus to the temple of the Lord in Jerusalem where he was praised by the people within the temple as the expected savior. By the time they were returning to Nazareth, Herod realized that the Magi had tricked him. He was furious that the Magi had left without telling him where he could find the baby Jesus.

Herod did find out when the child was born. He issued a decree that every baby boy that was born in or around Bethlehem was to be put to death. He ordered his guards to kill every boy under two years of age. Herod was such a ferocious and evil ruler that everyone feared him. None of his guards dared defy his orders, no matter how horrible.

Before the guards started carrying out Herod's orders an angel appeared in Joseph's dreams. "Take the child and his mother," the angel said. "You must flee immediately to Egypt, where you will be safe. You must stay there until I tell you, for the evil king of Judea is searching for the child and wants to kill him."

Joseph awoke, and that very night got his wife Mary and the baby Jesus and fled Bethlehem. Egypt was a long journey for the young family to take. It was a three-day trip through a harsh desert. It was the same desert Moses and the Israelites had gone through so many years before when escaping Egypt. Egypt was a much more peaceful place where people would often go for refuge. Joseph and Mary, with the baby Jesus, made it to Egypt safely because God protected them on their journey. They were now far from Herod's grasp and would be safe until it was time to return.

Many years before, the Lord through the Prophet Hosea said, "Out of Egypt I will call my son." Joseph and Mary's journey to Egypt fulfilled that prophecy. When Herod died, an angel of the Lord again appeared to Joseph in a dream. "Get up and return to your homeland. The people who were trying to kill the child are now gone."

Joseph did as the angel of the Lord commanded. He took Mary and Jesus back to the land of Israel. Once there, he found out that Herod's son Archelaus was the new ruler in Jerusalem of the land of Judea. He was afraid of the son of Herod. Again the Lord sent Joseph a dream telling him what he should do.

So Joseph took Mary and young Jesus to the land of Galilee, north of Judea. They settled in Nazareth, where Joseph and Mary had both lived before they were married. Jesus spent most of his youth growing up in Nazareth, which is why he is sometimes referred to as "Jesus of Nazareth."

68. Young Jesus in the Temple of the Lord

Luke 2

When Herod died, an angel of the Lord appeared to Joseph in a dream. "Get up and return to your homeland. The people that were trying to kill the child are now gone." Joseph did as the angel of the Lord commanded. He took Mary and Jesus back to the land of Israel.

Archelaus, the son of Herod, was the new ruler in Jerusalem of the land of Judea. Joseph took Mary and young Jesus to the land of Galilee, north of Judea, to be out of the son of Herod's domain. They settled in Nazareth, where Jesus spent most of his youth.

While Jesus was growing up, he went with Mary and Joseph to the Temple of the Lord in Jerusalem during the Feast of the Passover every year.

When Jesus was twelve, he went with Mary and Joseph to the temple as was their custom. When the feast was over, Joseph and Mary set off for home. Every year they traveled with many relatives and friends, so the procession was quite large. Joseph and Mary had seen Jesus before they left Jerusalem, so they were not worried during their first day of travel when they did not see him. They assumed he was somewhere in the group of travelers.

That night, Joseph and Mary got a little worried when they still had not seen Jesus. In the morning they searched throughout their traveling group asking if anyone had seen him. None of their relatives and friends had seen him.

Joseph and Mary became very worried as any parent would. They were already halfway back to Nazareth. Joseph and Mary left their group of friends and relatives and headed back to Jerusalem.

For three days they looked everywhere in Jerusalem for Jesus, but could not find him. Feeling desperate, they went to the temple to pray. When they arrived they saw young Jesus sitting among the temple elders and teachers!

Jesus was sitting with several wise men. The wise men and teachers were asking Jesus questions. Jesus was listening to their questions, giving answers, and asking questions of his own. The temple elders were astounded by the wisdom of this boy who was only twelve years old.

When Joseph and Mary saw their son they were shocked. When Mary saw her son she walked up to him. "My son," she asked, "why have you done this to us? Did you not know that we've been so worried about you? We have been looking everywhere for you for three days."

"Why did it take you so long to find me?" Jesus asked. "Didn't you know that I had to be in my Father's house?" Joseph and Mary were confused and did not understand what the young Jesus was saying. However, they were just so very happy to have found their son.

Jesus then went back to Nazareth with Mary and Joseph and always obeyed their wishes from that day on. Although not fully understanding everything that was going on, Mary still treasured every moment that happened, because she knew it was God's will.

As Jesus grew up to be an adult, he grew in both size and wisdom, and both God and his neighbors looked at Jesus with great admiration and favor.

69. John the Baptist

Matthew 3; Mark 1; Luke 3; John 1

n the time of Herod's rule, the priest Zechariah and his wife Elizabeth were very good people, and always obeyed God's laws. Elizabeth and Zechariah were sad because they were old and did not have any children.

One day when Zechariah went inside the Temple of the Lord to burn incense an angel of the Lord appeared before him. Zechariah had never seen an angel and was scared. "Do not be afraid, Zechariah, the Lord is with you. Your wife will bear you a son, and you will name him John. He will be filled with the Holy Spirit even at the time of his birth, and the people of Israel will follow him back to the ways of the Lord."

Even though Zechariah's wife had never been able to have children, and was by then well beyond child-bearing age, she did have a son. Zechariah and Elizabeth named their son John as the angel commanded.

John grew up and became strong in spirit. When he was on his own he lived out in the desert. This was about twenty years after the day Jesus appeared in the Temple of the Lord as a boy. Pontius Pilate, a Roman, was the new governor of Judea, while the offspring of Herod were ruling the surrounding lands.

While John was in the desert, God called out to him. John began preaching in the desert. He wore a tunic made out of camel hair with a leather belt around his waist. He ate locusts and wild honey.

John would preach for the forgiveness of people's sins. People from all over would come to John to confess their sins. After their confessions, John would baptize them in the Jordan River.

Crowds and crowds of people would come to John. John yelled at them. "Just because you are descendents of Abraham, do not think that you are special! God can raise new children of Abraham out of these rocks! Be warned, the axe is already at the root of the trees. Those that do not bear good fruit will be cut down and thrown into the fire!"

"What should we do?" the people in the crowd asked.

"The man with two pairs of shoes should give one to the man with none," John answered. "The person with plenty of food should feed those who are hungry."

Among the crowd was a group of tax collectors. "Teacher, tell us what we should do," they asked.

"Collect only the money you are required to, and not any more," John answered.

"And what should we do?" asked some soldiers.

"Do your duty and be content. Do not threaten innocent people nor take bribes."

News of John's wisdom quickly spread through the land. The people in the crowds around him quietly wondered to themselves if John was the Messiah.

John knew what the crowds were thinking. "I am but a man. While I baptize you with water, there is another to come after me who will baptize us all in the Holy Spirit. The true Christ is more powerful than any of us can imagine. I am not even fit to untie his sandals." John continued for some time, preaching about what joys awaited them.

"Then who are you?" the crowd asked.

"I am the forerunner of Christ," John replied. "I have been called to prepare the way for our Savior!"

The next day, John saw Jesus approaching. John and Jesus had never met, although, their mothers were together when they were still carrying their sons in their wombs. When John's mother came into the presence of Mary, Jesus' mother, she had felt the child within her leap for joy. When John saw Jesus this time, he felt within him his heart leap for joy in the same way.

"Look!" John called. "Here comes the Lamb of God who will take away all of our sins. It is he I spoke of when I said, 'There is another to come after me who will baptize us all in the Holy Spirit!' I have never seen him before, but as I laid eyes on him I knew that the reason I am here to baptize you with water was so that he might be revealed to us all!"

Jesus approached John the Baptist and asked to be baptized in the Jordan. "I have no right to baptize you," John said to Jesus. "You are the one who should baptize me."

"Let us do what is the will of the Lord," Jesus replied. John bowed down in agreement and they both went into the river.

John baptized Jesus. As Jesus and John walked out of the river, the heavens opened up above them. A bright golden light shone down on John, Jesus, and the hundreds of people gathered near the river. The Holy Spirit descended from heaven in the shape of a dove. The Holy Spirit rested on Jesus. Then everyone there heard the voice of God. "This is my son," the voice of the Lord said, "whom I love."

His baptism marked the beginning of Jesus' life as the Savior. 📖

70. The Temptation of Christ
Matthew 3–4; Mark 1; Luke 3–4

 hen Jesus was about thirty years old he went to John the Baptist, who was preaching in the desert by the Jordan River. Jesus went to John to be baptized.

Once Jesus was baptized, the heavens opened up above them. A bright golden light shone down on John, Jesus, and the large crowd gathered by the river. The Holy Spirit descended down from heaven in the form of a dove. Then the voice of God was heard by everyone. "This is my beloved son who pleases me greatly," the voice of the Lord said.

After his baptism, the Holy Spirit led Jesus away from the crowd at the Jordan River and deep into the desert. Jesus remained in the desert alone for forty days. While there he prayed, meditated, and fasted. Jesus did not eat a thing the entire time he was in the hot and barren land. Vultures flew over his head, and the sun beat down hard on his head. After forty days he was faint with hunger, and greatly weakened.

As Jesus prepared to return to his people, the devil appeared before him. The devil wanted to test Jesus. "If you are the son of God," he said to Jesus, "end your hunger! Turn this stone into bread."

"It is written that people cannot live on bread alone," answered Jesus. The devil was tempting Jesus not only to end his hunger, but also to prove his power. The devil wanted to show that Jesus did not trust that God would take care of him.

"It is the word of God that people need to live and be happy," said Jesus.

Undeterred, the devil then took Jesus into Jerusalem. He took Jesus to the Temple of the Lord and went to one of the highest towers. There high above the city, they looked upon the great city. "If you truly are the son of God, prove it to all these people," the devil said to Jesus. "Throw yourself off of this tower, for is it not written, 'He will command his angels to protect you—they will lift you up with their hands so that not even your foot will touch stone'?"

"It is also written, 'Do not put the Lord, your God, to the test'," Jesus answered to this challenge. Jesus knew that the people had to be drawn to God not by miracles, but by their own faith and choice.

The devil would not give up easily. He led Jesus up to the highest mountain in the land. At the top of the mountain they could see far off into the distance in every direction. "Look all around you," the devil said to Jesus. "From here you can see all the kingdoms of the world." He paused and let Jesus look about. "All this I will give to you! You must simply bow before me and worship me." Jesus was destined to become the king of all of God's people for all time, but he had barely begun what he knew would be a long and trying journey. The devil was offering him everything instantly.

"Away with you!" Jesus shouted. "It is written, 'Worship only the Lord your God, and serve only him.'"

After Jesus finished speaking the devil left his presence. Immediately afterwards, the Lord sent angels down to attend to Jesus.

Jesus had been tired, weak, and weary. Yet even though the devil tempted him with several great rewards—to satisfy his hunger, to prove to the people that he truly was the son of God, and even the giving him the whole world as his kingdom—he did not give in to temptation. Even through these most difficult tests and trial, Jesus remained pure and true to God's will.

71. Jesus Begins His Life as a Preacher and Healer

Matthew 4; Mark 1; Luke 4

fter being baptized by John, Jesus spent forty days in the desert fasting and praying. Afterwards the devil presented Jesus with three temptations, which Jesus overcame. Jesus sent the devil away and was then cared for by angels of the Lord.

Filled with the Holy Spirit, Jesus returned to Galilee, the country in which he had spent his youth. He went from place to place teaching people about God. Wherever he went, Jesus was praised, until he finally returned to the town of his youth—Nazareth.

It was the day of the Sabbath—the day of prayer and rest according to the Ten Commandments. Jesus went to the synagogue in Nazareth, as did everyone else in the town. He got up in front of everyone to read.

Jesus read from the scroll of the prophet Isaiah. "'The Spirit of the Lord is on me,'" Jesus read out loud to the people in the synagogue, "'because he has anointed me to preach the good news to the poor, to heal the sick, give sight to the blind, to release the oppressed, and to proclaim the year of the Lord's favor.'"

Jesus handed the scroll back to the priest and sat down. Everyone looked at him and was happy. They were amazed at what Jesus had said. "But isn't this the son of Joseph?" someone asked.

"I will tell you," Jesus said to the people, "no prophet is accepted in his own town." Jesus scolded the people for being proud and questioning him.

Jesus also spoke of things in the scriptures that the people did not understand. They thought he was speaking ill of them.

The people became furious with Jesus. The got up and grabbed Jesus. They dragged him out of town and brought him to the edge of a hill, where they planned to beat him, to teach him a lesson. However, when they reached the outskirts of the town, Jesus simply walked through the crowd. No one was able to stop him.

From Nazareth, Jesus headed to Capernaum, another town in Galilee. While preaching to a group of people in that town, a man possessed by an evil spirit appeared in the crowd.

"What are you doing here?" the possessed man taunted Jesus. "Have you come to destroy us? I know what you are up to, Holy One of God!"

"Quiet!" Jesus said to the man. "I command you to leave this man!" As Jesus spoke these words, the evil spirit threw the man down on the ground and left his body. The man stood up, completely unharmed.

All the people were amazed. "Who is this man? What is his teaching?" they all asked one another. "With nothing more than his words he was able to drive out an evil spirit from a man." All the people who witnessed one of Jesus' first miracles were amazed and quickly the news about him spread.

Jesus wasn't done yet that day. He left the group of admirers and went to the home of a man named Simon. Simon's mother-in-law was very sick with a high fever, Simon and the others in the house asked Jesus if he could do anything to help her.

Jesus took her by the hand and lifted her up. Immediately her fever went away and she began to serve them. All the people in the town brought their sick to Jesus that day, and he healed them all. After a long day, Jesus walked to a quiet part of the town to be alone.

The people of Capernaum followed Jesus and asked him not to leave. "I must preach the word of God to the people in other towns too, because that is why I am here." With that, Jesus got up and left Capernaum to preach to all the people of Israel.

72. Jesus Calls His Disciples

Matthew 4; Mark 2; Luke 4–5; John 1

esus preached throughout the land of the Jewish people. One day, while walking by the Sea of Galilee, Jesus saw two brothers. The older brother was Simon Peter and the younger was named Andrew. The two brothers were in a small fishing boat by the shore. They were both fishermen and had had a bad day—they hardly caught anything. When Jesus arrived, they were cleaning up their nets and getting ready to call it a day.

Jesus got into the boat with Simon Peter and Andrew. He preached to the people the word of God, and many gathered around him to listen. When he finished speaking to the people, he turned to Simon Peter and Andrew. "Now, let's go out to deep waters and let out your nets for a catch," he said to them.

"Master, we have been fishing all day and are very tired," Simon Peter answered, "and we haven't caught a thing. However, we will do as you say."

Simon Peter and Andrew threw out their nets into the water. After a few moments, they began to pull the nets in, but they were so full of fish that they couldn't lift them! They called to the other fishermen around who brought their boats near to help them. When they were done, they had caught more fish in that one haul than they ever had in an entire day!

Simon Peter got down on his knees in front of Jesus. "Lord, I am not worthy of your presence!" he said, astonished at the miracle of such an enormous catch. Two fishermen in a nearby boat, brothers named John and James, were also amazed at what they had seen.

"Do not be afraid," Jesus said to Simon Peter. "Come with me, now you will be fishers of men." Simon Peter and Andrew rowed their boat to the shore and went with Jesus, leaving everything behind without a thought.

As they left, Jesus saw John and James in their boat. They were with their father, Zebedee. Jesus called to them to follow. Without hesitation, the brothers got up and left their boat and father to follow Jesus.

The next day Jesus decided to head back into Galilee. With his disciples he set off and met a man named Philip. Philip was from the town of Bethsaida, and knew about what happened the day before.

"Come and follow me," Jesus said to Philip. Philip immediately ran to find his brother, Nathanael.

"We have found him, the one written about by the prophets!" Philip said to Nathanael when he found him. "It is the savior, Jesus of Nazareth!"

"Nazareth?" Nathanael replied, "What good could come from there?"

"Come and see," Philip told him.

When Nathanael approached, Jesus said, "Here is Nathanael, an Israelite pure of spirit and true of heart."

"How do you know me?" Nathanael asked.

"I saw you sitting under the fig tree before Philip called you."

"Teacher, you truly are the son of God," Nathanael said.

"You believe me because I have shown to you that I knew where you were," Jesus told Nathanael. "Follow me, and you will see even greater things."

While preaching the next day, Jesus saw Levi, a tax collector standing off away from the crowd. Because Levi was a tax collector, the people did not like him. Jesus approached Levi. "Come and follow me," he said to the tax collector. Levi got up and followed Jesus without a word.

Levi took Jesus to his house for dinner. The other disciples and many of the people in the crowd followed and sat with them. Many of the people in the crowd were know to be criminals, beggars, and other "low lifes" of society.

The Pharisees, high elders among the Jewish people, were also there and saw Jesus sitting with these sinners. The Pharisees felt threatened by what Jesus said and challenged those following him. "If this man is the 'Son of God,' then why does he sit and eat with tax collectors and sinners?"

Jesus heard what they had said. "Would a doctor go to see a healthy person?" he asked the elders. "I have come not to help the righteous, but those who are weak in spirit, sinners. They are the ones who need me most."

Jesus climbed up to a mountain with a great crowd below him. He called out to the people he wanted to have as his disciples. Jesus wanted his disciples to preach to others and to appoint them apostles. That way he gave them powers over evil and the ability to heal others. The twelve he chose were: Simon Peter (who was renamed Peter); James and John, sons of Zebedee (Jesus called them Boanerges, the "Sons of Thunder"); Andrew; Philip; Nathanael (renamed Bartholomew); Levi (renamed Matthew); Thomas; James, son of Alphaeus; Thaddaeus; Simon; and Judas Iscariot.

73. Jesus Changes Water into Wine

John 2

hortly after Jesus had chosen his twelve disciples, a wedding was held in the town of Cana, not too far from the Sea of Galilee. Mary, the mother of Jesus, was invited. Jesus and his twelve disciples were also invited to the wedding.

Wedding feasts were a very important gathering, where the father of husband-to-be would show off his family's great wealth by being as lavish as he could.

Midway through the feast Mary noticed that the big wine casks were empty. She whispered to Jesus, "They have no more wine."

In the corner of the banquet room stood six large stone jugs. The jugs were empty. The jugs were normally used for holding water for ceremonial washing. Each jug was tall and round, and weighed over 100 pounds empty.

"Fill those jars with water all the way to the top," Jesus told the servants. As fast as they could, the servants filled each of the six jugs to the brim with water.

"Now," Jesus said to the servants when they were done, "draw out from the jugs and take some to the chief steward." The servants did as Jesus instructed. One servant took a small clay pitcher and filled it from the large stone jug. He took it to the steward and filled his cup.

The steward did not know where his drink had come from. The water in the stone jugs had been turned into wine. After taking a drink, the steward went to the bridegroom, the man who was just married.

"Most hosts would serve the best wine first, and when everyone had had some of it, then the host would bring out cheaper wine. But you, you have saved the best wine for last. This is the finest wine I have ever tasted!" The steward smiled and drank some more wine.

This was the first true miracle Jesus performed. The servants and the disciples saw what Jesus did and realized that he was great in power. The steward also made a premonition without realizing it. Just as he thought the host of the feast had saved the best wine for last, Jesus was to save his greatest miracle for last. On that day, the disciples' faith in Jesus was strengthened.

74. The Parables

Note to reader: This story is actually a collection of several of Jesus' parables. They can be read as individual mini-stories, or all together.

When Jesus preached to the people, he often spoke in parables. A parable is a kind of story with a special, heavenly meaning. Jesus would use stories about real life events—things that would be very easy for the people to understand and relate to—to teach lessons about the ways of God. Also, when Jesus spoke in parables, and then explained their full meaning, the stories often touched the people's hearts more deeply.

In all, Jesus told fifty-one parables during his three years of preaching to the people. Only a few of the more famous ones are recounted here.

The Sower
Matthew 13; Mark 4; Luke 8

Jesus was teaching by the lake. However, the crowd around him was so large that he could not see everyone, and most of the people in the crowd could not see him. So Jesus got into a boat and went out on the lake, while the people stayed at the water's edge. From here, everyone could see Jesus and hear what he had to teach.

"Listen!" Jesus began. "A farmer went out to sow his seeds in the fields. As he was scattering the seed around, some fell along the path. The birds came down and ate it. Some seeds fell on rocky places, where the soil was shallow. These seeds sprouted quickly, but when the sun came up, the plants withered because

227

their roots were not deep enough. Other seeds fell among the thorn bushes. When these seeds sprouted they were choked by the thorns, so that they did not bear grain. Other seeds made it on to good soil. These seeds sprouted and bore a lush and bountiful crop." Jesus then said, "Everyone who has ears to hear, let them hear."

Later that day, when Jesus was alone, the twelve disciples asked him about the parable. "You don't understand this parable?" Jesus asked. "How will you be able to understand any of them then? I sow the word to the people, as the farmer sows seeds to the soil. Some people are like the seeds along the path. As soon as they hear the word, Satan comes and takes away

the word because they are too hard to accept the word. The soil of the path was too packed to accept the seeds. Others, like seed sown on rocky places, hear the word and at once receive it with joy. But since they are not rooted deeply, they last only a short time. When trouble or persecution comes because of the word, they quickly fall away. Still others are like the seeds sown among thorns. They hear the word, but cannot free themselves from the desire for wealth and other worldly things. But those like the seeds that were sown on good soil hear and accept the word and produce a lush and bountiful crop."

The Weeds in the Wheat

Matthew 13

"The kingdom of heaven is like a man who sowed good seed in his fields. But while he and his servants were sleeping, a neighbor who hated the man came and sowed weeds among the wheat.

"When the wheat sprouted and formed heads, the weeds appeared as well. 'Master, didn't you sow only good seeds in your field? Where did those weeds come from?' asked the servants who worked in the field.

"'An enemy did this in the night,' he replied.

"The servants asked him, 'Do you want us to pull the weeds up?'

"'No,' the man answered, 'If you go out into the field and pull the weeds, you may uproot some of the good wheat as well. Let both grow together until it is time to harvest. At that time I will tell the harvesters to collect the weeds and tie them in bundles to be burned; then gather the wheat and bring it into my barn.'"

Jesus left the crowd and went into the house where he was staying. His disciples followed him. "Can you explain the parable you just told?" they asked.

"The one who sowed the good seed is the Son of Man, the field is the world, and the good seed are the good people of the earth. The weeds are the evil people of the earth, and the enemy who sows them is the devil. The harvest is the end of the age, and the harvesters are angels. Just as the weeds were pulled up and burned in the fire, so it will be at the end of the age. But the righteous will shine like the sun in the kingdom of their Father."

The Mustard Seed and the Yeast
Matthew 13; Mark 4; Luke 13

"The kingdom of heaven is like a mustard seed," Jesus said to the gathered crowd, "which was planted in a field. Even though it is the smallest of all seeds, when it grows it becomes a tree so large that birds come and perch on its branches."

Jesus looked at the crowd and continued, "What shall I compare the kingdom of God to? It is like yeast that has been mixed into a large amount of flour until it has worked its way through all the dough."

Jesus was showing the people that the word of the Lord would spread from a very small source to encompass the entire world. Just as the yeast spreads throughout dough, the kingdom of God will spread throughout the world.

The Good Samaritan
Luke 10

One day when Jesus was preaching to a group of people, a man who worked as a lawyer approached him. The man wanted to test Jesus in the same way that he tested people who had committed crimes.

"Teacher," the man asked, "what must I do to go to heaven and have eternal life?"

"What is written in God's Laws?" Jesus replied. "How do you interpret it?"

"Love the Lord with all your heart, strength, mind, and soul; and love your neighbor as you love yourself," the man answered.

"That is correct," Jesus said. "If you do this you will have eternal life."

The man wasn't satisfied yet. He asked Jesus, "Who then is my neighbor that I must love as I love myself?"

"A man was walking from Jerusalem to Jericho," Jesus replied. "On his way he was attacked by a gang of thieves. They took his clothes, beat him horribly, and ran off, leaving him near death.

"Later on, a priest walked down the same road. When he saw the man, he passed by on the other side of the road so he wouldn't have to be near the beaten man. A Levite, one of the men who help the priests in the temple, came by shortly after. When he came upon the beaten man, he did the same thing the priest had done, and went along his way.

A third traveler came by. He was a Samaritan. When he came to where the man was and saw him in his poor condition, he took pity on him. The Samaritan bandaged the man's wounds and then put him on his own donkey. The Samaritan took the wounded man to an inn and cared for him the whole night. The next day he gave two silver coins to the innkeeper and said, 'Look after him, and when I return, I will reimburse you for any extra expenses you might have.'

"Which of these three do you think was a neighbor to the man who fell into the hands of robbers?" Jesus asked.

"The one who had mercy on him," the lawyer answered.

"Go and do the same," Jesus told the lawyer.

The Lost Sheep
Matthew 18; Luke 15

While Jesus was preaching, several people who were known to lead sinful lives were gathering around him. The Pharisees—elders among the Jewish people—saw this and muttered to each other about how Jesus was welcoming the presence of the sinners and not even acknowledging them.

"Suppose a shepherd has a hundred sheep and one of them wanders off," Jesus said to the Pharisees. "Wouldn't he leave the ninety-nine unattended and go after the lost sheep until he finds it? And, when he finds the lost sheep, he would embrace it and gently bring it home with great joy.

"Later, he would call his friends and neighbors together and say, 'Rejoice with me, I have found my lost sheep.' In heaven, it is the same way. There will be more rejoicing over one sinner who repents than over ninety-nine righteous people who have no need to repent."

Jesus told the parable to point out how important it was for those who had fallen into sin to repent. He let everyone know that God loves sinners and that he would not treat them harshly if they repented. Just as the shepherd did not treat the lost sheep harshly when he found it, God welcomes people to repent and follow his word.

The Lost Coin
Luke 15

"Say a woman has ten silver coins and loses one," Jesus continued to the same crowd and the Pharisees after telling the parable of the lost sheep. "She would light a lamp, sweep the entire house, and search carefully until she found it. When she does, she'd call her friends and neighbors together and say, 'Rejoice with me. I found my lost coin.'

"In the same way, the angels in heaven rejoice when even one sinner repents."

Jesus told this story to reinforce his parable of the lost sheep. Jesus was saying that he would never give up in his quest for bringing lost souls back to the word of the Lord.

The Prodigal Son
Luke 15

After telling the parable of the lost sheep and the lost coin, Jesus continued with another parable about finding something precious that had been lost. "There was a man who had two sons. One day, the younger one said to his father, 'Father, give me my share of the estate, so I might go out into the world.'

"So the father divided his property between them.

"Not long after that, the younger son got all his belongings and wealth together and set off for a distant country. There, he wasted all of his wealth having fun. After he had spent everything, there was a severe famine in the whole country. Suddenly, the younger brother found himself hungry and without friends or family to help him. He went and got a job working on a farm. He was so hungry he was jealous of the food the pigs got.

"Eventually, he came to his senses. 'How many of my father's hired men have plenty of food, while I am here starving to death!' he thought to himself.

"He headed back to his father's house. He was going to tell his father that he was no longer worthy of being called his son, but would like to become one of his hired men to work for his living.

"But, when the younger son was still a long way off, his father saw him and was filled with joy. He ran to his son, threw his arms around him, and kissed him.

"'Father, I have sinned against the Lord and against you. I am no longer worthy to be called your son.' Before he could finish, his father said to the servants, 'Quick! Get the best robe you can find and put it on him. Prepare a feast and we will all celebrate! My son of mine was dead and is alive again. He was lost and now is found.'

"The celebration occurred that night. The older son was working in the field while this all happened. When he got near the house, he heard music. He called one of the servants and asked him what was going on. 'Your brother has returned,' the servant told the older son. 'Your father has thrown a feast to celebrate his return.'

"The older brother was angry and refused to go in. His father went out and begged him to come inside and greet his brother. 'All these years,' the older son said to his father, 'I've been obedient to you and have served you faithfully. Yet, I have never gotten a party! But when my brother comes slinking back after wasting all your money partying, you throw a feast!'

"'My son,' the father said, 'you are always with me, and everything I have is yours. But we have to celebrate and be happy that your brother has returned! He was dead and is alive again. He was lost and now is found'."

This parable reflects on the life Christ has given us. Everyone who has sinned against the Lord has wasted something in their lives. Jesus' parable of the prodigal son told the people that no matter how far from God they had gotten, they would still be welcomed back.

The Hypocritical Servant
Matthew 18

One day, Peter went to Jesus and asked, "Lord, how many times should I forgive a man who has done something wrong to me? Up to seven times?"

"I say, not seven times," Jesus answered, "but seventy-seven times." The other disciples were there and were listening to Peter and Jesus speaking.

Jesus turned to his disciple. "There once was a king who often loaned out money to his servants," Jesus said to them. "When he wanted to settle some of the accounts with his servants, a man who owed him a large amount of money was brought before him. The man owed the king so much he had no hope of repaying the king.

"Since he was not able to pay, the king ordered that the man, his wife, his children, and his property be sold to repay the debt.

"The servant was full of despair. He fell on his knees before the king. 'Be patient with me, my lord,' he begged, 'I will find a way to pay you back everything I owe.'

"The servant's master saw how distraught the man was and took pity on him. The king cancelled the servant's debt and let him go free. The servant thanked the king profusely and ran out into the streets shouting with joy.

"A few days later the same servant was walking along and met up with a man who owed him a small amount of money. 'Give me the money you owe me,' he said to the man.

"'I don't have it on me right now, but soon I promise,' he replied.

"The servant grabbed the man around the neck and began to choke him. 'Pay back what you owe me!' he shouted out angrily.

"The man fell to his knees. 'Be patient with me, I will pay you back soon!'

"But the servant refused. He went off and had the man arrested and thrown into prison until he could pay the debt.

"When the other servants saw what happened, they were very upset and went and told their master, the king, everything that had happened.

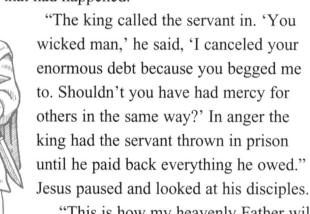

"The king called the servant in. 'You wicked man,' he said, 'I canceled your enormous debt because you begged me to. Shouldn't you have had mercy for others in the same way?' In anger the king had the servant thrown in prison until he paid back everything he owed." Jesus paused and looked at his disciples.

"This is how my heavenly Father will treat each of you unless you forgive others of their sins, as the Lord forgives you of your sins."

75. The Sermon on the Mount

Matthew 5–7; Luke 6

esus preached the word of the Lord to the crowds. He also healed many people. He gave the blind sight, he made the sick healthy, he made the paralyzed able to walk, and for those who were possessed he freed them from evil spirits. He became well known throughout the land of Galilee. Enormous crowds followed him, asking him to cure their ills and wanting to hear his wisdom.

As Jesus was walking near the Sea of Galilee, he saw how immense the crowds around him had become. He went up a little ways on a mountainside and sat down. His disciples followed him. Jesus then began one of his most famous sermons, the Sermon on the Mount, primarily to his disciples. But many of the masses of people could also see and hear him.

"Blessed are the gentle, they will inherit the earth. Blessed are those who mourn, for they will find comfort. Blessed are those who seek out the Lord, their wish will be filled. Blessed are those who show mercy, for they will be shown mercy. Blessed are the pure in heart, for they will see God. Blessed are those who suffer for the Lord, for theirs is the kingdom of heaven. Be rejoiceful, your reward in heaven will be immense.

"You are the light of the world. When people light a lamp they do not hide it under a bowl, they

237

put it on its stand, and it lights up the entire room. In the same way, let your light shine before all, so they might see your good deeds and praise your Father in heaven.

"Don't think that I have come to abolish the Law or the Prophets; I have not come to abolish them but to fulfill them. Not the smallest letter, not the least stroke of a pen, will by any means disappear from the Law until everything is accomplished. Anyone who breaks even one of the smallest of God's Laws and teaches others to do the same will be called the smallest in the kingdom of heaven. Whoever practices and teaches these commands will be called great in the kingdom of heaven.

"You know that it is written, 'Do not murder,' but I am telling you that anyone who wishes harm or thinks about killing is just as evil. You must keep violent thoughts out of your mind.

"You have heard it being said, 'an eye for eye, and tooth for tooth.' I tell you now, do not resist an evil person. If someone hits you on your right cheek, turn so they can have your left as well.

"It has been said, 'Love your neighbor and hate your enemy.' I tell you now, love your enemies and pray for those who wish you harm. How hard is it to love only those who love you? And if you greet only your brothers, what are you doing that anyone else might do?

"Do not show off your faith by praying out in front of everyone. When you give to the needy, do not announce it to everyone, just so people know you are generous. When you pray, do not be like those who pray on the street corners just to be seen by others. They have already received their rewards.

"When you pray, go into your room and close the door. Pray to your Father, who is unseen. This is how you should pray: 'Our Father in heaven, hallowed be your name, your kingdom come, your will be done on earth as it is in heaven.

Give us today our daily bread. Forgive us our sins, as we have forgiven those who have sinned against us. And lead us not into temptation, but deliver us from evil.' If you forgive someone who sins against you, the Lord will also forgive you. But if you do not forgive the sins of others, the Lord will not forgive your sins.

"Do not live only to gain wealth, these things do not last. Instead, collect treasures in heaven, which will serve you forever. No one can serve two masters. Either you will hate one and love the other, or be devoted to one and despise the other. You cannot serve both God and money.

"Do not judge others, or you too will be judged. Do not criticize the speck of sawdust in your neighbor's eye and pay no attention to the plank in your own. Take the plank out of your eye first, and then you will see clearly to help remove the speck from your neighbor's eye.

"Ask and it will be given to you; seek and you will find; knock and the door will be opened to you. Those who ask will receive, those who seek, will find; and to those who knock, the door will be opened.

"Enter through the narrow gate. For wide is the gate and broad is the road that leads to destruction, and many enter through it. But small is the gate and narrow the road that leads to life, and few find it. Being full of sin is easy, while leading a good life is difficult.

"Everyone who hears these words I speak of and puts them to use is like a wise man who built his house on the rock. When the storms and floods came the house remained standing, because it had its foundation on the rock. But everyone who hears these words of mine but does not put them into practice is like a foolish man who built his house on sand. When the same storm and flood came, it fell with a great crash."

When Jesus had finished, the crowds were amazed at what he said because he taught as one who had authority, and not as a simple teacher of the law.

76. The Roman Centurion
Matthew 8; Luke 7

esus was now well known as a healer and teacher throughout the land of Galilee. Enormous crowds would follow him, asking him to cure their ills and wanting to hear his wisdom.

One day, as Jesus was walking near the Sea of Galilee, he saw how immense the crowds around him had become. He went up a little ways on a mountainside and sat down with his disciples. Jesus began a sermon to everyone that later became known as the Sermon on the Mount.

In the Sermon on the Mount Jesus preached God's laws—The Ten Commandments, and gave the people many new views on what God expected of them. Jesus taught with such confidence and authority, and not as a simple teacher of the law, that the crowds gathered were amazed.

When he came down from the mountainside, large crowds followed him. A man with leprosy, a horrible disease that caused sores to cover his entire body, came and knelt before him and said, "Lord, if it is in your heart to do so, I believe you have the power to heal me."

Jesus reached out his hand and touched the man. "It is in my heart," he said. "Be healed!" Immediately the man was cured of his disease.

"Do not tell anyone what has happened. But go, show yourself to the priest in the temple and make an offering to the Lord."

After Jesus healed the sick man, he headed to Capernaum, a town near the Sea of Galilee. When he had entered Capernaum, everyone in the town recognized him and knew about how he healed the sick and performed miracles.

In Capernaum, a man was so ill he was going to die soon. The man was a faithful servant to a centurion or commander in the Roman army. The Roman centurion was a very good man and was sad that his servant was so ill. He had heard that Jesus had come into the town, so he sent some of the Jewish elders in the town to go to Jesus and ask for help.

"Lord," the elders said, "the servant of the Roman soldier in charge of this town is on his death bed." The elders pleaded with Jesus to go to the centurion's house to heal the sick man. "The centurion is a good man, he treats everyone fairly and had the temple in the town built."

"I will go," Jesus replied. He followed the Jewish elders of the town to the Roman centurion's house. When the centurion saw Jesus coming, he ran out to meet him.

"Lord, I do not deserve to have you come under my roof," the centurion said to Jesus, kneeling down, "I do not even deserve to stand before you. I know that if you just say the word, my servant will be healed. I myself understand, being a man in the military with both superiors and subordinates. I tell one soldier, 'Go,' and he goes. To another I say, 'Come,' and he comes. I say to my servant, 'Do this,' and he does it."

When Jesus heard what the centurion said, he was astonished. Jesus turned to those who had been following him, "In all my travels, I have not found anyone in Israel with such great faith." Then Jesus said to the Roman centurion, "Go. It will be done just as you believed it would." And when the centurion returned to his home, his servant was already healed and feeling well.

77. The Death of John the Baptist

Matthew 14; Mark 6; Luke 3

 ohn the Baptist was born to parents who would normally be considered too old to have children. His birth was a miracle and blessing that God had given his parents. John grew up and became strong in spirit. He became a great prophet. He lived out in the desert.

While John was in the desert, he preached to the people about repenting from their sins so that God's might forgive them. People from all over the land came to John to confess their sins. After their confessions, John would baptize them in the Jordan River.

News of John's wisdom quickly spread through the land. People wondered whether John might be the Messiah. This was before Jesus had shown himself to the world through his many miracles.

John knew what the crowds were thinking. "I am but a man," he told them. "While I baptize you with water, there is another to come after me who will baptize us all in the Holy Spirit. The true Christ is more powerful than any of us can imagine. I am not even fit to untie his sandals." John continued for some time, preaching about what joys awaited them.

"Then who are you?" the crowd asked.

"I am the forerunner of Christ," John replied. "I have been called to prepare the way for our Savior!"

John criticized Herod, the ruler of the lands, because Herod had married his brother's wife. (This Herod was the son of King Herod, who had tried to have

Jesus killed as a baby.) Herod was furious that anyone dared speak out against him. He had John locked up in prison.

Because John spoke out against their marriage, Herodias, Herod's wife, was very angry and wanted to kill him. But she was not able to because Herod feared John and protected him. Herod knew John was a righteous and holy man who was well respected by the people of the land. Herod would visit John in prison. He was amazed and often confused by the things John said. Yet he liked to listen to him.

Finally the perfect moment came for Herodias to get her vengeance. Herod gave a great banquet for his high officials and military commanders and the elders of Galilee to celebrate his birthday.

The daughter of Herodias came in and danced for everyone. She was so beautiful and such a good dancer that everyone was very happy and enjoying themselves. Herod was pleased that his party was going so well thanks to his wife's daughter. "Ask me for anything you want," he told the girl, "and I'll give it to you. I swear that whatever you ask I will give you, up to half my kingdom."

The girl had never had such a big choice to make. "What should I ask for?" she asked her mother in private.

"Ask for the head of John the Baptist," Herodias answered.

The girl hurried in to the king. "If I can really have anything I want," she said to Herod, "I want you to give me the head of John the Baptist on a platter."

Herod was upset. Because he had made an oath in front of all his dinner guests, he did not want to refuse.

He sent an executioner orders to bring John's head. The man went, beheaded John in the prison, and returned with John's head on a platter. He presented it to the girl, and she gave it to her mother.

John's followers found out about his death and came to get his body. They put John's body in a tomb, and sent word to Jesus, to tell him what happened. Jesus was very sad to hear about his friend, and went off by himself to mourn for the man who had baptized him.

78. The Great Miracles of Jesus

Matthew 8, 14–16; Mark 4, 6–8; Luke 8–9; John 6, 13

One day, while Jesus was walking along the Sea of Galilee with his disciples, he decided to get away from the crowds of people who were following them. Jesus had been preaching his parables to the crowds and everyone was eager to hear more of his wisdom, but Jesus wanted to get away from the crowds so he could speak with his disciples alone.

"Let's go over to the other side of the lake," Jesus said to his disciples. So they got into a boat and began to sail for the other side of the Sea of Galilee. Jesus fell asleep because he had been preaching long and hard with little rest.

While they were sailing, a great storm came out of nowhere. The sea was becoming rough, and the little boat rocked violently. The disciples were terrified and woke Jesus up.

"Master!" they yelled, "How can you sleep? We are going to drown!"

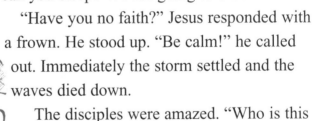

"Have you no faith?" Jesus responded with a frown. He stood up. "Be calm!" he called out. Immediately the storm settled and the waves died down.

The disciples were amazed. "Who is this man?" they asked one another. "Even the wind and the sea obey him!"

When John the Baptist was killed, his followers gave him a proper burial and sent word to Jesus. When Jesus heard what had happened, he got on a boat and went to a soli-

tary place, to be alone with his sadness and mourn the death of his friend. The crowds followed him on foot from the towns around the Sea of Galilee to the place where Jesus was.

When Jesus landed he saw the large crowd waiting for him. Several people who were sick had come to be healed. Jesus had compassion for them and healed the sick, and spoke to them all.

"This is a remote place," the disciples said to Jesus, "and it's already getting late. Send them away, so they can go and buy themselves food. "

"They do not need to go," Jesus replied. "You give them something to eat."

"It would take a year to earn enough money to buy everyone here food!"

A boy overheard them. He walked up to the disciple Andrew and gave him five loaves of bread and two fishes, hoping to help. "Teacher, this boy has five loaves of bread and two fishes," Andrew said to Jesus. "But how far will this go? There must be over 5,000 people here."

"Give them to me," he said. "Have the people all sit around us on the grass." He took the five loaves and the two fish and, looking up to heaven, gave thanks to the Lord and broke the loaves into pieces. Then he gave them to the disciples. "Give this out to everyone."

The disciples began handing out pieces of bread and fish. However, no matter how much they gave away, there was always some left over! The disciples then gathered the

leftover food and were able to collect twelve basketfuls of leftovers!

Jesus then told the disciples to get back into the boat and go on ahead of him to the other side, while he dismissed the crowd. After, Jesus went up on a mountainside by himself to pray. When evening came, he was there all alone. The boat with the disciples was already far from the shore.

In the middle of the night, the disciples had thrown out their anchor to rest. They had left late and would need to spend the night on the water before making it across. In the starlit night, they saw a figure of a man walking toward them, walking on the water! When the disciples saw this, they became terrified. "It's a ghost!" they cried.

It wasn't a ghost. It was Jesus. "Be brave! It is I. Don't be afraid."

"Lord, if it's really you," Peter replied, "tell me to come to you on the water."

"Come," he said. Then Peter stepped out of the boat. He walked on the water and went toward Jesus.

The wind began howling, and Peter became afraid. He began to sink. "Lord, save me!" he cried out.

Jesus reached out his hand and grabbed him. "You of little faith," he said, "why did you doubt?" When they both climbed aboard the boat the wind died down.

"Truly you are the Son of God," all the disciples said in awe.

Jesus continued to preach and perform miracles. The Pharisees, the high priests and leaders of the Jewish people, were becoming worried. They saw Jesus as a threat to their power. All around them people were flocking to Jesus. They also heard what Jesus said and saw it as a challenge to what they interpreted God's laws to mean.

The Pharisees took every opportunity to criticize Jesus. They challenge him at every chance they got, demanding he prove himself by performing a miracle, and asking him trick questions to trip him up. No matter what they tried, however, they could not outwit him.

Several times, Jesus explained to his disciples that he must go to Jerusalem and suffer many things at the hands of the elders, chief priests, and teachers of the law. He also said that he must be killed, but then on the third day he would be resurrected.

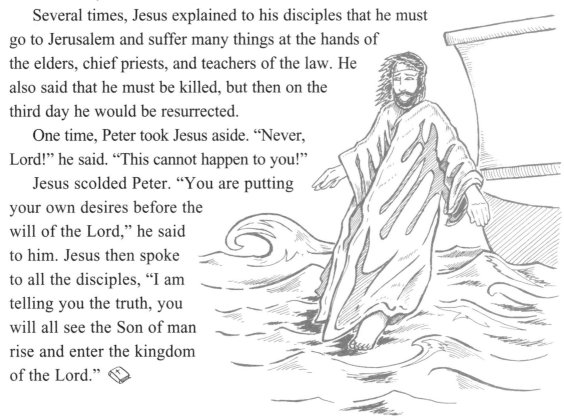

One time, Peter took Jesus aside. "Never, Lord!" he said. "This cannot happen to you!"

Jesus scolded Peter. "You are putting your own desires before the will of the Lord," he said to him. Jesus then spoke to all the disciples, "I am telling you the truth, you will all see the Son of man rise and enter the kingdom of the Lord."

79. The Transfiguration
Matthew 16–17; Mark 8–9; Luke 9

esus told his disciples that he would be killed, but then three days later he would rise and live again. Peter tried to argue with Jesus, begging him to keep this from happening. Jesus simply replied that this was the way God had planned things.

Six days later, Jesus took Peter, James, and John up a high mountain. The three disciples watched in amazement as the appearance of Jesus changed right before their eyes. His face became as bright as the sun, and his clothes became as white as fresh snow.

Moses and Elijah appeared next to Jesus. They began talking with him.

"Lord, thank you for bringing us here to see this miracle!" Peter said. "I will set up three shelters if you want me to—one for each of you." While he said this, a bright, glowing white cloud appeared above them all.

"This is my son," a voice from within the cloud said, "whom I love and with whom I am pleased. Listen to what he says!"

When the disciples saw the cloud and heard the voice of God, they fell down on the ground, terrified. Jesus came to them and said, "Get up, there is nothing to be afraid of." When the disciples looked up, only Jesus was with them. The cloud was also gone.

As they all went down the mountain, Jesus instructed them, "Don't tell anyone what you saw, until I rise from the dead."

"Why do the teachers of the law say that Elijah will come first?" they all asked.

"Yes, Elijah will be first," Jesus replied. "But I tell you. Elijah has already come, and no one recognized him. They treated him cruelly. In the same way they will make the Son of man suffer." The disciples realized that Jesus was talking about John the Baptist.

When they were down the mountain, a man approached Jesus and knelt before him. "Lord, please help my son," he said. "He is possessed by an evil spirit. I brought him to your disciples, but they could not heal him." The boy was beside his father, acting in a crazed manner.

Jesus touched the boy and ordered the evil spirit to leave him. That very moment the boy was healed and back to his normal sweet self.

"Why couldn't we drive it out?" the disciples asked Jesus.

"Because you have so little faith. If you had faith as small as a mustard seed, you could say to this mountain, 'Move over there,' and it would move. Nothing would be impossible for you."

As they walked along the road to Capernaum, three men caught up with them and knelt before Jesus. "I will follow you wherever you go," the first man said.

"You may do so," Jesus replied, "but you will need to give up everything, even your home."

"Come and follow me," Jesus said to the second man.

"First let me go and bury my father," the man replied.

"Let the dead bury their own. Go and proclaim the kingdom of God."

The third said, "I will follow you, Lord, but first let me say goodbye to my family, for I will miss them."

"No one who looks back in sadness is fit for service in the kingdom of God. You must joyously follow in the way of the Lord." Many said they were willing to follow in the ways of Jesus, but few were willing to do what it took.

Jesus and his disciples returned to Capernaum, where they had a house to stay in. The tax collectors saw them and recognized who they were, and knew they had been living in the town. They went to the house Jesus and the disciples were staying in. "Doesn't your teacher pay the temple tax?" they asked Peter.

"Of course," he replied.

Peter went inside the house. Before he said a word, Jesus asked, "From whom do the kings of the earth collect taxes—from their own sons or from others?"

"From others," Peter answered.

"Then the sons are exempt," Jesus said to him, meaning that because he was the Son of God, the tax did not apply to them.

"But, just so we don't upset anyone, go to the lake and cast your fishing line. The first fish you catch will have a four-drachma coin in its mouth. Take it and give it to the tax collectors to pay for us both."

80. Jesus Raises Lazarus from the Dead

John 11

 man Jesus knew named Lazarus was very sick. He lived in Bethany, a village not far from Jerusalem. Lazarus had two sisters, Mary and Martha.

Mary and Martha sent a messenger to Jesus. "Lord, your servant Lazarus, who loves you with all his heart, is terribly ill," the messenger told Jesus.

"Lazarus will not die," Jesus replied. Jesus stayed where he was for two more days.

"We must go to Judea," he said to his disciples. "Our friend Lazarus has fallen asleep, and I must go there to wake him up."

"Lord, if he sleeps, he will get better," his disciples replied. Jesus meant that Lazarus had died, but his disciples thought he meant natural sleep.

"Lazarus is dead," Jesus responded. "Perhaps when you see what I do you will finally believe."

It was a long journey to Bethany. When they got there, Lazarus had already been in the tomb for four days. Many people had already come to Martha and Mary to comfort them over the loss of their brother.

When Martha heard that Jesus was coming, she went out to meet him. "Lord," she said to Jesus, "if you had been here, my brother would not have died. But I know that God will give you whatever you ask."

"Your brother will live again," Jesus replied.

"I believe that you are the Christ, the Son of God, who has to come into the world to save us." Martha went back and found Mary, her sister.

"The teacher is here," she told Mary. "He is asking for you." When Mary heard this, she got up and went to him immediately. Jesus hadn't entered the village yet, he was still where Martha had met him. Those who were comforting Mary in the house thought Mary was going to the tomb to mourn her brother there, so they all followed her.

When Mary reached the place where Jesus was and saw him, she fell at his feet. "Lord, if you had been here, my brother would not have died," she said, sobbing.

When Jesus saw her weeping, and then saw the others who had come with her also weeping, he was deeply moved and saddened. "Where is he now?" he asked them.

"We will take you to his tomb," they replied.

They all arrived at the tomb. It was a cave with a large stone in front of the entrance. "Take away the stone," Jesus said.

"But, Lord," replied Martha, "he has been there four days."

"Didn't I tell you that if you believed, you would see the glory of God?"

The men of the village moved the stone away from the entrance to the tomb. When this was done, Jesus looked up to heaven and praised God. Then he called in a loud voice, "Lazarus, come out!"

Lazarus then walked out of the tomb! His hands and feet were wrapped with strips of linen, and there was a cloth wrapped around his face. This was the most amazing thing anyone had seen Jesus do up to this point. Soon everyone in the village was talking excitedly about the miracle. News got to Jerusalem, which wasn't far away, quickly.

The Pharisees and other Jewish elders in Jerusalem heard what Jesus had done. Then the chief priests and the Pharisees called a meeting of the Sanhedrin—a special council of Jewish elders. These elders were both the leaders of the Jewish people and judges in the courts for the Jews. The Roman Empire often allowed local areas within the empire to have take care of local matters. For the Jewish people around Jerusalem, the Sanhedrin took care of these matters.

"This man is performing miracles before all the people. If we let him go on like this, everyone will believe in him, and then the Romans will come and take away our power and our nation."

"It is better for you that one man die, rather than the whole nation be destroyed," said Caiaphas, the high priest of the Sanhedrin. The group of elders plotted to take the life of Jesus.

Jesus knew what the Sanhedrin was plotting. As a result, he no longer moved about freely. He went to a remote region near the desert, a village called Ephraim, where he stayed with his disciples.

When it was almost time for the feast of Passover, many people went to Jerusalem for their ceremonial cleansing before the Passover, as was the tradition. Many people looked around for Jesus. "Isn't he coming to the feast?" they asked one another.

The chief priests and Pharisees had given orders that anyone who found out where Jesus was, should report it so that they could arrest him. ✒

81. Zacchaeus in the Tree

Luke 19

The chief priests and Pharisees of the Sanhedrin had given orders that anyone who found out where Jesus was, should report it so that they could arrest him. They were afraid of Jesus because he was becoming so well known. The Pharisees did not want to give up the power they had. They were all members of the Sanhedrin—a council of Jewish elders who were both the leaders of the Jewish people and judges in the courts for the Jews.

Jesus knew what the Sanhedrin was plotting. As a result, he no longer moved about freely. He decided to go to a remote region near the desert, a village called Ephraim. Ephraim was near the city of Jericho.

One day, Jesus and his disciples were passing through Jericho. Crowds of people still followed him around wherever he went, despite the fact that Jesus now had many enemies looking for him.

A man named Zacchaeus wanted to see who Jesus was. He was a chief tax collector in Jericho and was very wealthy. But Zacchaeus was short and could not see over the crowd.

So, he ran ahead of the Jesus and the crowds, and climbed a sycamore tree. Jesus was walking in that direction. When Jesus walked under the tree, he looked up and saw Zacchaeus.

"Zacchaeus, come down immediately," Jesus said. "I would like to stay at your house today."

Zacchaeus came down at once. He was overjoyed and rushed home to prepare a welcome for Jesus. The people in the crowds began to mutter to one another when they saw what happened. "He is going to be a guest in the house of a sinner." People disliked tax collectors. Many tax collectors were dishonest and collected more money than they were supposed to. The people could do little to stop this from happening, because a tax collector had the power to put them in prison if they didn't pay or he said they hadn't paid, even if they had paid.

When Jesus arrived at Zacchaeus's house, he was welcomed. While they were eating, Jesus told everyone there about the word of the Lord. Zacchaeus stood up and said to Jesus, "My Lord, I will I give half of my possessions to the poor immediately, and anyone whom I have cheated in any way will be paid back four times the amount."

"Salvation has come to this house today," Jesus said joyously, "because this man is now truly a son of Abraham. I came to this house today to seek out and to save what was lost."

Zacchaeus had many people in his house, including the disciples and some of the people from the crowds. Jesus began to tell them a parable that would help explain the coming kingdom of God. The people thought that the kingdom of God was going to appear at once and they would not have to wait long.

Jesus said, "A man of noble birth went to a distant country to have himself appointed king and then to return. He summoned ten of his servants and gave them ten minas. 'Put these ten pieces of silver to work until I return,' he said to them.

"He was made king, and returned home shortly afterwards. Then the new king sent for the servants to whom he had given the money to find out what they had done with it.

"The first one that came said, 'Sir, I invested your money and was able to double its value.'

"'Well done, my good servant!' the king replied. 'Because you have proven yourself with this small task, I am putting you in charge of ten cities.'

"A second servant came and said, 'Lord, your mina has earned five more.'

"To this the king answered, 'Well done, you will be put in charge of five cities.'

"Another servant came to the new king and said, 'Lord, I have kept your money safe and hid it in a piece of cloth in my house. I was afraid of what you might do if I made extra money. You have taken the crops of people who worked hard for them, even though you did nothing to help.'

"'You wicked servant! You say that I am a hard man, taking what I did not help with, and reaping crops I did not sow. Why didn't you put my money on deposit, so that when I came back, I could have collected it with interest?'

"The king turned to the other servants nearby. 'Take the money I gave him away and give it to the first servant who came to me, the one who earned ten minas.'

"'But my lord,' they said, 'he already has ten!'

"'I tell you that to everyone who takes what they have and makes it grow, more will be given to them. But for those who do nothing, even what they have will be taken from them.'"

After Jesus completed the parable, he got up and left the house with his disciples. "It has come time for us to go to Jerusalem," he said.

82. Jesus Goes to Jerusalem

Matthew 21; Mark 11; Luke 19–20; John 2, 12

 esus had performed many miracles. He had even brought someone who had died back to life! Soon, many, many people were following Jesus around, listening to him preach, and praising him as a great healer. The chief priests and Pharisees of the Sanhedrin had given orders that anyone who found out where Jesus was, should report it so that they could arrest him. They were afraid of Jesus because he was becoming so well known. The Pharisees did not want to give up the power they had. They were all members of the Sanhedrin—a council of Jewish elders who were both the leaders of the Jewish people and judges in the courts for the Jews.

Jesus knew what the Sanhedrin was plotting. He knew it was not yet time for him to face them, so he decided to go to a remote region near the desert, a village called Ephraim. Ephraim was near the city of Jericho.

One day, while in Jericho he met a tax collector who was so impressed with Jesus, he mended his sinful ways and became righteous and generous. After this, Jesus knew it was time to go to Jerusalem.

As Jesus, his disciples, and a large crowd of followers approached Jerusalem, they went near a small village called Bethphage. "Go to the village," Jesus said to two of his disciples, "you will find a colt tied up right near the village entrance that has never been ridden. Untie it and bring it here. If anyone says anything to you, tell him that the Lord needs them, and he will return them soon."

The disciples went and did as Jesus had instructed them. They brought the colt to where Jesus was waiting. They placed their cloaks on the animals, and Jesus sat

259

on the colt, which had never been ridden before. The colt was not nervous to have a person sitting on it, as most young donkeys would be. They usually need to be trained. In those days, kings would ride around on donkeys during peaceful times, because a horse was a symbol of war to them. Jesus rode on the young donkey as a message to the people of Jerusalem that he came in peace.

As Jesus rode the donkey into Jerusalem, the large crowd with him spread their cloaks on the road. Others who were there cut branches from the trees and spread them on the road. Crowds of people ran ahead of him shouting, "Praise to the son of David! Blessed is he who comes in the name of the Lord! Glory to God in heaven!"

When Jesus entered Jerusalem, the whole city shook with the noise of the crowds. The people of Jerusalem saw Jesus riding in on the young donkey. They asked one another, "Who is this person being honored like this?"

"It is Jesus, the prophet from Nazareth in Galilee," people from the crowds answered jubilantly.

Jesus entered the temple area. In the courtyard of the temple many merchants had set up little shops. Jesus got off his donkey and knocked the tables over and kicked the merchant's merchandise so hard it scattered all about. "My house is a house of prayer," Jesus said to the merchants, "but you are making it a den of thieves!"

The sick, blind, and injured people of Jerusalem all flocked to the temple. When they came before Jesus, he healed them of their suffering. Everyone outside the temple was rejoicing.

However, the chief priests and the teachers of the law inside the temple were not rejoicing. They saw the amazing things Jesus did. There were many children around all shouting and dancing joyously in the temple area. "Blessed is the son of David," they sang out. The priests and temple elders were angry at the disturbance.

"Do you hear what these children are saying?" they asked Jesus.

"It is said, 'from the lips of children and infants you will receive the greatest praise,'" was all Jesus said to them. He then left with his disciples to Bethany, a smaller city not far from Jerusalem, where they spent the night.

They woke up early in the morning to go back to Jerusalem. Jesus was very hungry. He saw a fig tree a short distance from the road and went to it. However, when he reached it, Jesus found nothing on it except leaves. "May you never bear fruit again!" Jesus said out loud at the tree. Immediately the tree withered and its leaves fell off.

When the disciples saw this, they were amazed. "How did the fig tree die so quickly?" they asked.

"If you have faith and do not doubt, not only could you do what was done to the fig tree," Jesus answered them, "but you could say to this mountain, 'go and throw yourself into the sea,' and it would obey. If you believe, you will receive whatever you ask for in prayer."

Jesus entered the temple courts. While he was teaching the people who had gathered around him, the chief priests and the elders of the temple came to him. "By what authority are you doing these things?" they asked. "Who gave you this authority?" They were particularly upset when they heard that Jesus was forgiving people of their sins. They thought only God had that power.

"I will ask you one question. If you answer me, I will tell you by what authority I am doing these things. Regarding John's baptisms, where did his right to baptize come from? Was it from heaven, or from men?"

The priests discussed the question among themselves. "If we say, 'from heaven,' he will ask, 'why didn't you believe him?' But if we say, 'from men,' the people will be angry with us, because they believe John was a great prophet."

"We don't know," they finally answered, not knowing what else to say.

"Then I will not tell you by what authority I am doing these things. However, listen to this story.

"There was a man who had two sons. He went to the first and said, 'Son, go out and work in the vineyard for me today.'

"'I don't want to,' the son answered. However, the son thought about it and changed his mind and went without telling his father.

"The father then went to his other son and said the same thing. The second son said, 'Of course I will, Father.' However, when it came time to go, the other son went off with his friends instead.

"Which of the two sons did what his father wanted?" Jesus asked the priests and elders.

"The first one," they answered.

"Correct!" Jesus said. "And just as the first son did what was right by his father, these people whom you think of as sinners are doing right in the eyes of the Lord. John came to you to show you the way of righteousness, but you did not believe him. However, these people did. Even after you saw this, you did not repent and believe him. You claim out loud that you obey the will of the Lord, but your actions do not."

83. The Last Supper

Matthew 26; Mark 14; Luke 22; John 12–13

While Jesus was in Jerusalem with his disciples, he said to them, "As you know, the Passover celebration is only two days away. During that time I will be handed over to the Pharisees and will be crucified."

At the same time the chief priests and the elders of the people assembled in the palace of the high priest. They plotted to arrest Jesus in secret and kill him. "But not during the Feast of Passover," they said, "or the people will riot against us."

While Jesus was in Bethany in the home of a man known as Simon the Leper, a woman came to him with an alabaster jar of very expensive perfume, which she poured on his head as he was reclining at the table.

"Look at that waste," they said. "That perfume could have been sold at a high price and the money given to the poor."

"Why are you bothering this woman?" Jesus asked. "She has done a beautiful thing to me. You will always have the poor with you, but you will not always have me. When she poured this perfume on my body, she did it to prepare me for burial. What she has done will be told for years to come and she will always be remembered."

Then Judas Iscariot, one of Jesus' twelve disciples, went to the chief priests. "What will you give me if I hand Jesus over to you?" he asked them. They counted out thirty silver coins and gave it to him. From then on Judas watched for an opportunity to hand him over. The faith of Judas was weak and he doubted that Jesus was who he said he was. Jesus had promised great things for those who followed him, and Judas was upset because he felt like he had received nothing but the trouble of following Jesus all over the desert. He did not realize that the followers of Jesus had a reward greater than he could ever imagine waiting for them in heaven.

On the first day of Passover, the disciples asked Jesus. "Where do you want us to make preparations for you to eat the Passover?"

"Go into the city. You will see a man carrying a clay jar full of water. Tell him, 'The teacher says his appointed time is near and wants to celebrate the Passover with his disciples at your house.'"

The disciples did as Jesus had directed them and prepared the Passover at the man's house. The man was eager to offer his house to Jesus and made a room ready for them.

That night, Jesus was sitting at the table with his twelve disciples. "Soon," he said, "one of you will betray me."

They were very sad and began to say to him one after the other, "I would never do such a thing, Lord"

"One of you will. The Son of man will go just as it is written. But pity the man who betrays the Son of man! It would be better for him if he had never been born."

Then Judas, the one who was actually plotting to betray Jesus, said to him, "Surely not I, teacher."

"Yes, it will be you," Jesus answered quietly.

While they were eating, Jesus took the bread of the Passover feast. He gave thanks and broke it. He gave the bread to his disciples, saying, "Take this bread and eat it, this is my body."

Jesus then took his cup of wine, gave thanks, and passed it to them, saying, "Drink from it, all of you. This is my blood. The blood of promise to the world, which is poured out to many for the forgiveness of their sins."

They all prayed together and then went outside to the Mount of Olives, a small mountain which lay just outside the city.

84. Judas Betrays Jesus

Matthew 26; Mark 14; Luke 22; John 18

esus and the twelve disciples celebrated the Feast of the Passover quietly together in a man's house in Jerusalem. He had predicted that Judas would betray him and hand him over to his enemies. After this Judas slipped away into the night by himself. The rest of them all prayed together and then went outside. They walked to the Mount of Olives, a small mountain that lies just outside of the city of Jerusalem.

"This very night you will all scatter in fear when they take me and you will deny knowing me," Jesus said to his disciples once they reached the small mountain. "It has already been prophesized. But after I have risen, I will return to Galilee and wait for you."

"Even if everyone else runs away from you, I will never leave your side," replied Peter.

"I tell you the truth," Jesus replied, "this night, before the rooster crows, you will deny knowing me three times."

"Even if I have to die with you," Peter cried, "I will never disown you." All the other disciples said the same thing.

On the Mount of Olives was an olive grove called Gethsemane. Jesus went with his disciples to the beautiful gardens of Gethsemane. "Sit here while I go over there and pray," he said to his disciples.

Jesus took three of the disciples, Peter, James, and John, along with him to a quiet part of the garden.

"I am feeling overwhelmed with sorrow," Jesus said to the three men. "Stay here and keep watch over me while I pray." Jesus knew his greatest challenge was coming.

Jesus moved a little bit away from the three disciples. He fell with his face to the ground and prayed, "My Father, if it is possible, may this suffering be taken from me. But I shall obey your will above mine."

When Jesus returned to his disciples he found them sleeping. "You could not even keep watch over me for one hour?" he asked Peter. "Now, watch me and pray that you will not fall into temptation. Your spirit is willing, but your body is weak."

He went away and prayed again. When he came back, he again found them sleeping, because they were very tired. He woke them again and scolded them for being so weak.

He left them once more and prayed a third time. He returned to the disciples and said to them, "Are you still sleeping and resting? Look, the hour has come and the Son of man has been betrayed. Get up! Here comes my betrayer!"

Judas then appeared from behind a thick patch of shrubs. With him was a large group of soldiers armed with swords and clubs. They were sent from the chief priests and the elders of the people.

Judas had already arranged a signal with them. He told them, "The one I kiss is the man you are looking for and must arrest."

Judas walked up to Jesus. "Greetings, teacher!" Judas said. He then embraced Jesus and kissed him on the cheek.

"Do what you have come for, my friend." Jesus replied. Then the soldiers stepped forward from the bushes and grabbed onto Jesus, arresting him.

Peter rushed to the men who were holding Jesus. He drew out his sword and struck the servant of the high priest, cutting off his ear.

"Put your sword back in its place," Jesus said to Peter. "He who draws the sword will die by the sword. Don't you realize I could call on my Father, and he would at once send down an army of angels to my aid? But how would the Scriptures be fulfilled that say it must happen in this way?" Jesus then reached out his hand and covered the ear of the injured man. Immediately the ear was healed.

"Am I leading an army against you," Jesus asked the crowd, "so that you have to come out with swords and clubs to capture me? Every day I sat in the temple courts teaching, and you did not arrest me then. This has all taken place so that the writings of the prophets would come true." The crowd grew angry. The disciples all ran away.

The men who arrested Jesus took him to Caiaphas, the high priest.

85. The First Trial of Jesus

Matthew 26–27; Mark 14–15; Luke 22–23

efore Jesus was arrested, he had told his disciples that they would all abandon him when the moment of his arrest arrived. All his disciples, especially Peter, said they would not run away.

A little later, Jesus was arrested by an angry mob of men with swords and clubs. They were sent by the high priests in Jerusalem to get Jesus. Those who had arrested Jesus took him to Caiaphas, the high priest. The disciples, as Jesus said they would, all ran away, scared for their lives.

At first Peter ran away with the other disciples, but then turned around and followed the crowd that took Jesus to the high priest's house. Peter followed all the way up to the courtyard of the house. He entered the courtyard and sat down with the guards to see what would happen.

Jesus was put on trial before the Sanhedrin, the council of Jewish elders who were the judges and leaders of the Jews in Jerusalem. They were determined to find Jesus guilty of something, of some crime against God's laws. For a long time they did not find anything against Jesus, even though many witnesses came forward with wild claims and told a lot of lies about Jesus. The false witnesses were easily proven wrong, however, and the priests were getting frustrated.

Finally two men came forward as witnesses. "This man said, 'I have the power to destroy the temple of God and rebuild it in three days.'"

The high priest stood up and looked down at Jesus. "How do you answer to this? What is the meaning of the statement that these men are saying against you?"

269

Jesus remained silent. The high priest said to him, "I demand you answer under oath before the living God. Tell us if you are the Christ, the Son of God."

"Yes," Jesus replied. "And someday you will see the Son of man sitting at the right hand of the Lord among the clouds of heaven."

The high priest became angry. "He has spoken blasphemy!" he shouted. "We need no more witnesses. You have all heard his blasphemy. No mere man can be a son of God. It is an insult to his glory!"

"He must die!" the people in the court shouted. They spit in his face and hit him. "Prophesy to us now Christ," they jeered at him. "Who hit you?"

Peter was sitting out in the courtyard with the high priest's men waiting for the trial to end. A servant girl walked by and saw him. "You are one of the men who was with Jesus of Galilee," she said. She had seen them at the temple days before.

"I don't know what you're talking about," Peter replied.

Peter got nervous that someone recognized him. He left the courtyard through the front gateway. There was a large group of people waiting by the gate. "This fellow is one of the disciples of Jesus of Nazareth," a girl in the crowd said.

"I swear, I do not know the man!" Peter shouted.

Peter didn't want to leave the area, because he was still worried about what was going on in the trial. He stood as far away from everyone as he could. After a little while, a few of the people in the crowd went up to Peter. "You must be one of them, your accent gives you away. You are definitely from the land of Galilee."

Peter yelled at them and sword an oath. "I am telling you, I don't know the man!" Just then a rooster crowed.

The sound of the rooster immediately reminded Peter of the words Jesus had spoken to him, "This night, before the rooster crows, you will deny knowing me three times." Peter ran away from the crowd and began crying bitterly.

Early the next morning, all the chief priests and the elders of the people got together and discussed what to do next. They decided to put Jesus to death. Jesus was tied up and led to Pontius Pilate. Pontius Pilate was appointed by the Roman Empire to serve as the governor of Judea.

When Judas saw that Jesus was condemned, he became overwhelmed with remorse. He went to the chief priests and the elders who had used him to capture Jesus. "I have sinned," he said to them. "I have betrayed an innocent man." He tried to return the thirty silver coins that he was paid to betray Jesus.

"What is this to us?" they replied. "Keep your money and deal with your guilt on your own."

Judas threw the money into the temple and left. Then he went away and hanged himself from a tree.

The priests picked up the tiny silver coins off the temple floor. "We cannot put this back into the temple treasury," one of them said. "It is blood money."

The priests discussed what to do with the money. They decided to use the money to buy the field a local merchant was selling. They could use the field as a burial place for foreigners. Afterwards, the field became known as the Field of Blood.

86. Jesus Is Taken to Pontius Pilate

Matthew 27; Mark 15; Luke 22–23; John 18–19

esus was taken to stand trial before Pontius Pilate. Although the Sanhedrin was given power to rule over and judge the Jewish people, everyone in all of Judea still had to answer to the governor who was there to represent the interests of Rome. Also, the Sanhedrin did not have the power to have anyone put to death. Only the governor did.

Pilate went outside to meet the high priests who had come with Jesus. "Why are you bringing me this man," he asked them. "What has he done?"

"He has been causing all kinds of trouble," the high priests answered. "He opposes payment of taxes and claims to be Christ, King of the Jews."

"Then why bring him to me? I am not a Jew, you should punish him yourselves."

"We have, and decided he must be put to death," they answered. "Only you can approve of this." They reported everything about Jesus' trial before the Sanhedrin.

Pilate went back inside the palace. He had the guards bring Jesus before him. "Are you the king of the Jews?" he asked.

"Is that what you believe?" Jesus asked, "or did others say this to you?"

"I am not Jewish and do not know anything about you," Pilate replied. "Your people and your chief priests handed you over to me. What is it you have done?"

"My kingdom is not of this world. If it were, my followers would have fought to prevent my arrest by the Jews. My kingdom is in another place."

"You are a king, then!"

"What you say is right, I am a king. That is the reason why I was born. I have come into the world to testify to the truth. Everyone on the side of truth listens to me."

"What is truth?" Pilate said quietly. He went out again to the crowds. "I have not found him to have committed any crime."

"He rallies the people all over Judea by his teachings, which oppose us. He started in Galilee and has come all the way here."

Pilate asked if Jesus was a Galilean. When he learned that Jesus was, he sent him to Herod, who was also in Jerusalem at that time on a visit. Herod was the king over Galilee.

Herod had heard about Jesus and hoped to see him perform a miracle. He asked all sorts of questions, but Jesus gave no answers. The chief priests and the teachers of the law were also there. They accused Jesus of all sorts of crimes. Jesus said nothing.

Herod became angry and wanted Jesus punished. He and his soldiers ridiculed him. They thought he was a sham. As a joke they dressed him in royal robes. They then sent him back to Pontius Pilate.

The governor knew the high priests of the Sanhedrin sent Jesus to him only because they were jealous of how popular he was with the Jewish people. In those days, at the end of the Passover Feast, it was a custom to release one

Jewish prisoner who had been sentenced to death. The people were allowed to choose who would be pardoned. At that time the only other Jewish prisoner that was sentenced to death was a man named Barabbas. He was a wicked man who had killed many people and tried to take control of the city with a small army.

Earlier, while Pilate was sitting on the judge's seat, his wife sent him a message. Her message told him that she had horrible dreams about what was being done to Jesus and that Pilate should not have anything to do with his punishment.

Not wanting to cause unneeded confrontation with the Sanhedrin, Pilate decided to let the people decide whether or not Jesus should be killed. He summoned the Jewish people to his palace courtyard where he would ask them who should be freed. Pilate was sure that the people would choose to free Jesus, over the murderous Barabbas.

When the crowd had gathered, Pilate asked them, "Who do you want me to release, Barabbas or Jesus?"

But the chief priests and the elders knew of Pilate's plan. They went to work immediately, persuading everyone in the crowd to ask for Barabbas.

"Release Barabbas!" the crowd answered.

"What should I do with Jesus then?" Pilate asked.

"Crucify him!" they all shouted.

"Why? What has he done?" asked Pilate.

"Crucify him!" they shouted even louder.

Pontius Pilate saw that that the crowd was becoming rowdy, and appeared ready to erupt in violence. He went to a basin of water nearby and washed his hands in front of the crowd. "I wash my hands of this man's blood," he said.

Barabbas was released to them. All the people cheered. Jesus was handed over to be crucified. The governor's soldiers took Jesus into the prison and gathered the whole company of soldiers around him.

87. The Crucifixion
Matthew 27; Mark 15; Luke 23; John 19

esus was handed over to be crucified. The guards took Jesus into the prison and guarded him. They made fun of Jesus, putting a scarlet robe on him and laughing at how absurd it was that he would claim to be a king. Then they twisted together some branches from a thorn bush into the shape of a crown and set it on his head. They put a staff in his right hand and knelt in front of him laughing. "Hail, King of the Jews!" they said mockingly. The guards were abusive until it was time to lead him off to be crucified.

When the time came, they took the scarlet robe off of Jesus and put his own clothes back on him. Then they led him away to crucify him. They forced Jesus to carry the horizontal beam of the cross, which was a big heavy wooden pole. Everyone who was crucified had to carry his own cross. However, Jesus had been beaten so badly that he was too weak to carry the cross beam.

As they were going out, the soldiers crossed paths with a man named Simon. They forced him to carry the beam of the cross instead. The crucifixions took place on a hill called Golgotha (meaning the place of the skull). On the way, one of the soldiers offered Jesus some wine but he refused to drink it.

When they reached the hill, the soldiers crucified Jesus. Above his head, they carved the words, "This is Jesus, the King of the Jews." Many of the people there to witness the crucifixion laughed. The

soldiers all sat down, to guard Jesus while he died. To be crucified was one of the cruelest ways of being executed. It took a long time to die. The guards had to make sure no one came to his rescue. While the guards sat there, they played games to see who would win what little property Jesus had with him.

Two men were also crucified with Jesus that day. They were both thieves. One was on his right, and the other on his left. One of the thieves yelled at Jesus. "If you are the Son of God, then save yourself and us!"

"Be quiet," the other thief said to the first. "Have you no compassion? He is under the same sentence as us, yet he is innocent! We have earned our places up here." He then said to Jesus, "Remember me, Lord, when you enter your kingdom."

"By the end of this day, you will be with me in heaven," Jesus told him.

People passed by and hurled insults at Jesus, shaking their heads in disgust. "You said you were going to destroy the temple and rebuild it in three days! If you are so mighty, then save yourself! Come down from the cross, if you are the Son of God!" one person shouted at Jesus.

The chief priests, the teachers of the law, and the elders also came by and ridiculed him. "He saved others," they said, "but he can't save himself! He says that he is the King of Israel! Let him come down from the cross, and then we will believe in him. He says he trusts in God. If he really were the Son of God, wouldn't God rescue him?"

"Father," Jesus called out, "forgive them. They know not what they say."

Then, at only midday, darkness covered the land. After about three hours Jesus cried out in a loud voice. "My God, my God, why have you forsaken me?" he cried.

"He's calling Elijah," someone standing nearby said. One of the other witnesses ran and got a sponge soaked in vinegar. He put it on a stick and raised it for Jesus to drink. Jesus cried out again in a loud voice. His spirit left him. Jesus had died.

At that exact moment when Jesus died, the curtain that stood behind the altar in the temple was torn in two from top to bottom. The earth shook with a deep rumbling, and the rocks crumbled before everyone's eyes.

When the men who were guarding Jesus felt the earthquake and saw all that had happened, they became terrified. "He really was the Son of God!" one of them shouted. Many of the people who were gathered around became afraid.

Many women who believed in Jesus deeply were also there, watching from a distance. They had followed Jesus from Galilee to care for his needs. Among them were Mary, the mother of Jesus and Mary Magdalene. While the others ran away, they remained.

As evening came, a rich man from Arimathea, named Joseph, came into Jerusalem. Joseph had become a disciple of Jesus long before. He went to Pontius Pilate and asked for Jesus' body. The governor ordered that it be given to him.

Joseph went and got the body, wrapped it in a clean linen cloth, and placed it in his own new tomb that he had carved out of the rock. After Jesus was placed in the tomb, a large stone was rolled in front of the entrance of the tomb. Once this was done, Joseph returned home.

Mary Magdalene and the other women who had followed Jesus followed Joseph and watched him put the body of Jesus in the tomb. After, they went home and prepared spices and perfumes to honor Jesus. However, before they finished, the Sabbath day arrived and they rested, in obedience to the fourth commandment.

88. The Resurrection

Matthew 27–28; Mark 16; Luke 24; John 20

esus had been crucified. After he died, Simon, a wealthy follower of Jesus from Arimathea, took Jesus' body down from the cross. Simon took the body to a tomb he had just had carved into a rock cliff. After wrapping the body in linen and placing it in the tomb, Simon had his servants roll a large rock over the entrance to the tomb.

After, Mary and the other women went home and prepared spices and perfumes to honor Jesus. However, before they finished, the Sabbath day arrived and they rested, in obedience to the fourth commandment.

The next day, the chief priests and the Pharisees went to Pontius Pilate. "Sir," they said, "while Jesus was still alive he said, 'after three days I will rise again.' We would like the tomb to be guarded until the third day."

"Take a guard," Pilate answered. "Make the tomb as secure as you can."

They put a seal on the tomb, so it couldn't be opened. They also left a guard there to keep people out of the tomb.

Very early the next morning, Mary Magdalene took the spices and oils she had prepared and went to the tomb. The guard that was left there was gone. There was no one there. She found the stone that had been covering the entrance to the tomb rolled away. She looked into the tomb, but did not find the body of Jesus.

While she was wondering what was going on, suddenly two men in clothes that shined like lightning appeared inside the tomb. The woman fell down to the ground with her face down.

"Why do you look for the living among the dead?" the two angels asked. "He has risen! Remember how he told you, while he was still with you in Galilee, 'The Son of man must be delivered into the hands of sinful men, be crucified and on the third day be raised again.'"

Mary remembered the words of Jesus and realized what happened. She got up and suddenly was face to face with Jesus!

"My Lord," she cried out in joy.

"Go to the disciples," Jesus said to her. "Tell them what has happened."

Mary went back to tell the eleven disciples. But they did not believe her, because everything she said sounded impossible. All except Peter. He got up and ran to the tomb. When he got there it was deserted. He saw the strips of

linen that Joseph had used to wrap Jesus' body with lying on the ground. He went away, wondering to himself what had happened.

Later that same day, two other followers of Jesus were walking to a village called Emmaus, a few hours' walk from Jerusalem. They were talking about everything that had happened. As they talked, Jesus came up and walked along with them, but they did not recognize him.

"What were you two talking about?" he asked them.

One of them, a man named Cleopas, asked him, "You do not know the things that have happened in Jerusalem the past few days?"

"What things?" Jesus asked.

"About Jesus of Nazareth," they replied. "He was a great and powerful prophet of the Lord. The chief priests and our rulers handed him over to be sentenced to death, and they crucified him. We had hoped that he was the one who was going to save us all. Also, this morning a woman went to the tomb, but didn't find his body. She said she saw Jesus alive, but when we got there we saw the tomb broken open and empty. There was no sign of anyone.

"How foolish you are, and how slow you are to believe the prophecies! Hasn't all of this been written down by the prophets?"

As they approached the village, Jesus acted as if he was not going to the village, but somewhere farther away. "Stay with us," the two men said to Jesus, whom they still did not recognize, "it is nearly evening and you should not be traveling alone at night." He agreed and went in.

Later that night, they all sat at a table for dinner. Jesus took some bread, gave thanks, broke it, and gave some to them. At that moment, the two men recognized who he was. Once they realized this, Jesus vanished.

They got up and immediately ran back to Jerusalem. There they found the eleven disciples and the other followers of Jesus all assembled together. "It is true! The Lord has risen. He appeared to us this very night!" They told the group everything that happened, including how Jesus broke the bread exactly as he did during the Passover feast and how he completely vanished without a trace.

Suddenly, Jesus himself was standing there. "Peace be with you!" he said.

They were all startled. They thought they were seeing a ghost.

"Why are you afraid, and why do I sense doubts among you? Look at my hands and my feet. It is I! Touch me. A ghost does not have flesh and bones, as I do." He showed them his hands and feet, which still showed the wounds from the crucifixion.

Everyone was amazed. "Do you have anything to eat?" Jesus asked.

They gave him some broiled fish. Jesus took it and ate it in front of them. "I told you all before that everything must be fulfilled that is written about me in the Law of Moses, the Prophets, and the Psalms. It has all happened as it was written. You are all witnesses of these miracles."

Thomas, one of the original twelve disciples, was not with the group when Jesus had visited. The others went and found him. "We have seen the Lord!" they all said joyously.

"Unless I see him myself," Thomas replied, "and see the nail marks in his hands, I will not believe it."

A week later, the disciples were together, including Thomas. Even though the doors were locked, Jesus appeared among them. "Look at my hands, Thomas," Jesus said. "Stop doubting and believe."

"My Lord and my God!" Thomas said when he saw Jesus.

"Because you have seen me, you believe. Blessed are those who have not seen me, yet still believe."

89. The Ascension

Luke 24; John 21; Acts 1

 ne day, some of the disciples, including Peter, Thomas, Nathanael, James, and John were walking by the Sea of Tiberius. "I'm going out on the boat to fish," Simon Peter told them. The others said they would go too, so they all got into the boat and went out a ways from the shore.

They fished through the night until the sun rose, but still hadn't caught a thing. Early in the morning, as they were heading toward shore, they saw a man standing on the land. It was Jesus, but they couldn't recognize him.

"Friends, have you caught any fish?" Jesus called out.

"Not a one," they answered.

"Throw your net on the right side of the boat and you will find some." They all shrugged and figured it would be worth a try. When they tried pulling the net back in after throwing it out to the right, they were unable to because it was full of so many fish.

"It is the Lord!" the disciples all exclaimed.

Without hesitation, Peter jumped out of the boat into the water and swam toward Jesus. The others followed in the boat, towing the net full of fish. When they landed, they saw Peter and Jesus sitting by a fire. They had some fish cooking on it, and some bread nearby.

"Bring some of the fish you have just caught," Jesus told them.

Peter got up and climbed aboard the boat. He grabbed the net and dragged it ashore by himself, even though it was full of more fish than all the disciples could pull into the boat. Even with so many fish, the net did not tear.

"Come and eat," Jesus said to them. Jesus took the bread and gave it to them, and did the same with the fish that had already been cooked.

When they finished eating, Jesus said to Peter, "Simon Peter, son of John, do you truly love me more than anything?"

"Yes, Lord," Peter replied, "you know that I love you."

"Look after my followers," Jesus said to Peter.

"Peter, son of John," Jesus said, "do you truly love me?"

"Yes, Lord, with all my heart."

"Look after my flock," Jesus said to him.

"Peter, son of John, do you love me?" Jesus asked a third time. Peter was hurt because Jesus asked him so many times.

"Lord, you know all things. You know that I love you."

"Look after my followers. I tell you, when you were younger you dressed yourself and went wherever you wanted. Now that you are old you will stretch out your hands in my name, and then someone else will dress you and lead you where you do not want to go."

"Follow me!" Jesus said to Peter. The other disciples followed.

The day that the disciples were waiting for came. It was the day Jesus had promised they would see something amazing, and the day of their salvation. They all stood on the Mount of Olives, where Jesus had been betrayed. "Lord," they asked Jesus, "Are you going to restore the kingdom to Israel today?"

"It is not for you to know God's plan in that matter," Jesus replied. "Today you will receive power when the Holy Spirit comes on you. You will be witnesses of what is about to happen, and you must go out into the world and spread the news of God's glory."

After Jesus said this, he was lifted up into the sky. The disciples watched as Jesus rose up in a bright light until he became hidden by a cloud.

While this was happening two angels appeared among the disciples. "Men of Galilee," they said, "why do you stand here looking into the sky? Jesus will come back to you some day, in the same way you see him going into heaven now."

The eleven disciples returned to Jerusalem and went upstairs to the room where they were staying. They all prayed together, along with the others who believed in Jesus as their savior. This meeting was very early in the beginnings of the Christian church, when about 120 followers remained loyal to Jesus.

90. The Twelfth Disciple
Acts 1–3

ecause Judas Iscariot had betrayed Jesus and then killed himself, there were only eleven disciples left. The disciples, who became known as the apostles (or messengers of Christ), decided that they should replace him.

Two men were suggested: Barsabbas and Matthias. The apostles prayed for God to guide them in choosing and then they cast lots. Matthias was chosen from the lots, so he became the twelfth apostle.

It was the day of the Pentecost festival. The twelve apostles were all together. Suddenly, they all heard something that sounded like a violent storm coming from up above. All through the house they were in, the sound could be heard.

Then, the disciples saw flames flickering over their heads. Each of the apostles felt the Holy Spirit within him and began to speak in other languages. Remarkably, they understood each other as well.

The disciples ran into the streets of Jerusalem speaking of the glory of Jesus and the Lord. During Pentecost, Jewish people from all over the world would gather to celebrate. These people spoke many different languages, and when they heard the disciples speaking about God, they could understand what they were saying. A crowd gathered around the disciples, who were telling everyone about the miracles Jesus had performed. Everyone was astonished because they all heard the disciples speaking in a language they understood.

"Aren't these men who are speaking Galileans? How is it that we all can understand them?" the people in the crowd all asked each other. Amazed, they asked one another, "What does this mean?"

Some, however, made fun of them. "They must be drunk!" they said while laughing.

Peter stood up with the other eleven, raised his voice, and addressed the crowd. "Fellow Jews and other citizens of Jerusalem, let me explain what has happened. These men are not drunk, as you are thinking. It's only nine in the morning! We are servants of the Lord, and it is in fulfillment of the prophecies that you can understand what we are saying. We have been filled with the Holy Sprit and have come to preach in the name of the Lord, Jesus Christ. Jesus of Nazareth was sent to us by God. And you, with the help of wicked men, put him to death by nailing him to the cross. Then God raised him from the dead, freeing him from the agony of death, because it was impossible for death to keep its hold on him. Therefore, let it be known that God has made this Jesus, whom you crucified, both Lord and Christ."

When the people heard this, they were moved and believed everything Peter had said. "What should we do?" they all asked.

"Repent your sins and be baptized in the name of Jesus. Then you will receive the gift of the Holy Spirit." Peter continued to preach to everyone there, warning them to confess their sins and pray for forgiveness. Everyone was amazed at the power behind Peter's words. Almost three thousand people were baptized that day and became followers of Jesus.

They all sold their property, and gave the money to whoever was in need. They prayed together in the temple courts. Soon, many others joined with them, and their numbers grew.

91. Peter Follows in Jesus' Footsteps

Acts 3–5

ne afternoon, Peter and John were on their way up to the temple to pray. They found a man at the temple gate begging for money. The man had been unable to walk since he was born. When the man saw Peter and John about to enter the temple, he asked them for money.

Peter looked straight at him, as did John. The man kept his head to the ground. "Look at us!" Peter said to the beggar.

The man looked up at Peter, thinking he was going to get some money. He held out the bowl he had with him.

"I do not have silver or gold or any other money. But, I will give you what I can give. In the name of Jesus Christ, walk!" Peter reached out and took the man's hand. He helped him up, and the man was able to walk! He jumped and walked around singing with joy. Then the man went with Peter and John into the temple courts, praising God.

The people in the temple saw the man walking and praising the Lord joyously. They recognized him as the man who sat begging at the temple gate every day.

"People of Israel, why are you so surprised? asked Peter. "Do you think we were able to make this man walk with our own powers? No! It was through Jesus that we have healed this man! You handed him over to be killed, yet God brought him back to life, we were witnesses."

When the priests heard Peter preaching about Jesus to the people in the temple they became upset. They ordered the temple guards to arrest the two apostles. The man who was healed was also taken by the guards.

The next day the rulers, elders, and teachers of the law met in Jerusalem. They had Peter and John brought before them. "By whose authority were you acting yesterday?" they asked Peter.

"It is in the name of Jesus Christ of Nazareth, whom God raised from the dead, that we healed the man who could not walk," answered Peter. "It is also through Jesus, the Son of God, that I preach to the people."

The members of the Sanhedrin could see the man who had been healed standing there with them, they knew that a miracle had been performed. They had the guards take the men away so they could discuss what to do.

"What are we going to do with these men?" one of the high priests asked. "Everybody living in Jerusalem knows they have performed a miracle, and there is no way we can deny it."

They summoned Peter and John again and commanded them not to speak or teach in the name of Jesus.

"Judge for yourselves whether it is right to obey your order rather than God's will," Peter replied. "We cannot help speaking out."

The Pharisees and elders tried to threaten them again, but could not convince Peter or John to stop preaching in the name of Jesus. They could not figure out a way to punish them either, because all the people were praising God for what had happened. They decided all they could do was let them go, and to keep an eye on what they did.

More and more men and women believed in the Lord. People brought the sick into the streets and laid them on beds and mats so that at least Peter's shadow might fall on some of them as he passed by. Peter healed every one that came to him.

The high priests of the temple became filled with jealousy. The elders saw the disciples preaching to a large crowd of people. They sent soldiers to get them. The soldiers asked the apostles to come with them to the temple elders. The apostles went with the guards.

"We gave you strict orders not to teach in the name of Jesus," the high priest said. "Yet you have filled Jerusalem with your teaching and are determined to make us look bad."

"We must obey God's will over that of men!" Peter replied angrily.

When the high priests and elders heard what Peter said, they became furious and wanted to put them to death. One of the Pharisees, Gamaliel, stood up and ordered that the men be put outside for a little while.

"Men of Israel, consider carefully what you intend to do to these men. We have seen this kind of thing before. A radical or two rally up the people, but eventually they turn on him and scatter. My advice is to leave these men alone. Let them go! If they have any intentions, they will eventually fail. However, if it truly is God's will they are doing, then you will not be able to stop these men. Not only that but you will find yourselves fighting against God."

His speech persuaded them. They called the apostles in and had them whipped as punishment. They ordered them again to not speak in the name of Jesus, then let them go. The apostles never stopped teaching about Jesus.

92. Stephen the Martyr
Acts 6–8

The number of followers and believers in Jesus increased as time went on. These followers were known as the disciples, or students, of Christ. However, as the number and crowds grew, problems among the people began to occur. Some groups were complaining that they were not getting their fair share of the food. The apostles started to hear complaints.

The twelve apostles got together to discuss the matter. "We need to devote our time to the word of the Lord, and not spend all our time feeding the people. But it also must be done. Let's have other men appointed to be in charge of taking care of the people."

They decided to let the people themselves decide who it would be. "Choose seven men from among you who are wise, good, and honest. We will turn this responsibility over to them."

Everyone thought this was a great idea. One of the seven they chose was a man named Stephen. Stephen was a good man who was wise and strong in faith. The other men chosen were Philip, Procorus, Nicanor, Timon, Parmenas, and Nicolas. The disciples presented these men to the twelve apostles. The apostles prayed over them so that they could serve the followers of Jesus as best they could.

Now that the twelve apostles had more people helping them care for the disciples, they were now able to spread the word of God more easily. The number of disciples in Jerusalem increased rapidly.

Stephen performed many miracles. He also preached with a large amount of strength and power and was well respected among the people. As Stephen's popularity grew, however, some of the people were jealous of him. These men tried to argue with Stephen, but they could not stand up against his wisdom.

Then they secretly persuaded some others to say that they had heard Stephen say evil things against Moses and against God. When this was done, many people got angry and the false rumor was spread, all the way up to high priest. Stephen was arrested and brought to stand trial before the Sanhedrin.

False witnesses were brought in to lie about Stephen. "He never stops speaking against this holy place and against the law," one man said. "We have heard him say that Jesus will destroy this place and change the customs Moses handed down to us."

The members of the Sanhedrin looked at Stephen intently. They noticed that his face was pure, like the face of an angel.

"Are these charges true?" the high priest asked.

Stephen responded by telling the members of the Sanhedrin the history of the Jewish people. He told them the entire story of Joseph and Moses leading the people out of Egypt. He told them about the building of Israel as a nation and its collapse. Stephen tried to explain to the Sanhedrin that Jesus was the fulfillment of God's plan for their people. However, the members of the Sanhedrin would not listen to what Stephen was saying.

"Was there ever a prophet your fathers did not persecute?" Stephen went on. "They even killed those who predicted the coming of Jesus. Now you have betrayed and murdered him—you who have received the law of the Lord but have not obeyed it."

When the members of the Sanhedrin heard this, they became so furious at Stephen that the shouts of anger they made sounded like angry wild animals snarling. Stephen, full of the Holy Spirit, looked up toward heaven.

"Look," he said, "I see heaven open and Jesus standing at the right hand of the Lord."

They all covered their ears and yelled out in anger at the top of their voices so they wouldn't hear what Stephen was saying. They rushed at him, dragged him out of the city and threw stones at him.

While they were stoning him, Stephen prayed, "Lord Jesus, receive my spirit." Then he fell on his knees. "Lord, do not hold this sin against them!" he cried out. When he had said this, God put him in a deep sleep. Stephen was the first person to die in the name of Jesus. Stephen's faith was so great that he was willing to die for it, and he was rewarded with eternal life in heaven.

Witnessing everything that happened was a young man named Saul. Saul was happy when Stephen was killed. On that day a terrible persecution broke out against the Christians in Jerusalem. Everyone, except the apostles, had to run away and the followers became scattered throughout Judea and Samaria.

93. The Journey of Philip
Acts 8

When Stephen was killed for his belief in Jesus, he became the first Christian martyr. A martyr is a person who dies because of, or in defense of, his or her beliefs. A young man named Saul witnessed the death of Stephen and then became the biggest enemy of the early Christian church. He went from house to house, dragging off men and women he suspected were Christians, and put them in prison.

Because the Christians had so many enemies in Jerusalem, they all fled to other lands, except for the apostles, who stayed in the city. Those who fled preached about Jesus wherever they went.

Philip, one of the seven chosen by the disciples to look after feeding the people, went to the city of Samaria north of Jerusalem. Philip preached about Jesus, healed the sick, and performed many other miracles. When the people of the city saw the amazing things Philip did, they all paid close attention to what he said. Philip healed everyone who was sick or impaired in the city. He gave the blind back their sight; the dying became healthy again; and those who could not walk were able to stand on their feet. There was great joy in Samaria.

Simon was a sorcerer in Samaria. He boasted that he had great power, and the people followed him because he had amazed them for a long time with his magic.

However, when Philip arrived, everyone began to follow him. Soon, everyone in the city was baptized and began following in the ways of Jesus. Even Simon believed and was baptized. He followed Philip around everywhere, astonished by what Philip was able to do. Simon no longer thought his power was anything special.

When the apostles in Jerusalem heard that the city of Samaria had accepted the word of God, Peter and John went out to them. When they arrived, they prayed that the Samaritans would receive the Holy Spirit, because the Holy Spirit had not yet come upon any of them; they had only been baptized.

Peter and John placed their hands on each person one by one. When they did this, each person felt the Holy Spirit fill her or him. When Simon saw what the apostles were doing, he offered them money and said, "Give me this ability, so that everyone I lay my hands on will receive the Holy Spirit."

"May your money be destroyed with you!" Peter said to Simon angrily. "You think you can buy the gift of God with money?" You have no place in this church because your heart is not in the right place. Repent and pray to the Lord. Maybe he will forgive you for having such a thought. I can see that you are full of bitterness and sin."

"Please pray to the Lord for me as well," replied Simon humbly, "so nothing you said happens to me."

When they had finished, Peter and John returned to Jerusalem. Along the way back to Jerusalem, they preached in many of the Samaritan villages.

Philip stayed behind, not knowing what to do next. Just then an angel of the Lord appeared to him. "Go south to the desert road that goes down from Jerusalem to Gaza," the angel said to Philip.

Philip obeyed the angel. He began walking toward the road. On his way he met an Ethiopian man riding in an extravagant chariot. Ethiopia was a country far off on the other side of Egypt. The Ethiopian was an important official of the queen of the Ethiopians. He was on his way home from Jerusalem. While in Jerusalem, he got a copy of the book of Isaiah the prophet, which he was reading.

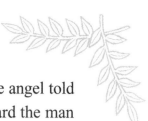

"Go to that chariot and stay near it," the angel told Philip. Philip ran up to the chariot and heard the man reading Isaiah the prophet. "Do you understand what you are reading?" Philip asked.

"No," the Ethiopian answered. "It is confusing, can you explain it to me?" He invited Philip to sit with him in the chariot.

Philip and the Ethiopian man spent a long time riding in the chariot. They took turns reading passages from the book of Isaiah, and Philip explained each passage's meaning. Philip also told the man about the life of Jesus.

As they traveled along the road, they came near a river. "Look, here is water," the Ethiopian said. "I would like you to baptize me."

The chariot came to a stop. Philip and the Ethiopian went down into the water and Philip baptized him. When they came up out of the water, the spirit of the Lord suddenly took Philip away. The Ethiopian went on his way rejoicing.

Philip, however, was put in another village in Samaria. He continued to travel about, preaching the gospel in all the towns on his way to Caesarea, another city in Samaria along the ocean. 📖

94. The Conversion of Saul

Acts 9, 11

aul was one of the greatest enemies of the Christian church in the beginning of its life. He searched throughout the streets of Jerusalem for disciples of Jesus and had them arrested and thrown into prison.

Soon, all the disciples had fled from Jerusalem. Many of them went to Damascus, a city far to the north of Jerusalem. Saul decided to pursue the Christians there. He went to the high priest and asked him for letters that would give him permission to arrest followers of Jesus wherever he found them.

The high priest granted Saul's request. Saul immediately headed north toward Damascus. Just as he was almost in Damascus, Saul saw a brilliant white light from heaven flash around him. He fell to the ground.

"Saul, Saul, why do you persecute me?" the voice of the Lord called out.

"Who are you, Lord?" Saul asked, terrified.

"I am Jesus, whom you are persecuting," he replied. "Get up and go into the city, and you will be told what you must do."

The men traveling with Saul stood there speechless. They could hear the voice but did not see anyone.

Saul got up from the ground, but when he opened his eyes he could see nothing. His companions had to lead him by the hand into Damascus. For three days he remained blind. During that time, he did not eat or drink anything.

In Damascus was a disciple named Ananias. The Lord called to him in a vision.

"Yes, my Lord," Ananias answered.

"Go to the house of Judas on Straight Street and ask for the man from Tarsus named Saul," the Lord said to Ananias. "He is praying. In a vision he has seen a man named Ananias come and place his hands on him to restore his sight."

"Lord," Ananias answered, "I have heard about this man and all the harm he has done to your saints in Jerusalem. He has come here with authority from the chief priests to arrest all who call on your name."

"Go!" the Lord's voice boomed. "This man is my chosen instrument to carry my name before the gentiles and the people of Israel. I will show him how much he must suffer for my name."

Ananias went to the house and entered it. He placed his hands on Saul. "Brother Saul, the Lord has sent me so that you may see again and be filled with the Holy Spirit." As Ananias said these words, a scaly skin fell off of Saul's eyes, and he could see again. He got up and was baptized. After eating, he regained his strength. Saul spent several days with the disciples in Damascus.

Saul began to preach in the temples that Jesus was the son of God.

All those who heard him were astonished. "Isn't he the man who raised havoc in Jerusalem among those who follow Jesus? And hasn't he come here to take them as prisoners to the chief priests?"

Saul grew more and more powerful as he preached in the name of Jesus. The Jewish elders living in Damascus were baffled by Saul's actions. After a time, they came up with a plan to kill him. They instructed the guards at the gates to kill him once he left the city through the gate.

Saul learned of the plan against him. He went to each gate in secret, but saw the extra men waiting there for him.

297

One night, a group of men who had become followers of Saul approached him. They told him they had a plan for helping him escape from the city. They took Saul to an opening in the city wall, and lowered him in a large basket tied to ropes.

When Saul returned to Jerusalem, he tried to join the disciples, but they were all afraid of him. They did not believe that he really was a disciple. But the apostle Barnabas believed him and took him to the rest of the apostles. He told them how Saul had seen the Lord and that the Lord had spoken to him, and how in Damascus he had preached fearlessly in the name of Jesus.

Saul stayed with them and moved about freely in Jerusalem, speaking boldly in the name of the Lord. He talked and debated many of the people of Jerusalem. But, one day some of them tried to kill him.

When the apostles learned of this, they took Saul to Caesarea and sent him off to Tarsus. The Christian church throughout Judea, Galilee, and Samaria then enjoyed a time of peace. It was strengthened and grew in numbers.

Until this point, the disciples were mainly Jews. Around this time, some of the disciples began preaching to non-Jews, or gentiles, about Jesus. The gentiles were baptized and became members of the Christian church as well. When this began, a great number of people joined with the disciples.

95. Peter and the Gentile
Acts 9–11

fter Saul converted to Christianity, the church throughout Judea, Galilee, and Samaria enjoyed a time of peace. The number of members of the church grew.

One day, while Peter was traveling about the country, he decided to visit some disciples he knew in the town of Lydda, which was between Jerusalem and Joppa on the southeast coast of the kingdom of Judea. He met a paralyzed man named Aeneas.

"Aeneas," Peter said to him, "in the name of Jesus Christ be healed. Get up." Aeneas got up out of bed for the first time in eight years.

Everyone in the town was amazed at what happened. They all immediately converted to Christianity.

Further along, in Joppa, lived a disciple named Dorcas, who was always doing good deeds and helping the poor. When Peter was traveling in the area, she became sick and died. When the family of Dorcas heard that Peter was nearby in Lydda, they sent two messengers to him to asking him to go to Joppa immediately.

Peter went to Joppa. When he arrived he was taken upstairs to the room where the body of Dorcas was laying. Peter was surrounded by Dorcas's family and neighbors, who were all crying and showing him the robes and clothing that Dorcas had made for them while she was still alive.

Peter sent them all out of the room. He got down on his knees and prayed. "Dorcas, get up," he said to the body of the woman. She opened her eyes, and seeing Peter she sat up.

Far north of Joppa, was a city called Caesarea. In Caesarea lived Cornelius, a centurion in the Roman Army. Cornelius was a gentile—a person who is not Jewish.

One afternoon, Cornelius had a vision. He saw an angel of God standing in front of him. "Cornelius!" the angel shouted.

"What is it, Lord?" Cornelius asked.

"You must send messengers to Joppa to bring back a man named Peter," the angel commanded. "He is staying with Simon the tanner, whose house is by the sea."

When the angel left, Cornelius summoned two of his servants and a soldier. He told them everything that happened and sent them to Joppa to get Peter.

In the middle of the following day, as the three messengers of Cornelius were on their journey to Joppa, Peter went up on the roof to pray. He became hungry and asked his host for something to eat. While the meal was being prepared, he fell into a trance. Peter saw the sky open up above him and something that looked like a large sheet was being lowered by its four corners to the earth. Inside the sheet were all kinds of wild animals and birds.

"Get up Peter, and eat," the voice of the Lord said.

"Surely not, Lord," Peter replied. "I have never eaten anything impure or unclean."

"Do not call anything impure that God has made clean," the Lord said.

While Peter was wondering what his vision meant, the men sent by Cornelius arrived at the gate of the house.

Peter was still thinking about the vision. "Simon, three men are looking for you," the voice of the Lord said. "Get up and go with them."

Peter went down and greeted the three men. "I'm the one you're looking for," he said to them. "Why have you come?"

"We have come from Cornelius the centurion. He is a righteous and good man, who is well respected by all the citizens of Caesarea. An angel told him to have you come to his house so that he could hear what you have to say."

Peter invited the men into the house to stay for the night. The next day they walked to Caesarea. Some of the people of Joppa went along as well.

Cornelius was expecting them and had called together all of his relatives and friends. As Peter entered the house, Cornelius greeted him and fell at his feet out of respect.

"Stand up," Peter said to Cornelius. "I am only a man myself. No different from you." Peter went inside the house and saw a large gathering of people.

"God has shown me in a vision that all people are equal in his eyes. It does not matter if you are a Jewish person or not. No one is to be considered inferior or unclean. This is why when I was sent for, I came without raising any objection, even though it is against Jewish law to visit a house of a gentile.

"I now realize how true it is that God does not show favorites among the different races of people. He accepts people from every nation who are kind." Peter told them all about the life, death, and resurrection of Jesus. Everyone in the room became filled with the Holy Spirit, proving to them that God loves everyone.

The apostles and the other disciples throughout Judea heard that Peter had preached to the gentiles. When he arrived in Jerusalem, the disciples criticized him. "You went into the house of non-Jews and ate with them." Peter explained everything to them exactly as it had happened. When they heard his explanation, they were no longer upset with Peter. They praised God, saying, "God has granted even the gentiles salvation."

96. Peter in Prison

Acts 12

od had spoken to Peter in a vision. At first, Peter did not understand what the vision meant. He saw a large sheet lowered from the skies. In the sheet were every sort of wild animal and bird on earth. Peter heard the voice of God tell him to eat the animals he saw. Some of the animals were considered unclean to the Jewish people, and therefore against Jewish law for them to eat. Peter had never eaten an unclean animal before, and said so to God. The Lord then scolded Peter, telling him that he had made them clean.

Peter did not understand his vision at first. Then he was taken to the house of a gentile—a person who is not Jewish. It is also against their laws for Jews to eat with gentiles. However, Peter then realized that his vision was meant to tell him that God loved everyone—both gentiles and Jews. Peter returned to the rest of the apostles and told them what happened, and then the Christian church began welcoming gentiles into their faith.

While Peter began preaching to everyone, both Jews and gentiles, King Herod began to arrest Christians. Herod was an enemy of the church and did everything in his power to persecute the disciples. He had the apostle James, the brother of John, put to death. When he saw that the Jewish people were happy that he did this, he had Peter arrested during the Passover feast.

Herod had Peter thrown in a prison cell that was guarded by four squads of four soldiers each. The king was planning to put Peter on trial after the Passover was over. While Peter was in prison, the disciples all prayed to God for him.

On the night before the trial. Peter was sleeping between two soldiers. His arms and legs were shackled in chains. Two guards stood at the entrance to the

cell. An angel of the Lord suddenly appeared, and a light shone in the cell. He tapped Peter on his side and woke him up.

"Quick Peter, get up!" the angel said. As the angel spoke, the chains fell off of Peter. "Put on your clothes and sandals. Wrap your cloak around you and follow me."

Peter did as the angel commanded, and then followed him out of the prison. Peter had no idea that what the angel was doing was really happening. He thought he was seeing a vision in his sleep.

Peter and the angel walked right by the guards and up to the iron gate at the prison's front entrance. The gate opened for them all by itself. Once they had walked about a block away from the prison, the angel left Peter.

Peter realized that God had saved him. He immediately went to the house of Mary, the mother of John, where many people had gathered and were praying.

Peter knocked on the door. A servant girl named Rhoda answered it. She recognized Peter's voice and became so overjoyed she immediately ran back without opening the door and exclaimed, "Peter is at the door! He's here!"

"You're crazy," everyone in the house told her. Peter kept on knocking, so everyone got up to see who it really was. When they opened the door and saw Peter standing there, they were all amazed.

Peter described to them how the Lord had brought him out of prison. "Tell James and the brothers about this," he said, and then he left the house without saying where he would go.

The next morning all the guards were in a tizzy trying to figure out what happened to Peter. Herod had a thorough search made for him, but no one found him. Herod had each of the guards working that night interrogated, but no one knew what happened to Peter. In his anger, Herod had all the guards that worked that night put to death.

Herod was very evil, but he was not long for the world. He had been quarreling with the people of Tyre and Sidon—two lands that bordered Herod's country. The people of these lands joined together and went before King Herod to ask for peace. They asked for peace because they depended on the king's country for their food supply.

The day came that Herod was scheduled to meet the people of Tyre and Sidon. He wore his royal robes, sat on his throne, and gave a speech to the people.

"This is not a man speaking before us, but a god!" the people listening all shouted.

Herod was pleased with this compliment. However, because Herod did not give praise to the Lord, an angel of the Lord came down and touched King Herod. The king immediately fell over dead.

97. The Early Adventures of Paul

Acts 13–16

aul was once one of the fiercest enemies of the early Christian church. Then, after witnessing the miracles of the disciples and being spoken to by God, he converted and became strong in his faith in Jesus. Saul became known by his Roman name, Paul.

Many of the disciples and early teachers were gathered in the city of Antioch. They were worshiping the Lord and fasting together. Then they felt the Holy Spirit among them. "I have chosen Barnabas and Paul to do special work for me," the Holy Spirit said, "They must leave you and go on by themselves to where I lead them."

Barnabas and Paul obeyed the Holy Spirit and went to Seleucia and sailed from there to Cyprus, an island in the Mediterranean Sea. They traveled through the whole island until they reached the small town of Paphos. In Paphos lived a Jewish sorcerer and false prophet named Bar-Jesus, who was an attendant of the proconsul of the town. A proconsul was the leader of the town government. The proconsul asked for Barnabas and Paul to come to him because he wanted to hear what they were preaching.

The false prophet tried to stop them from entering the proconsul's presence by lying to him. However, Paul made it in and confronted the false prophet. "You are an enemy of everything that is good and right!" he said to Bar-Jesus. "You are full of all kinds of deceit and trickery. Will you never stop twisting the meaning of the ways of the Lord? Now the hand of the Lord is against you.

Because of your sins, you are going to be blind." The false prophet immediately saw a mist cover his eyes, which got thicker and thicker until he could see nothing. He reached out and stumbled, then cried out for someone to help him.

When the proconsul saw what happened, he believed and listened to what Barnabas and Paul had to say. He was amazed at their teachings about the Lord.

From Paphos, Barnabas and Paul moved on and sailed away. They traveled about from place to place all around the coastline and islands of the Mediterranean Sea, teaching the word of the Lord to everyone who would listen. They performed many miracles, and more and more people who had heard their message began to believe in Jesus.

One night, while he was sleeping, Paul had a vision of a man from Macedonia standing before him. "Come to Macedonia and help us," Paul heard the man beg. Paul woke up and immediately got ready.

When Paul, who was now traveling with Silas (Barnabas had gone with the apostle John to preach in another land), arrived in Macedonia, they went to a river, where a group of women were gathered. They spoke to the women and told them about Jesus. They also told them about their adventures. One of the women was Lydia. She had with her large bundles of purple cloth, which she sold in the cities around the area. When she heard Paul's words, she asked him to baptize her. After he did this, she insisted that he and Silas stay at her house.

Paul and Silas stayed at Lydia's house. They often went to the river to preach to whoever would come to listen. One day they met a slave girl who could predict the future. Her owners had made a lot of money by charging people who wanted their fortunes told. When Paul saw her, he realized she was possessed by an evil spirit, which was why she could predict the future.

This girl followed Paul and Silas everywhere, shouting out wildly. She kept this up for many days. Paul became troubled by her and felt sorry for her.

"In the name of Jesus Christ I command you to come out of her!" Paul commanded the evil sprit within the slave girl. The spirit left her.

When the evil spirit left the slave girl, she lost her ability to know the future. When the girl's owners realized they couldn't use her to make money any more, they became angry at Paul and Silas. They seized Paul and Silas and dragged them into the marketplace to face the magistrates—the policemen of the town.

"These men are throwing our city into an uproar," the owners said to the magistrates. The magistrates ordered them thrown in jail. The jailer was ordered to guard them carefully because they were a danger to the town. The jail guard put them in the inner cell and locked their feet in chains.

That night around midnight, Paul and Silas were praying and singing hymns to God. Suddenly a violent earthquake shook the foundations of the prison. All the prison doors flew open, and everybody's chains fell off.

The jailer was awakened by the earthquake. When he saw the prison doors open, he became very distressed. He assumed the prisoners escaped, which would be very bad for him. The jailer grabbed a torch and rushed inside the cell. He fell trembling before Paul and Silas when he saw them.

The jailer brought them out of the cell. "What must I do to be saved?" He knew that the men had been arrested because of their preaching.

"Believe in the Lord Jesus, and you will be saved," Paul replied.

The jailer took them to his home. He and all his family were baptized that night. The jailer prepared a meal for them and they all ate together.

The next morning, the magistrates sent an order to the jailer to have Paul and Silas released. The jailer told Paul that he and Silas could leave. "Go in peace," the jailer said to them.

Before leaving the city, Paul and Silas went to Lydia's house. They said goodbye to her and her family, then left.

98. Paul Returns to Jerusalem

Acts 18–23

Paul and Silas continued to travel in the area of Macedonia and places nearby. Macedonia was in Greece, which was part of the Roman Empire. At one point, they ended up in the city of Corinth on the coast.

In Corinth, Paul met a Jewish man named Aquila, who had recently moved from Italy with his wife Priscilla, because the Roman Emperor, Claudius, had ordered all the Jewish people to leave Rome.

Paul stayed with Aquila and his wife while he was in Corinth. Aquila was a tentmaker, which was a job Paul had done when he was younger, so Paul worked with Aquila. Paul went to the synagogue every Sabbath trying to teach the people about Jesus. However, the Jewish people of the synagogue opposed Paul and everything he stood for.

"Let your fate be your own!" Paul shouted to them in distress. "I have tried my best with you. From now on I will teach to the gentiles." Paul left the synagogue and went next door to the house of Titius Justus, who worshiped God. Crispus, the synagogue ruler, and his entire household believed in the Lord and went to Paul to be baptized, as did many other Corinthians. Some of the Jews chose to follow Paul, but most were angry with him.

So Paul stayed in Corinth for a year and a half, teaching them the word of God. He eventually moved on and continued to travel from place to place in the Roman Empire, preaching to anyone who would listen.

One day he spoke to the crowd that was gathered around him. After many years of traveling around, thousand upon thousands of people became followers of Jesus after hearing Paul preach. He was well respected and loved by many.

"I must return to Jerusalem," Paul said to the crowd. "None of you will ever see me again most likely. I speak here today to let you know life will not always be easy for you. I know that after I leave, men like savage wolves will come in among you and will be cruel. Even among you, some will rise up and distort the truth in order to collect their own power. Be on your guard! Remember that for three years I never stopped warning each of you of the dangers of sin."

After Paul spoke, he knelt down with all of them and prayed. Everyone was sad because they would never see him again. Afterward, they all went with him to the ship that would take him to Caesarea.

When Paul and his companions arrived in Caesarea, a prophet named Agabus approached them.

"Do not go to Jerusalem," Agabus warned. "If you do you will be arrested, abused, and sent to Rome."

"I am prepared for more than suffering abuse and captivity for Jesus," Paul replied. "I would die in his name. Let the will of the Lord be done."

Paul and his companions then got themselves ready and left for Jerusalem. When they arrived, the disciples and apostles who were there welcomed them.

The next day they all went to went to see the apostle James. All the elders of the followers of Jesus were there as well. Paul reported in detail everything that had happened on his journey. He made a special point to talk about how God told him to seek out everyone, not just Jewish people, to join with them in the ways of the Lord.

When they heard this, they praised God. They then warned Paul that many of the Jewish elders in Jerusalem were spreading rumors about him. "They will hear that you are here, and they will come for you," they said to Paul. "However, there are four men with us who are going to the temple to purify themselves according to the laws of Moses. Go with them and join in their purification rites. When everyone sees this, they will know there is no truth in these reports about you. They will see that you are living in obedience to the law."

Paul agreed. The next day Paul took the men and went to the temple. The ritual of purification was complicated and took seven days. While Paul and the other four men were performing these rituals, some Jewish men who had seen Paul in his travels noticed him in the temple. These men were among the ones who had rejected what Paul was preaching, and were jealous of the following he had. They also despised the fact that he preached to both Jews and gentiles.

When they saw Paul talking with some gentiles outside of the temple, they came up with a plan to have Paul arrested.

When Paul left the temple, after the ritual of purification was completed, his enemies swarmed around him. "Men of Israel, help us!" they shouted to everyone in the streets. "This is the man who teaches people everywhere to be against us and our laws. He has also brought Greeks into the temple and defiled this holy place!"

Everyone who heard the accusations became angry. People came running from all directions and seized Paul. They dragged him out of the temple area and shut the gates. They started beating Paul and the people became so enraged a riot broke out in the streets. People were yelling and screaming everywhere.

The commander of the Roman troops saw that the whole city was in an uproar. He immediately took some officers and soldiers and ran into the crowd. When the rioters saw the soldiers, they stopped beating Paul.

The commander had Paul arrested. He ordered a soldier to put chains on Paul so he wouldn't escape. Then he asked the crowd, "Who is this man and what has he done?" Everyone in the crowd shouted something different. The commander could not figure out what was going on because of the uproar, so he ordered that Paul be taken to the police station until everything was sorted out.

By the time they had led Paul to the steps of the station, the violence of the mob intensified. The guards were forced to carry Paul into the police station. "Away with him!" the crowd chanted.

As the soldiers were about to take Paul inside, he asked the commander, "May I make a request? Please let me speak to the people." Paul told the entire story of everything he had done, and everything God had told him in visions. He also told them how God had sent him to save the gentiles as well as the Jews.

The crowd listened quietly to Paul until he mentioned gentiles. When they heard that he was preaching to gentiles as well as Jews they became angry. "Rid the earth of him! He doesn't deserve to live!" they shouted. As they were shouting they all threw off their cloaks and flung dust into the air.

The commander ordered that Paul be taken back into the police station and beaten until he revealed why the crowd was so angry with him.

The soldiers got ready to beat Paul. Just then, Paul said to the captain of the soldiers, "Is it legal for you to flog a Roman citizen who hasn't been found guilty?" Paul knew it was illegal in the Roman Empire for a citizen to be abused; in fact, Roman citizens had many protections in the Empire.

When the captain heard that Paul was a Roman citizen, he went to the commander and reported it. The commander went to Paul. "Are you a Roman citizen?" he asked.

"Yes, I am."

"I had to pay a lot of money to get my citizenship," said the commander. "How is it that someone like you, with no money, was able to become one?"

"I was born a citizen," Paul answered.

Those who were about to abuse Paul left the room immediately. The commander himself was a bit scared when he realized that he had put a Roman citizen in chains.

The next day the commander released Paul. He still wanted to find out exactly why Paul was being accused by the Jews, so he ordered the chief priests and the Sanhedrin to assemble. Then he took Paul before them and had him stand trial.

Paul stood before all the Sanhedrin. "My brothers," Paul said, "I have fulfilled my duty to God as best I could to this day."

When Ananias, the high priest, heard this he ordered those standing near Paul to hit him on the mouth.

"God will strike you, you simple fool!" Paul shouted. "You sit there to judge me according to the law, yet you yourself violate the law by commanding that I be struck!"

"You dare to insult God's high priest?" asked the members of the Sanhedrin standing near Paul.

"I did not realize that he was the high priest or I would not have said that. For it is written, 'Do not speak evil about the ruler of your people.'"

The Sanhedrin could be broken down into smaller factions. Two of the most powerful factions were the Pharisees and the Sadducees. The Pharisees believed in spirits, that God can resurrect the dead, and in angels. The Sadducees did not believe in any of those things. Paul knew all of this because his father had been a Pharisee. Paul came up with a plan to confuse the trial.

"My brothers, I am the son of a Pharisee, and a Pharisee myself. I am on trial today because of my belief in the resurrection of the dead."

The Pharisees and the Sadducees began arguing about this point, and the debate became chaotic, with different groups shouting at each other. There was a great uproar, and the Pharisees stood up and shouted at the Sadducees. "We find nothing wrong with this man," they said. "What if a spirit or an angel has spoken to him?" This remark caused the Sadducees to yell back angrily because they did not believe in spirits or angels and thought the Pharisees were talking nonsense.

The dispute became violent, with scuffles between the elders breaking out all over. Scrolls and rocks were being hurled back and forth. The commander was afraid that Paul would be torn to pieces by them. He ordered the troops to take Paul away from the Sanhedrin and take him back to the police station.

99. The Shipwreck

Acts 23–28

aul had been arrested in Jerusalem. Because he was a Roman citizen the commander of the Roman forces in Jerusalem was careful to treat Paul fairly. Many of the members of the Sanhedrin wanted to put Paul to death.

Paul was sleeping in the police station. Many people outside wanted to kill him, so the commander wouldn't let him leave until everything was figured out. While Paul was lying in bed, God appeared beside him. "Take courage," the Lord said. "You will now go to Rome and testify in my name there as you just did here in Jerusalem."

Paul's enemies, outraged that he was still alive and being protected, got together and formed a plan. They announced to the Sanhedrin, the commander, and all of Jerusalem that they would not eat, sleep, or drink until Paul was killed. They then went to the Sanhedrin. "Ask the commander to bring Paul back here. Tell him you want to ask Paul more questions. We will be waiting along the way, ready to kill him before he gets here."

Paul's nephew heard about the plan. He went to the police station and told Paul. Paul called for one of his guards. "Please take this young man to the commander. He has something to tell him."

Paul's nephew was taken to the commander. The guard told the commander about Paul's request. "What is it you want to tell me?" the commander asked the nephew.

"The Sanhedrin have agreed to ask you to take Paul back before them tomorrow. They will say they want to ask him more questions. Don't do it! More than forty men will be waiting for him along the way. They have sworn an oath to kill him."

"Don't tell anyone that you told me this," the commander said as he dismissed him. He then summoned two of his officers and ordered them to muster a large force of two hundred soldiers along with several horsemen and other members of the Roman Empire to escort Paul to Caesarea. The commander wanted Paul to be taken to his trusted friend Governor Felix.

The commander wrote a letter to Governor Felix explaining the entire situation. He made sure to mention that Paul was a Roman Citizen. He wrote that he didn't think Paul deserved to be put to death. The commander also wrote that he was sending Paul's accusers there, to present their case against Paul to him.

The soldiers took Paul and the letter during the night toward Caesarea. It was too long a journey to complete in one night, so they made camp once they were safely away from Jerusalem. The next morning, the soldiers let the horsemen take Paul the rest of the way, while they returned to Jerusalem. When they arrived in Caesarea, they delivered the letter to the governor and handed Paul over to him.

The governor read the letter. He told Paul that he would wait for his accusers to arrive, and he ordered that Paul be kept under guard in Herod's palace.

Five days later the high priest Ananias went to Caesarea with some of the elders and a lawyer named Tertullus. They told the governor all the charges that they believed Paul was guilty of. The lawyer gave a long speech, constantly giving the governor compliments on his wisdom to gain his favor. He told the governor that Paul was causing all kinds of trouble among his people, including starting riots and turning people away from the traditional laws of God. The others who also came to accuse Paul all shouted out in agreement.

The governor turned to Paul and asked him to reply to his accusations.

"I know that you have been a judge of this land for a long time," replied Paul, "so I gladly present my defense to you. Twelve days ago I went up to Jerusalem to worship. My accusers did not find me arguing with anyone at the temple, or stirring up a crowd in the synagogues or anywhere else in the city. They cannot prove any of the charges they are making against me. However, I admit that I worship the God of our fathers as a follower of Jesus." Paul then told the governor everything that had happened over the past few years. The whole time Paul remained calm and even said he hoped that his accusers would find their way to salvation.

Felix ended the trial. He said he would speak to the commander before making a decision. He ordered that Paul be kept under guard, but allowed some freedom. He also permitted Paul's friends to take care of his needs.

Felix did not make any decisions. He did not want the enemies of Paul to turn against him, but he also didn't want to do anything to Paul. For two years Felix kept Paul under guard.

After two years Festus was appointed as governor of Caesarea. Festus brought Paul before him for another trial, which ended up virtually the same as the one conducted by Felix. Paul's enemies had secretly asked Festus to send Paul back to Jerusalem for a new trial. They were planning on killing him on the way back.

"Your accusers have requested that you be sent back to Jerusalem to stand trial in their courts," Festus said to Paul. "Do you agree to this?"

"I am now standing before Caesar's court," Paul replied. "As a Roman citizen, this is where I ought to be tried. I have not done any wrong, as you know very well. If I am guilty of doing anything deserving death, I do not refuse to die. But if the charges brought against me by my enemies are false, I should not be handed over to them. I appeal my case to Caesar!"

Festus conferred with his council to figure out what to do. "You have appealed to Caesar. Therefore, you will be sent to Rome to stand trial!"

Paul and some other prisoners were handed over to a Roman officer, a centurion named Julius. The centurion took Paul and the prisoners on a small ship and sailed out onto the Mediterranean Sea. After a few days, they came across another ship that was heading for Rome. The ship had several Roman soldiers aboard. Julius paid the ship's captain to take on the prisoners, and gave the officer of the soldiers the responsibility of getting the prisoners to Rome for their trials.

The ship headed for Rome. It moved slowly because the wind was not blowing well. They were taking much longer than they should. It was also just after Yom Kippur, a Jewish holy day that involved fasting. All of the men aboard the ship were Jewish, and none of them had eaten anything because of the holiday.

As they moved on, a gentle wind began to blow. Everyone was happy be-cause the wind was blowing directly toward Rome. However, before long the wind picked up and began blowing furiously. The ship was caught in the storm. The storm lasted all night. The next morning the crew began throwing the cargo over-board, to lighten the load on the ship. They were near a small island but it had no safe place for the ship. The ship's captain ordered the anchor be dropped.

Three days after the storm began, it showed no signs of letting up. Everyone on board began throwing anything that wasn't absolutely crucial overboard. The crew lost all hope of surviving.

The men had gone a long time without eating. "Men, you should have taken my advice," Paul said to everyone. "Then you would have spared yourselves this damage and loss. But keep up your courage. Not one of you will be lost. Only the ship will be destroyed. We must run aground."

Two weeks after the storm had begun, the captain sighted land. It was so dark no one could see it clearly, but they headed for it. They dropped four

anchors to stop the ship when they were close to the shore. It was so dark they could not see if there were any rocks nearby. Everyone prayed for daylight.

Paul urged everyone to eat. "For the last fourteen days," he said, "you have been in constant fear and haven't eaten anything. I urge you all to eat some food. You need it to survive." After he said this, he took some bread and gave thanks to God in front of them all. He gave bread to everyone and they all ate.

When they had eaten as much as they could, they threw the grain into the sea. The ship needed to be as light as possible so it would float higher on the sea. They wanted to get as close to the land as possible.

When morning came, no one recognized the land. They saw a bay with a sandy beach, and decided to run the ship as close to the shore as they could. They cut the anchors and let them sink, making the ship even lighter. The sail was raised to catch the wind and the ship began to move toward the bay.

Before it got too close the ship hit a sandbar and got stuck. The wind pounded the ship so hard that the whole front end of the ship was crushed.

The soldiers wanted to kill the prisoners to prevent any of them from swimming away and escaping. The centurion stopped them. He wanted to spare Paul's life. He ordered everyone to get off the ship and swim to shore. Anyone who couldn't swim was to find a piece of wood and paddle toward the shore as best they could.

Everyone on the ship made it safely to the shore. They met some natives of the island who told them they were on Malta. The islanders were kind to the stranded men.

The chief official of the island, Publius, allowed everyone from the ship to stay in his house. He was wealthy and had a very large house and was able to take everyone in. Publius's father was very sick. Paul went in to see him and placed his hands on him and healed him.

When news of Paul's healing of Publius's father reached the rest of the island, everyone who was sick came to him. Paul was able to cure them all. Everyone on the island praised Paul and gave the shipwrecked men all the supplies they needed. They stayed on the island for the winter.

After three months, winter ended. Once the weather was nice, the shipwrecked men got on a ship that the islanders gave to them. It was a final thank you gift because of everything Paul had done for them.

From there, they were able to make it to Rome without any trouble.

100. Paul in Rome

Acts 28

hen Paul finally made it to Rome, he was allowed to live by himself in a house. The authorities in Rome guarded the house, and Paul wasn't allowed to leave until his trial.

Three days after arriving, Paul requested that the leaders of the Jews come see him. Paul wanted to discuss his case to them.

"My brothers, although I have done nothing against our people or against the customs of our ancestors," Paul said to the elders who had come, "I was arrested in Jerusalem and handed over to the Romans. They examined me and wanted to release me, because I was not guilty of any crime deserving death. When those who were against me objected, I was forced to appeal to Caesar. But, I had no charge to bring against my own people. This is why I have asked to see you and talk with you."

"We have not received any letters from Judea concerning you," they replied. "No one who has come from there has said anything bad about you either. We do want to hear what your views are, however. We know that people everywhere are talking against this sect of yours." They arranged to meet Paul later that week.

The entire day, from morning until night, Paul explained and declared to them the kingdom of God. He not only talked about Jesus, but also backed up everything with examples taken from the writings of the prophets.

Some of the people gathered were convinced by what Paul said, but others would not believe. They disagreed and argued among themselves.

For two years Paul stayed in his rented house and welcomed anyone who came to see him. He preached about the kingdom of God and taught about the Lord Jesus Christ without any fear.

Throughout his life, Paul wrote many letters. While the Christian church was still young, the Christians argued among themselves about a lot of issues. The church was also divided between those who were Jewish and those who were gentiles, or non-Jewish.

Christianity started as a religion within Judaism. Oftentimes Jewish people would force the gentiles to convert to Judaism before they could consider themselves Christian. Converting to Judaism was a long and complicated process, which required following strict rules. Christianity, however, primarily involved believing and receiving a baptism.

Paul wrote letters his entire life, and in many ways, he kept the Christian church together in its early years.

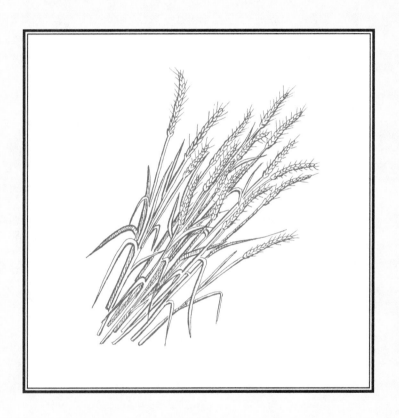

THE EVERYTHING MOTHER GOOSE BOOK

By June Rifkin

*T*he *Everything® Mother Goose Book* is a delightful collection of 300 nursery rhymes that will entertain adults and children alike. These wonderful rhymes are easy for even young readers to enjoy—and great for reading aloud. Each page is decorated with captivating drawings of beloved characters. Ideal for any age, *The Everything® Mother Goose Book* will inspire young readers and take parents on an enchanting trip down memory lane.

Trade paperback,
$12.95 ($19.95 CAN)
1-58062-490-1, 304 pages

OTHER *EVERYTHING®* BOOKS BY ADAMS MEDIA